ALSO BY ROSECRANS BALDWIN

You Lost Me There

PARIS, I LOVE YOU BUT YOU'RE BRINGING ME DOWN

PARIS, I LOVE YOU BUT YOU'RE BRINGING ME DOWN

ROSECRANS BALDWIN

FARRAR, STRAUS AND GIROUX NEW YORK

Farrar, Straus and Giroux
18 West 18th Street, New York 10011

Distributed in Canada by D&M Publishers, Inc.
Printed in the United States of America
First edition, 2012

Portions of this book have previously been published
in substantially different form in *The Morning News*.

Library of Congress Cataloging-in-Publication Data
Baldwin, Rosecrans.
Paris, I love you but you're bringing me down / Rosecrans Baldwin — 1st ed.
p. cm.
ISBN 978-0-374-14668-9 (alk. paper)
1. Baldwin, Rosecrans. 2. Baldwin, Rosecrans—Homes and haunts—France—Paris. 3. Americans—France—Paris—Biography. 4. Couples—France—Paris—Biography. 5. Paris (France)—Biography. 6. Paris (France)—Description and travel. 7. Paris (France)—Social life and customs. I. Title.

DC718.A44 B35 2012
944'.36108412092—dc23
[B]

2011045886

Designed by Jonathan D. Lippincott

www.fsgbooks.com

1 3 5 7 9 10 8 6 4 2

To my parents

Paris, as much as I love Paris, feels to me as though it's long since been "cooked." Its brand consists of what it is, and that can be embellished but not changed.

—William Gibson

CONTENTS

THE GODDESS P.

SUMMER

—A cubicle in Versailles—Everything I know about Paris I learned in seventh grade—Job interviews in France are brief—The hunt for a room for sport or pastime—Young Jeezy is the Frenchest—A life in ten duffel bags—The main difference between the French and American economies explained while I apply for a credit card—The Paris Flu—Rachel passes a breast exam—Bruno and I embrace for the first time—

1

The sun above Paris was a mid-July clementine. I bought copies of *Le Monde* and the *Herald Tribune* at a kiosk and climbed the stairs to my new office on the Champs-Elysées. For three hours, I mugged at a laptop, trying to figure out how the e-mail system worked. My fingers were chattering. I spent long, spacey minutes trying to find the @ key. They'd given me a keyboard mapped for French speakers, with the letters switched around.

For the rest of the day, strangers approached and handed me folders, speaking to me in French while I panicked inside. A sentence would begin slow, with watery syncopation, then accelerate, gurgling until it slammed into an *ennnnnnh*, or an *urrrrrrr*, and I'd be expected to respond.

What did they want from me?

Why was every question a confrontation?

First day on the job, my French was not super. I'd sort of misled them about that.

The advertising agency occupied three floors of a building located a few blocks east of the Arc de Triomphe, next to a McDonald's. Our floor might have been a wing from Versailles. Chandeliers everywhere. Gold-flaked moldings. Long rooms walled by spotty mirrors. There were fireplaces like cave mouths, and high ceilings painted with frescoes. A cherub's little white gut mooned my desk.

For a long time I'd thought Paris had the world's best everything.

Girls, food, the crumble-down buildings. Even the dust was arousing. Coming out of the Métro that morning, I'd been so full up my throat constricted.

Basically, I'd been anaphylactic about France since I was ten.

So I was trying to seem cool and unruffled.

My new boss, Pierre, was an old friend. We knew each other from New York, where Pierre and his wife had lived before returning to Paris, their hometown. In March, I'd received an e-mail that Pierre had sent around looking for someone to join his agency who could attend meetings in French but write English copy.

We spoke the next day. Pierre said, "You're good in French . . ."

I said, "How good in French?"

Around lunchtime, Pierre introduced me to André, his co-creative director. They shared an office. André was stocky, long-haired, orthodontic. He grinned like Animal from the Muppets. I liked him right away. Probably ate scissors for lunch.

"André doesn't speak English," Pierre said.

"Fuck that," André said in English, staring at me. He added, smiling, "But no, do not."

A computer monitor attached to André's laptop showed two nude women sixty-nining. André had on a pink Lacoste shirt and a blazer with two lapels, one folded up. It was the first jacket I'd ever seen that included a constantly popped collar, suggesting, *Dude, let your clothes handle the boil, you're busy musing*. At that moment, André's boots were perched on an Italian racing bicycle. People informed me later that he never rode it—it was parked there only to keep beauty in near proximity.

I told André I liked his office. André grinned, then his BlackBerry began to chirrup. André ignored it and said in English, "So, where you come?"

"Come from," Pierre corrected him.

"New York," I said.

The BlackBerry kept ringing. André grabbed it like it was a

burning club and screamed down the line while rampaging out of the room.

In a short while, I'd figured out the e-mail system and how to remap my keyboard; as long as I didn't look too closely at what I was doing, it would perform like a QWERTY layout and communicate my intentions. Perhaps this will become a metaphor, I thought. Then my calendar program started making a boingy sound. It said I was late for a *réunion* on the sixth floor.

Getting my *étages* wrong, I wound up in a law firm. The receptionist was prickly: I was due for a meeting where? With whom?

On the proper floor, I asked an IT guy for directions. He said a bunch of things and gestured with his arm. Tried a hallway: dead end. Backtracked, tried another hallway. Oh, you're dead, I told myself. Around me people were speaking French into headsets, wearing scarves despite the heat. Finally I found a conference room, took an empty chair, and apologized to a horseshoe of elders who were watching a PowerPoint presentation—"*Désolé*," I said, catching my breath, "*désolé*."

A woman wearing a white suit and white eyeglasses said in English, "Excuse me, who are you looking for?"

Kind of bold, I thought, matching your pantsuit to your glasses.

Finally, down the hall, in the right conference room, I met Claude, a senior account director, who assured me I was where I belonged.

"Dude, you're from, like, New York? So cool, man," Claude said in English. Claude was skinny and smelled of cigarettes, with arms sunburned to the color of traffic cones. "I love New York," he said. "Why did you leave? You know, no one goes New York to Paris."

Claude said he'd recently returned from the beach. "Just the total best, dude, Antibes. You haven't been? You must go with me sometime."

Behind me, a breeze suckled the blinds from a large open

window. The view spanned Paris, one of those views that came with sunshine and clarinets, from the Eiffel Tower to the Grand Palais, to the fondant of the Sacré Cœur.

I wanted to levitate right out of the room.

Claude asked if I was married and what girls were like in New York. "They're easy, right, easy pussy? Like you're just going down the street"—Claude mimed a drum major swinging his arms; he found it hilarious and exciting—"and there's one! And there!"

Slowly, about a dozen young French people turned up—art directors, copywriters, project managers, programmers—nodding with afternoon fatigue. They helped themselves to Coke and Coca Light from plastic bottles shaped like petite scuba tanks, and Claude began the meeting. "Okay, so hey, meet this guy . . ." Claude paused before saying my name. Truthfully it was a pain in French, all those "R"s. Claude asked in French if I had any introductory remarks. I said, "*Excusez-moi?*" People laughed, and I laughed, too, a survival reflex or whatever. I said, "*Non.*" Claude explained to the group that I was there that afternoon only to listen. "*Mais demain matin, nous aurons un brainstorming* . . . with this dude." Claude gestured at me and winked.

An hour later, I had no idea what my assignment was, what I'd be called upon to do, or when I'd be required to do it.

In the beginning of my job, I had a look: toddler struggling with digestion. I saw it reflected back at me in people's sunglasses, absorbed by my coworkers' eyes. They weren't used to an American coming up so close, being such a worried listener—me pressing in with my nervous smile, my jaw clamped, my forehead rippling with humps like a Klingon's.

Why couldn't I have found a job in Sydney or Cape Town, where the surf brahs communicated by vibe?

What had I done?

2

My seventh-grade French teacher, Madame Fleuriot, wore brown nylons, high heels, and yielding sweaters. She had a bouffant hairdo of cotton candy that melted in the rain when she forgot her kerchief. Madame's bosom was substantial: a single body. I remembered it bobbing around the room. Who knows what the other boys thought about Madame, but there was something I found intriguing—her high laugh, her dismissive tone. When we didn't know a French noun's gender, Madame Fleuriot mocked us. Wasn't it obvious, the pen's masculinity? The crockery's curves?

In her class, we learned that most of life in France wasn't intended for children. Madame would sigh, "You are too young to understand."

At the end of the year, Madame Fleuriot threw us a party. She hung *tricolore* ribbons in the windows and taught us how to make crêpes. All the butter seemed to relax Madame's posture. She reclined on her desk and swung her feet. She told us, If ever we were lucky enough to visit Paris . . .

Just the word "Paris," she was undone a bit.

Around that time, my mother brought home *Charade*, a murder mystery set in Paris with Audrey Hepburn and Cary Grant. First time we watched it, in the den, my mother announced that *Charade* was her favorite movie.

It was the first time I'd heard her say she had a favorite anything.

Mom taught nursery school; Dad sold textiles. We lived in hell: suburban Connecticut. One year, when I was fourteen, my parents took me and my little sister, Leslie, for a week's vacation in Paris. Our hotel, near Place Saint-Sulpice, was minuscule. Leslie and I barely got our luggage into the room. That first morning, we were staggering from jet lag. Our mother was already in the dining room; she looked primed. Back at home, she'd said what she wanted most from Paris was the coffee, the morning coffee. She ordered *café au lait, très noir*. When the coffee was ready, the waiter brought it out on a silver tray and served it ceremoniously, pouring espresso from one little pot, milk from another, the two streams melding in the cup.

My mother held the coffee below her nose. Her cheeks flushed.

I'd never seen my mother as a woman before, a woman powerfully contented.

That's when I began drinking coffee. I was hung up on every little thing. I *loved* Paris, and felt straightaway at home. Not to be grandiose, but it seemed like the city had been waiting for me. The air was adhesive, hot, and fragrant, and we walked the city up and down and saw everything. Even my sister got into it: she ate from every crêpe stand we passed. My mother would say afterward, "I don't think she ate a single meal inside a building."

Toward the end of the week, at a men's store that resembled a cottage, my dad told me to choose something for myself, anything. I picked a red-and-white shirt with a button-down collar—the first piece of adult clothing I'd ever wanted to wear.

Too quickly, we were back in Connecticut.

In school, Madame Fleuriot's video days were notorious. Our lessons were based on a program, *Voix et Images de France* (Voices and Images of France), that featured a family in Paris called the Thibaults, who lived at number 10 Place d'Italie. Monsieur

Thibault was an engineer—*Monsieur Thibault est ingénieur.* Madame Thibault, a homemaker, took care of the children, Paul and Catherine, who looked miserable. There were two college students in the lessons, Robert and Mireille, who were also boyfriend-girlfriend. Mireille was a hot blonde, maybe nineteen. Every episode, she wore the same red skirt and white blouse—big tits, big hips, long hair, and if Robert was infatuated with Mireille, so were we.

For example, one day, visiting the Tuileries Gardens, Mireille took a table at an outdoor café. Spring in Paris, too good to be true, how lovely! But she was thirsty—well, who wouldn't be?—so Mireille ordered a kir royale. However, *ooh la la*, when the waiter returned with her drink, he spilled the whole thing down her front.

"What's so funny?" Madame Fleuriot said, pausing the VCR. She studied the screen, where Mireille's breasts and nipples were plainly showing through her blouse.

"Ah, you boys," Madame said, "please, grow up."

Madame laughed and relaxed, one hand perched on the TV cart. Mireille remained paused, pendulous.

"Now, a kir royale," Madame said. "You know this? It really is delicious. You're too young, of course." How we disappointed her. "In Paris, children do not drink to get drunk. Excuse me. Now, kir royale."

"Kir royale," we said.

"Mostly it's champagne," Madame said, "but with cassis, just a few drops? It's really wonderful. On a summer afternoon?"

Later in the year, Madame showed us a 1980s French movie called *La Boum*. At one point in the film, some teenagers go to the *cinéma*, and a boy sticks his penis into a popcorn box so the girl sitting next to him will jerk him off. But we weren't shocked. We were turning fourteen, we knew about those sorts of things.

Stuff like that happened in Paris. Plus, it wasn't cool to make a big deal about anything.

"French" became an umbrella term for me, describing things I liked before I knew why I liked them. But Paris was different. Paris was an umbrella, a dream I carried around in case the weather turned bad.

3

After college, I moved to New York City and began waking up early to write fiction. So far, I'd completed two novels—both were dreck—and set about writing a third, plus started an online magazine with a friend. But none of that paid much, so for the rest of the day I wrote anything that earned money. Pet-grooming articles. Real-estate brochures. At one point, I had a column in a magazine published exclusively for American Express "black card" members. They hired me to write what was characterized as luxury humor. "Oh, you know," a woman's voice said over the phone, from high above Sixth Avenue and Forty-third Street, "wine, châteaux, jokes about Greece. Can't you do that?"

Shortly after I replied to Pierre's e-mail, the agency flew me to Paris for an interview. It all happened pretty fast. Pierre let me crash on his floor and drove me to the office on his Vespa—at a stoplight he shouted, "There are handles under the seat, you do not need to hold me."

We had a meeting with Pierre's boss, Bernard. Bernard had long hair and chewed gum. He wore Beatle boots and a slim black suit and spoke perfect English, with a Valley girl's cadences.

During the interview, to compensate for my lack of credentials in advertising, Pierre said things like, "Luxury humor is the type of fresh thinking we need." I spoke a little French; Bernard suggested I stop. "You can learn this later." He wanted to know, Bernard said, how I felt about doing presentations.

"So, look, there's a lot of global business out there. We need, like, a hundred of you," he said. "English-speakers, I mean."

Bernard stared at me for a few seconds, snapping his gum. "Okay, well," he said, continuing in English, "so how do you feel about Paris, good?"

"*J'adore Paris*," I said.

"Who doesn't?" Bernard flipped through some folders for a moment, then looked up, as if he'd forgotten why I was there. "So . . . we'll see how it goes. Pierre, do we have any other business to discuss?"

That was the interview.

Three weeks later, I returned to Paris to find an apartment. The agency provided me with an HR representative and a real-estate agent to show me around. Extremely generous of them, I thought. We saw eleven apartments in nine hours. The agent was serious about her business. She rarely smiled, driving us in her small Peugeot. The HR rep was friendlier, with peachy skin and a high, screwy laugh. All day long, we crisscrossed the city, and I could barely keep track of the neighborhoods, the *arrondissements*.

Back in Brooklyn, I'd spent hours reviewing apartment listings on websites for expats. The descriptions were dreamy and confusing:

> Exclusive EXCLUSIVITY: Magnificent studio. Totally renewed, last floor, sight loosened on Paris. Beautiful room to be lived, with U.S.-equipped cooking (oven, patches, refrigerator). Public prosecutor's department. Very brilliant: several windows. SdE with wc. Close any conveniences. Immediate availability. To seize!

The first apartment was above a farmer's market near the Sorbonne, on the Left Bank. The location was Paris Magnificent. Many cheesemongers nearby, booksellers, and *tabacs*. It was the area known as the home of Sartre and Hemingway, the old boys you saw on postcards for €2.25. We waited for ten minutes to be let into the building, and the agent checked e-mail on her smartphone. A lot, I thought, had happened since the days of Hemingway. Luke Skywalker had happened. Supermarkets happened. Hip-hop happened and Joan Didion happened. E-mail happened. More relevant to Paris, there was 1968 and Les Halles razed, there were Mitterand's *grand projets* and Serge Gainsbourg buried in Montparnasse.

The landlord arrived and we climbed upstairs, where the apartment did not reflect the Left Bank's glory. It reflected us. It was a 1970s party pit and the owner had gone in for mirroring. Walls in the bedroom were mirrored. The headboard was mirrored and cabinets were mirrored. The breakfast bar would be good for doing cocaine.

"Do you like it?" the agent asked in French.

"*Ce n'est pas terrible*," I said, focusing on my annunciation.

She said, "What would you prefer to see?"

I glanced at a pair of chairs upholstered in red leopard. I did not want to seize them.

"*S'il vous plaît*," I said slowly, "*moins des chaises des animaux?*

"*Merci beaucoup*," I added.

The next two apartments were under construction. A fourth apartment, north of the Luxembourg Gardens on a demure, quintessential Parisian street, was all green. Green walls, green drapes, green furniture. Kitchen appliances in avocado. The only thing that wasn't green (the doorknobs were green) was in the bedroom, behind a chair: a large trompe l'oeil painting of women's lingerie hanging on knobs.

We were in a Folies Bergère dressing room.

"Not bad," said the agent. The HR representative agreed and went close to admire the work. The agent saw my face. "Wait, we're in Paris," she said. "It is creative, the capital of creative. Americans love this."

"*Je suis d'accord,*" I said. ". . . *Peut-être moins créatif?*"

Before we moved on, the HR rep said, "We thought you were creative."

Rue de Harlay. Sauf Accès Parc. Interdit. Honestly, even the street signs were nourishment; I was in a mood to drive around Paris all day long. First we went for lunch on Ile de la Cité, one of the islands on the Seine, where Paris had begun. The agent took us to Place Dauphine, behind Pont Neuf. We occupied a sidewalk table. The sun was so close we could have plucked it.

Just unbelievable, the idea I'd be living there soon.

The women required two minutes to confirm they would order different plates of charcuterie, then came wine selection:

"You think a Sancerre?"

"Oh no, not a Sancerre."

"No. Stupid of me."

"What about rosé?"

"But a good rosé."

"Yes, yes, a good rosé, it would be perfect. From where, though?"

"From Aix?"

"Ah, Aix . . ."

The next apartment, a loft nearby, was across the street from La Conciergerie, a fortress from the Middle Ages that once had been the "antechamber to the guillotine." The stairs we climbed were centuries old, tacky with black mold.

"Ah, the charm," the agent sighed. She paused on a landing for the HR representative to agree. The HR rep nodded, breathless from the climb.

Inside, I shielded my eyes, the loft was so bright. The apartment was wild. Windows overlooking Notre Dame's gargoyles, showing the Seine flowing east and west. *Sight loosened on Paris.*

The bathroom was all marble; it had a bathtub with a view and river breezes. And the rent, the agent said, was nothing.

Unfortunately, the apartment was about the size of the agent's car.

"Yes, it's too small," she said, patrolling the room in about four steps. "You will hit your head. And you are bringing your wife. You will need space."

The agent stopped dead next to the bathtub. Both of us took in the view of Notre Dame's spires. The agent tugged up her suede boots and said she had an idea.

"Listen," she confided, "now suppose you want to have an affair. Men in Paris . . . Just remember this place. It would be perfect for that."

The HR woman said, "The size would be just right."

She was sitting on the bed, patting the duvet. She smiled at me, blinked behind her glasses, and laughed. She said in English, "Nice bed, hey?"

My flight home was scheduled for early the next morning. Pierre and his wife, Chloe, said I shouldn't sleep, instead they'd invite six friends for dinner—it was the Parisian thing to do.

That night, I caught maybe 10 percent of the French spoken. Lots of talk about films and politics. Everyone knew one another from art school. Everyone smoked. Someone brought up the Minitel; I'd never heard of it. "It is a version of the Internet that the French invented," one guy told me in English. "No one beyond France desired it, for some reason."

Pierre and Chloe were native Parisians. Chloe was my age, Pierre was a little older. They had two young boys who were asleep upstairs, who were accustomed to their parents throwing noisy dinner parties. Pierre was big and tall, dark-haired, with glasses. Gregarious, upbeat, always laughing. Chloe was very pretty, slender, with short black hair and a tiny beauty mark.

Both were Parisian from two hundred feet: careless, chic, self-possessed; bon vivant in dress and manner; cigarettes, turtlenecks, et cetera.

Around midnight, we were finishing off the wine when one of Pierre's friends told a story about his grandmother, who lived in the countryside outside Paris, and how she recently had gone to the market in her village and bought a piece of cheese. When she brought it home, she realized the cheese was bad, and this made her furious, so she threw the cheese out the window and hit a cow.

People laughed. Pierre said to me in English, "Did you follow that?"

"Of course," I said. "About the cheese?"

"The cheese? What cheese?"

I recounted the whole story in English, which most of them understood: the grandmother, the cow. People exploded, laughing like a section of trombones. Pierre, who was crying he was laughing so hard, persevered to say that the story *actually* had been about his friend's *mother*. She'd been hiking and had been trampled by a runaway horse, breaking her leg. Ghastly news. The only funny bit had been something her doctor said to her in the hospital, how she should go back and break the horse's leg for revenge.

People started laughing all over again.

For the rest of the night, until two a.m., I sat next to Pierre and Chloe's stereo and didn't speak, pretending to be too stoned. Songs by the American rapper Young Jeezy were playing. He was "The Realest," and he could laugh about life's ups and downs with his trademark *Ahaaaaa*. Meanwhile I was counting my drinks, plunging into a long stare.

I thought: *Jeezy, I don't know what it's like to have my phone tapped by the feds, but I hear what you're saying. Literally: I understand every word. And I acknowledge that if we met in real life we'd have nothing in common. But right now you're all I've got.*

Or maybe I wasn't pretending to be too stoned.

Three-thirty in the morning, after Pierre and Chloe's friends had gone, I went out to the balcony. Paris below me was an empty chapel. No one was out. The big train station, Gare du Nord, was in sight, with tracks and cables like vines on the ground. Each neighboring building had a terrace for a headdress, and curved blue rooftops like hulls of ships upside down—and they'd stood there how long? Had stood above how many Americans in Paris passing through? I experienced a dizzy spell and clutched the railing. Below me, two girls floated home on bicycles cooing to each other. The sound of a scooter came around a corner, followed by its little dark sentry. No stores were open, the city was shut at that hour, and the air smelled of laundry that hadn't dried.

O Paris dawns . . .

That morning, sneaking out of Pierre and Chloe's apartment, hoisting my black travel bag on my shoulder, I knew again that I wanted all of it. No matter how many conversations I misunderstood. I couldn't imagine loving Paris less, only more.

4

The advertising agency paid for me to take three hours of French lessons before we moved, to acquaint myself with contemporary business vocabulary. I found an instructor, Gabrielle, who taught from a room overlooking a Manhattan parking garage. At the beginning of my first lesson, Gabrielle gave me a booklet of business vocabulary: *la souris*, the mouse; *l'ordinateur*, the computer; *le Mac*, the Macintosh computer. Gabrielle said this last term would be helpful, since I'd be working in advertising with *les créatifs*, creative people. Mostly we talked about Gabrielle. She was a frizzy-haired Belgian who wore a vest and a silk scarf in a manner of attempted, botched fashion. Gabrielle said she'd never worked in an office, she herself preferred to be mobile, *mobile*.

"*Ah*," I said, "*mais est-ce que vous avez une mobile?*"

Gabrielle took this as an affront. "Of course I do," she said, showing me her cell phone. "Don't you?"

At the end of our first lesson, Gabrielle said in English, "My boyfriend lives in Paris." When I asked what he did, where he lived in Paris, she said, "He is an Internet boyfriend."

During lesson two, Gabrielle told me she was tired of being a French-teaching mercenary. She'd taught in China and Romania. Now she lived with two other Belgians in a walk-up in Queens. Advertising could be a little break, she wondered. After all, she, too, had dreamed of living in Paris since she was little. If I could do it, why not she?

"Do you know," Gabrielle said, "if they are hiring more? Here is my personal e-mail," she said, scribbling it on her business card.

To finance the move, Rachel and I sold our bed, mattress, dresser, dining table, and stereo. We packed ten duffel bags, each weighing the maximum amount allowed on the plane, containing clothes, books, a nonstick frying pan, my tennis racquets, and a quarter of Rachel's shoes. At the airport, the check-in clerk said *ohnonononononono*. We'd been told wrong, she said, ten huge bags were too many, we'd need to leave at least two behind. After ten minutes and a phone call to her boss, she said *okayfinefinefinefinefine*, as long as we paid a bunch of fees, which were nearly the equivalent of a third ticket.

In Paris, when we landed, our luggage filled three carts. The horizon at five a.m., beyond the lights of Charles de Gaulle Airport, was densely black. Outside baggage claim, a man approached me holding a pair of cell phones. He wore two Bluetooth dongles: a plastic oyster squashed into each ear.

"You need a car to Paris?" He was glancing at some police officers.

"*Avez-vous une grande voiture?*" I said. "*Comme un camion?*"

But already he was pushing 180 pounds of our stuff toward a revolving door.

During the drive into Paris, my nerves were fizzy, so I took the opportunity to practice my French. *Where are you from? Do you own your own business? Would you recommend your cellphone provider to me? What kind of data plan do they offer?*

"Hey," he said, driving while texting, "*bequeil.*"

Oh, I couldn't place the word, I said.

"*Queil*," he repeated while typing, "*bequeil.*"

I apologized twice in French, adding, "*Je préfère que mon français est bon, mais je ne sais pas*—"

The driver put down his phone, looked at me, and touched my arm.

"Man, *be cool*," he said. "Okay?"

Beyond the highway, the outskirts of Paris came into view. Many billboards advertising cell phones and cars. Motels built on top of shuttered stores, and train platforms teeming with ants carrying shoulder bags. Some sooty buildings from the nineteenth century, though most were from 1972. We were still miles away from Paris proper, the Pont Neuf's splendid views; when traffic was bad, the airport could be an hour by car. Still, the deep blue dawn was somehow very French-seeming. On a billboard beside the highway, George Clooney smiled at us and held out an espresso.

When we pulled into the courtyard of our building, I didn't know how much to tip, so I gave the driver twenty euros. Way too much. He was about to return it, but gave me his business card instead, imprinting it into my palm. He made me promise to call him anytime for anything, day or night.

Rachel said, "We made it. Wow, even our luggage made it."

In fact, we were early. Our landlord wasn't scheduled to arrive for thirty minutes to let us in, so I moved our bags inside a ground-floor vestibule, then went out to buy cigarettes. The courtyard door buzzed and clicked, and now I was in Paris, our new home.

Our street, Rue Béranger, was narrow, one-way. Shops on the ground floor, apartments above. Stores were opening. Men and women zigzagged to work. The city smelled terrific, of the river and *boulangeries*, street-cleaning crews and summer mornings. I set out down the block. The closest *tabac*, around the corner, was full of commuters, coffee drinkers, plus a work crew in blue overalls drinking white wine out of delicate little glasses. I knew the phrase: *Un petit blanc sec*. On one TV, they were watching a horse race, the news on another.

I wore a gigantic smile and ordered *un café*.

When I returned, Rachel said she'd met someone, a tradesman with a message.

"I memorized it," Rachel said. "He told me, '*Je ne parle pas très bien français*.' "

I said, "Why would he tell you he didn't speak very good French?"

"What?" Rachel said. "No, he asked me some question in French. I had no idea, so I said what I'd memorized, *Excusez-moi, je suis desolée, je ne parle pas bon français*. Then he said, '*Non, je ne parle pas*—' "

"Right," I said, lighting a cigarette. "He was correcting you. Baby, I'm sorry, he was just telling you what you should have been saying."

The cigarette tasted disgusting. I squashed it underfoot and kicked it down a storm drain.

That night we went across the street to a glass-roofed passageway and took a table in the back of what seemed like a charming little bistro. It turned out to be an Australian bar; they served ostrich fillets in addition to *gigot d'agneau*. The air inside was sweltering. The walls were decorated with X-rated cartoons, with people shaped like sausages having an orgy on the beach. One table over, French office workers were crashing together beer glasses to celebrate someone's *anniversaire*. Rachel and I got two orders of *steak frites*, and a carafe of red wine to split. The food took forever to arrive and tasted horrible, daubs of gray on greasy plates. But I was too thrilled to notice—Rachel, too, from the look on her face. We couldn't see straight from all the smoke, but more from delight, because there we were, eating *steak frites* in Paris around the corner from our own apartment, ostrich meat be damned.

I was exhausted. So much was astonishing.

5

Paris's neighborhoods, the *arrondissements*, are organized like a twist. They spiral from the river like toilet water flushing in reverse and erupting out of the bowl—a corkscrew or what have you, a flattened pig's tail, a whorling braid notched one to twenty. But if you walk from one neighborhood to the next, there is little to suggest the numbers changing. So it was confusing. Anyway, if you began in the middle of the Seine and snaked around, we lived on the Right Bank in the top of the third arrondissement, called the *haut* Marais, the upper Marais, on Rue Béranger, a quiet little street curling down from Place de la République.

We'd chosen the apartment so we could be within walking distance of nearly everything. I'd overlooked its darkness and short ceilings for location's sake: fifteen minutes to Notre Dame; twenty-five to the Louvre.

Earlier generations of Americans wanted to live on the other side of the Seine, in the Latin Quarter, where artists and students rambled, but the Left Bank had long ago priced out the artists and students. Now it was home to the rich of Paris, the wealthy of the retired-expat class, and Russian moguls, while the youthful and creative tended to live on the Right Bank, especially in the higher, cheaper numbers, the nineteenth or the twentieth—if not the Right Bank of Berlin, or Toronto.

But we were very happy about our neighborhood, if not our quarters. Our apartment, located above a costume jewelry shop, was dismal and dark. The apartment above us was being renovated—I hadn't heard the noises during my initial visit. So during our first days—we had a solid week before I was required at work—we tried to get out as much as possible.

Behind our street was a village of elbow streets, sunny walls and filthy corners, and many tucked-away shops. A ten-minute walk south was the proper Marais, the former Jewish quarter that had become a trendy shopping zone, but our northern district was still untrafficked. There were tailors and art galleries. Cafés and butchers. A store that sold athletic trophies and one that sold model trains. A blood-samples lab, a computer-repair agency, a video rental. On a leafy corner was a brightly lit lingerie-and-sex-toy boutique.

And where roads didn't cross was an old covered market, the Marché du Temple, blue with a dirty glass roof. Some weekends, men trucked in what appeared to be stolen leather goods, but otherwise the market stood empty—Thursdays, maybe it was Tuesdays, a tennis league strung up nets inside—and the surrounding quadrant would be filled with people dawdling over café tables that they'd occupy for hours, chatting with friends. Then behind the market was Rue Bretagne, a picturesque street that wasn't trendy yet. It would be soon, but not yet. Rue Bretagne had a park with a playground, two bookstores, a boutique that sold vintage radios, a booth that sold found photographs—it was the Left Bank I'd seen in picture books, preserved in time. At the center stood the oldest Paris farmer's market still operating, Le Marché des Enfants Rouges, built in the 1600s, now ringed by food stalls that sold Moroccan tagines, huge piles of Turkish desserts, West African stews, even sushi.

It was fantastic.

Rachel and I tramped from dawn to late at night, and collapsed each evening. We also spent a lot of time having our pictures taken. Every service we signed up for in Paris—cell phones, Internet, electricity—required passport photos, with strict rules about their composure. On two separate occasions, we were asked to resubmit our photos; too much smiling. No visible happiness was allowed in official pictures—*pas de sourire, visage dégagé*.

To become Parisian was business *très serieux*.

Anyway, we set up home: bought dishes, stocked the larder, purchased a mop and broom. We ate cheaply so we could afford a few good meals, including an expensive lunch one day inside the Musée d'Orsay, under rows of dazzling chandeliers, where we drank too much wine. Later we got caught in a rainstorm, running for shelter alongside the Seine. That week we must have seen . . . we saw a lot. But there were also errands to do.

For example, we visited a bank to open a checking account and apply for a credit card. Well, France didn't have credit cards. Perhaps didn't grasp them, conceptually—it wasn't clear. The bank representative, who did not speak English, said I shouldn't be bothered, that yes, our accounts included debit cards.

"No," I said in French, "I apply for a card of credit."

"This is what you have, a debit card," she said.

"No. The debit card, it takes money, when I *have* money," I said, going slowly to find the words. "I want a card that does not have a need for money."

The banker rumbled it for a second. "Well," she said, "we have an option where the card does not remove the money until the end of the month. Is that what you want?"

"No," I said. "Something different." I smiled cheerfully and tried again. "I want the card when I do not have money."

"Maybe I do not understand," she said. "What type of bank has cards like these?"

"American banks," I said. "For example, if I want a computer for two thousand euros, but I do not have two thousand euros? I have a card. The card buys the computer. I give money to the card. Each month, a little money. Then: two thousand euros."

"Ah," the banker said, pleased now, "you would like to arrange a loan!"

"Yes, but no," I said. "I want a card. A card that gives a loan."

"I'm sorry, I don't understand, what kind of card again?" the clerk said.

"Its name is 'credit card,'" I said.

The clerk looked at me closely to make sure this wasn't all one big joke.

"I'm sorry," she said, "I do not think we have this in France."

Toward the end of our first week, Rachel and I were sneezing, dizzy, exhausted, light-headed, almost fainting, lacking jet fuel, and coughing up sea-green mucus.

"The Paris Flu," expats said. A persistent chest cold caused by French germs. "Everyone gets it," I was told over a drink in Beaubourg, by an editor at the *Herald Tribune*, a friend of a friend. "Trick is," he said, "you gotta eat the local honey. Go to that farmer's market near you, Enfants Rouges. Introduce antibodies to your system from the Paris bees. Make sure you look for the sticker that says the bees are from Paris, that's important."

The next day, after a morning rain, there was a huff of good weather, and Rachel and I went out and purchased the honey of local bees. Then our stove broke. I was eating honey off a Kit Kat when the repairman rang the buzzer.

The repairman looked at our stove and drew squiggles on a ticket. He made to leave, so I handed the ticket back to him and attempted to explain that I couldn't read his handwriting.

He wrote in block letters, CRÈME POUR LA PLAQUE.

So for lack of a creamy topping . . .

"The stove has plaque?" Rachel said from the doorway. She sniffled and went back into our living room, a cavern with dark beams.

I said quietly to the repairman, "Where do I find the cream for the plaque?"

But he'd already walked out. He was kind of a bastard.

In the hallway, he stopped in front of our neighbor's door. There were buzz-saw sounds, and sawdust pouring in through an open window from the apartment upstairs. The repairman snatched the paper back from me and scrawled in carpenter pencil, "BHV," then stomped downstairs, just avoiding a pregnant girl and her boyfriend.

"BHV," I announced, closing the door. "What's that?"

"Oh, the hardware store," Rachel said, "near Hôtel de Ville. *Bay-ash-vay*. It's the one with the lingerie section. I heard about it, I'll take you later."

Several letters arrived that week from the government. One said Rachel and I needed to be weighed, measured, and scanned for tuberculosis, immediately. Also, I'd be asked to pass a language test, since I'd be the one taking a job that could have gone to a French person.

Our appointment was the same day as the repairman's visit. The health clinic was located near Place de la Bastille, not far away. We were in that paunch of Paris summer when the heat ballooned at one p.m., and the weather was lovely in a vehement way, glares everywhere.

At the clinic, Rachel and I were assigned to different waiting areas. After X-rays and measurements, I was directed to a language examiner's office, for my French quiz.

"What do you do for a living?"

"I work in advertising."

"What do you do in advertising?"

"I write."

"What do you write?"

"I write for babies. Milk for babies."

"Where are you from?"

"New York City."

The examiner sat forward and said in English, "Wow, you are?" For five minutes she described to me how she was planning to visit Manhattan soon, it was a long-standing dream. "But isn't it very dangerous?" she asked in English, her consonants sharp as thorns. "Do blacks and whites really get along?"

We stopped for a bite to eat on the way home, in a café on the Boulevard Richard-Lenoir. We ordered some white wine and *frites*, which came served with awful ketchup—and here I'd thought Heinz was universal.

"So," Rachel said, "a lot of scientists have now seen me topless."

"Oh, I know the feeling," I said. I was holding my tuberculosis X-ray up to the window.

"Trust me, no, you don't," Rachel said.

She cinched her jacket, a green coat she'd bought especially for our move to France, and explained that things for women in Paris were quite different. "So the doctor is asking me questions. I have no idea what she's saying. I think she tells me to remove my top. I'm pointing—This, my bra, she wants off? Yes, she wants off. Then I'm instructed to leave. *Now that you're topless, please go out that door.* Only it's a door for a closet with a yellow bulb inside, and at the other end there's another door. I'm to go into the closet and wait for the other door to open."

Rachel drank some wine. "So I'm asking myself, do I cover up, or go out full-frontal? Because I want to do it right. Do it the French way. What would Chloe do? I figured, probably a Frenchwoman would just walk out, you know, breasts on parade."

"And?" I said.

"I went out French. The door opened, I checked my posture. It's a big room, like an operating theater, with three male technicians. But they barely notice me. I'm like, You're not even going to look? What does that say? Then I'm instructed to smoosh my chest against an upright X-ray machine, which was freezing, and they're saying, *Do it again, it's not quite right.* I mean, they're wearing lab coats, but they're also wearing jeans. How was I to know it wasn't some crazy French reality TV show?"

Friday evening of the weekend before my first day at work, Pierre and Chloe invited us over for dinner. In the same room where I'd slept during my interview weekend, we drank tequila and listened to Charles Trenet and Wu-Tang Clan until about three a.m., when Pierre and Chloe's downstairs neighbor complained about the noise.

Outside, the black sky combined Paris, summer, and the oncoming morning. Noises floated over our heads, but on Pierre and Chloe's street it was quiet enough to hear the traffic signals buzzing. To get home, we rented Vélibs. These were the new bicycles that Paris had installed in a bikes-for-rent program. They'd become the latest badge of chic. Misty mornings, columns of riders pedaled beside the river, and pictures were everywhere of bare-legged women cycling around town in Chanel. Columnists filed reports on Vélib trends, Vélib crime especially—how the city's bright young things rode Vélibs home after partying and crashed them into the Seine.

On the map, one street, the Boulevard de Magenta, appeared to run straight to our apartment. We looked down the hill, and there it was: four empty lanes plunging into blackness, flanked by gracefully decaying Haussmann slabs brambly with iron balconies. Rachel went first, her dress flapping in the wind. There was neon in her hair, then she was eaten up by the dark. I took off after her, twenty feet behind. Fifty feet behind. Soon she was gone. The boulevard flattened out, but for all my pedaling I was slowing down.

Rachel reappeared and found me gliding, kicking with my toes. The chain had come off my bicycle and was grinding on the road. There was no one around.

"We shouldn't have had the tequila," Rachel said, pedaling a circle around me.

"No, no," I said, stopping, "not the tequila."

We stood next to a bus stop and stared around. A Vélib stand was nearby. We parked the bikes and walked home. It was one of those moments when nothing could go wrong.

The next morning I tried to take out the garbage, but the shed door wouldn't budge. I yanked it, banged on it, was about to quit when Asif, the *gardien*, our building manager, whose rooms abutted the shed, rattled his shutters and yelled at me to shut up.

Asif came out, smoking. He wore an unbuttoned paisley shirt and blue jeans with embroidery on the seat. Asif appraised me and said something in French. I didn't understand and attempted a retreat. That just pissed him off more. He whipped back his hair and snatched my trash, unlocked the shed, and tossed the bag inside.

His hair had the slow-motion buoyancy of a mermaid's.

"I'm sorry," I said. "But I do not have a key."

"Give me your keys," Asif snapped in French, with a destabilizing Pakistani accent. I could barely understand him. He was tall and lank, posing like a model. He pinched the neck of a four-inch key on my key ring and handed it back to me with two fingers, like a silver snake.

"You're American?"

"From New York," I said. "My wife," I said, pointing at our bedroom window, just above his head.

"I love New York," Asif said. "I'm going soon. You'll tell me where your family lives?"

He pulled me inside his rooms. They smelled of sex. A cute brunette in a bathrobe was sautéeing peppers and chicken. She smiled at me. Asif downed some whiskey from a glass on top of a trash can, and poured us shots. We did a toast to New York City.

He gripped my arms, beaming. When I explained I needed to go run errands (*faire les courses*), Asif went slack. "Fine, then leave!" he shouted, frowning, and disappeared into the bedroom.

Over time, I'd learn that Asif gained and lost euphoria faster than anyone I'd ever met.

That same morning, Rachel and I walked down to BHV, the home-and-hardware store with a lingerie section—it also had a jewelry section, and cabinets of designer handbags, and a lumberyard in the basement, and a kitchen-items section with space for cooking classes—where we bought cream for our stove. Turns out the cream worked. Our coils didn't conduct electricity when they lacked moisturizer; apparently they'd gone dairy-free too long. And the same day, just when we couldn't face one more spoonful of honey, our flu vanished.

We lived in Paris, Paris being not only the city of milk and honey, but also the city where milk and honey were solutions.

No one wonders, because who needs to ask?

That afternoon, we walked halfway across the city and rode a bus home, and collapsed in bed. Lying there on top of the comforter, staring at the dark beams crossing the white plaster ceiling, suddenly I was anxious and out of breath, overpowered by homesickness.

I wanted out of that apartment, out of Paris, as fast as possible.

Rachel said something into her pillow about being hungry. Ice cream, I said, I'll go get ice cream.

I don't even like ice cream that much.

I ran outside, *le monde à mes pieds*, to Place de la République, the large traffic circle behind our apartment. République was a racetrack with four lanes of vehicles whipping around two parks. No square in America looked so majestic, yet in Paris République was considered a retail zone—hardly special except for being where protesters gathered whenever the government threatened to raise the retirement age. In the center was a statue of a robed woman. She was Marianne, symbol of the French Republic, proud and tall, perhaps unaware that her robe was slipping. In several ways, she reminded me of Mireille. I stood on an island in the middle of the Boulevard Saint-Martin, which flowed into République, and waited through several traffic lights, just watching. New, new, new, I was thinking. Our previous life would be reversed within twenty-four hours: me working in an office, in a language I barely spoke, and Rachel at home writing when she wasn't attending French lessons. Was this a good idea? Was it the right thing to do?

It seemed like a colossal mistake.

But would I really prefer to be anywhere else? Hadn't Rachel's breasts passed inspection by Parisian experts? As long as no one talked to me about topics other than New York, wouldn't I be fine?

I was scared. Well, so what?

I got the ice cream. We ate it in bed. Through the windows came fragrances from the trees outside and Asif's vegetable garden. We heard only birdsong. I remembered a letter Edith Wharton wrote about Paris in 1907 that I'd seen excerpted in a magazine back in the States: "The tranquil majesty of the architectural lines, the wonderful blurred winter lights, the long lines of lamps garlanding the avenues & the quays—*je l'ai dans mon sang!*" ("I have it in my blood!")

At the time, I'd thought I knew what she meant. But now I knew.

6

At the end of my first day at work, around seven p.m., Pierre introduced me to my new wife, Bruno. In advertising, copywriters and art directors work in pairs. Bruno and I would be overseeing an infant-nutrition account together, Pierre said.

Bruno approached me with a chuckling grimace. I tried to kiss him. No doing. For months I'd get that wrong. All day, I'd watched coworkers greet each other with a peck, the kissing version of Hey, what's up. But Bruno backed away. Instead we shook hands and grunted hello, *bonjour*, the way children do when one is new and the other has been asked to show him around school.

Still, Bruno offered me some madeleines he'd just bought from the vending machine.

No matter what happened, Bruno always meant well.

Bruno was a late-thirties Parisian, stocky and morose. Year-round, he was reddishly tan, with a rosy flush that became a glower the more he drank. Bruno was roughly good-looking. His lips were plump, and one ear was scarred from rugby. There was a good deal in Bruno—his sad confidence, his ponderous horniness—for women to get hooked on. Over time, we'd talk a lot about girls. Bruno liked a good time. He liked wine, photography, gourmet food, the sea, and the hours he spent on Sundays repairing antique furniture. For Bruno, cigarettes were life itself. Same for his Yamaha scooter.

In the beginning, Bruno's English was even worse than my

French. Pierre left the room, and Bruno tried to explain the project we'd be working on together. We didn't get far. Finally he said something like, Drinks? You like a glass? Glass of wine?

Hot summer evening outside, brightly yellow. A very windy Paris twilight, with dust pluming from cars going around the Arc de Triomphe. Bruno led us away from the Champs-Elysées to nearby Boulevard Haussmann, a regal side avenue of shops, restaurants, and white limestone buildings. We took seats at a sidewalk café. Gorgeous people walked by, going home, talking on their *mobiles*. Bruno sat under a machine shaped like a palm tree that sucked up smoke. He lit a cigarette, unpopped a shirt button nonchalantly, ordered Sancerre, and began talking over my head. After fifteen minutes, I understood that he'd worked on the infant-nutrition project for eleven months, ever since he'd joined the agency. They'd gone through four copywriters in the same amount of time; I was number five.

Bruno said, *Reservoir Dogs*, did I know this film?

"*Bien sûr*," I said, adding, "Mr. Pink?"

"Okay, good," Bruno said in English. "Then, Mr. Pink . . . do not be this. Do not be saying in the office, 'Fuck, fuck, fuck.' "

Evidently Bruno had overheard me swearing. He wanted me to know that cursing wasn't cool in Parisian office culture. It seemed to weigh on Bruno, speaking English like that, correcting my behavior. As though envisioning trials to come.

Bruno paid the bill in coins and wiggled out his cigarette.

Back in République, the day's heat was trembling, about to drop. Just like me. After nine hours of French, all I wanted was to snort some Excedrin, eat a meal *gargantuesque*, and sleep for two months.

Rachel and I decided on a café around the corner from our apartment, Café Crème on Rue Dupetit-Thouars. We managed to snag an outside table with a view of the blue market. But what a marvelous evening to be outside in Paris! Never-ending light. The buzz of *apéritifs*. Cafés full of disheveled girls smoking cigarettes and their boyfriends fluffing their hair once they'd set down their helmets. So many hello kisses—just another night in northern Europe. Back in the day, it might have been Le Dôme, or Deux Magots, only here everyone was twenty-first-century Parisian: dining on the Right Bank, and before they stacked their Camels and lighters on the table, first they laid down their Nokias.

After twenty minutes, a waitress turned up and propped a menu on the table. The day's dishes, in addition to traditional fare, included three types of cheeseburger.

Afterward, at home, a neighbor across the courtyard waved at me while he smoked a cigarette on his balcony. In the next window, a woman was preparing dinner in their kitchen. Two weeks later, I'd see him screwing her there while they both watched a news show on TV, and I'd be reminded of a Joan Rivers joke about the benefits of sex like that, how a woman's in a position to be productive and accomplish other things, like read a magazine.

Rachel and I both collapsed on top of the covers. I was asleep in two minutes.

A pattern emerged: whenever, wherever, I would glue my foot to the roof of my mouth.

Third day at the office, I was visiting the canteen to get two cups of water, one for me, one for Tomaso, who had the desk next to mine. The canteen wasn't so much a cafeteria as a Beaux-Arts salon with an enormous white cube in the middle, a sleek modern design structure that puzzlingly contained restrooms and a kitchen. From a distance it looked more like a contemporary art installation. Basically it was a nine-foot-tall white Rubik's Cube with secret toilets, situated in the middle of a ballroom. Anyway, it was where people got coffee and ate lunch.

"You must be delicate," Tomaso had warned me; "the pressure from the water fountain in the kitchen is very strong." So I slid into the kitchen—it was about the size of a closet—and carefully filled my two cups. I turned to find a man blocking my way out. We'd met that morning. He was senior VP of something. Systems administration? His name was Philippe. Philippe lurched past me into the closet, our chests scrubbing together while I said *bonjour*. Philippe grunted. Then he held out a cup and smashed the button—I guess he hadn't talked to Tomaso—and the water fountain blasted his cup out of the closet, across the room.

"Wow," I said. A second later, I said in French, "The water, it comes *very* hard."

Philippe didn't hear me. He asked me to repeat myself.

"The water," I said, "it comes forcefully?"

Philippe still didn't understand, so I tried louder, with my embouchure resembling a puckered "o," per Pierre's instructions—to sound more Parisian. I also gestured by waving my arms, which made one of my cups spill its contents on the floor.

The other cup went down the front of Philippe's suit pants, filling one cuff with a moat.

Philippe stared at me. Incredibly, some water had gotten trapped in his trouser pleats, so when he bent over to look at his shoes, even more water splashed out. For a dramatic conclusion. I didn't know what to do. What could I say? Some part of me decided to make a joke. It was my gut reaction whenever shame fluttered around my head. I stammered in French, "Well, when I come, I guess I come hard, too."

It wasn't until that afternoon when I wrote Rachel an e-mail that I realized what I'd said. Rachel replied, "I think you crossed a line in the workplace that even Parisians respect."

SEND IN THE CLOUDS

FALL

—Kiss and tell me how—I help the agency lose millions of euros—The art of communicating breasts—Parisian office workers eat McDonald's differently—Most days Bruno is SAD and ANGRY—Rachel meets her new best friend—Sarkozy gets divorced—A day of instruction in French history and genital piercing—Our "cartes d'identité" *arrive—Thanksgiving is for Italy; Christmas is for France—Do the Bruno—*

7

At the end of summer, *la morte saison* finished and *le rentrée* commenced, when Parisians came home from their vacations brimming with satisfaction. All my coworkers turned up eight shades nuttier; they tanned splendidly well. Their first day back, I'd watch them step out of the elevator like so many show ponies, glistening brown stallions, frosted bronze mares.

The best French word I found for the most prevalent tone was *bistre*, same spelling in English: "A brownish-yellowish pigment made from the soot of burned wood."

One lunchtime, an HR woman who was tanned to a Kit Kat told me that, when it came to sunbathing, she preferred the natural look. We were standing on a balcony while she smoked a cigarette—every *étage* of our building featured balconies overlooking the Champs-Elysées, where people would go to eat lunch or take smoke breaks. Some guys would ogle cleavage below, calling out like mountaineers when they spotted a deep crevasse.

"You see?" the HR woman said, indicating a girl below us on the sidewalk. "Around the eyes, how ugly she seems?"

Proper tanning was less a class issue, she suggested, and more a question of aesthetic commitment. The HR woman pointed out that fake tanning produced a Creamsicle glow. The bone she had to pick, between deep breaths, wasn't whether to tan, but if a person tanned outdoors—in Provence, for a hide of crackling; in Brittany, where the ocean bestowed a speckled salt crust—or applied self-tanner, or spray-tanned, or visited a tanning salon.

The lesson being that fake tanners didn't properly enjoy life.

In the beginning, people were always trying to give me lessons.

The creative department, all we *créatifs*—copywriters, art directors, graphic designers, illustrators, information architects, video editors, Web-animation mathematicians—sat in clumps. My unit had five desks pushed together, where I was one of two expatriates, me and Tomaso, the Italian, and the rest were French. My art director, Bruno, worked down the hall.

To start, I didn't understand four-fifths of what was said. It was a bitch. But the problem ran both ways, which made it worse. Two neighbors of mine, Julie and Françoise, both Parisiennes, would peer at my lips whenever I spoke in French, then explain they hadn't understood a word I'd said.

Julie was a twentysomething copywriter, wide-eyed and attractive, a romantic poet outside of the office. A poem of hers I found on the Internet was about flowers, the beauty of stars, and how she, any evening, might die in bed.

Julie asked one afternoon, "You said you live on Rue Béranger, is that correct?" She spoke perfect, if slightly formal English. "Béranger was a famous poet, you know," Julie said. "In *Madame Bovary*, Flaubert made Charles read Béranger so he would seem of his era. Béranger is forgotten now. But that is life."

Many days, Julie's style was low-cut trousers with a visible, high-riding thong. All men in the office were Julie's property to tease. She sang cheerily while she worked, except when her computer crashed, then she cursed—her computer being among the few things that Julie could not bend to her will.

But Julie was very nice. Frequently she helped me translate my electric bill.

Françoise, a graphic designer, sat across from Julie. Like Julie, she found my name ridiculous, all those "R"s to roll. When someone said my name in the office, Françoise would parrot it by clearing her throat.

Next to Françoise was Olivier. Olivier was a jovial, bitter art director in his fifties, who'd worked at the agency for twenty-plus years. All day long, Olivier listened to electronica through headphones to scare away project managers should they fancy him to work faster. He was tall, bald, and droll. His laugh went *hohoho*, and to the rest of the office, Olivier was Father Christmas. Beautiful women—the building was full of them—constantly stopped by to visit and flirt and kiss Olivier's cheeks.

For some reason, Olivier hated me from the start.

Tomaso was a handsome Italian from Venice who loved Paul McCartney and the Police. He had curly black hair and got along with everyone. In addition to French and Italian, Tomaso was fluent in English (he did a good Sting: "*Roooooooxanne*") and would help me when I couldn't follow the gossip at our desks. For example, Julie was upset one afternoon, shouting in high-speed French, it having something to do with André and a new account she'd been assigned. I poked Tomaso, whispering, "What did Julie just say?"

"Ah, my poor Rosecrans," Tomaso said loudly. He shook his head. "Julie say you are one sexy motherfucker."

I repeated my question. Tomaso repeated his translation. Julie was fuming, blushing underneath her tan.

"Come, it's a nice thing," Tomaso said, patting my shoulder. "A compliment for a beautiful gentleman. You know, maybe she will sleep with you this evening."

"Tomaso," Julie yelled, "please shut up!"

In a new office, you tried to play it clean. You kept your head down and went about your work while attempting to fit into the groove, pure and cool. Except here in Paris there were rituals beyond my understanding.

First off, I did not know whom to kiss.

Each day I'd wake up at five a.m. to work on my novel, eat a small breakfast with Rachel at seven, and be out the door in order to arrive at my desk by eight-thirty and be ready, fretting with low-lying dread, to give and to receive *les bises* (kisses).

Office culture in Paris held that it was each person's responsibility, upon arrival, to visit other people's desks and wish them good morning, and often kiss each person once on each cheek, depending on the parties' personal relationship, genders, and respective positions in the corporate hierarchy. Then you moved on to the next desk.

Not everyone did it, but those who did not were noticed and remarked upon.

So first a polite *bonjour*, walking through the room and repeating it at each chair, *bonjour, bonjour, salut, bonjour.* If someone arrived late and needed to get straight into a meeting, they might let out a big *bonjour* for the group. For example, André did this a lot, blazing through the office at ten a.m. with his collar popped, shouting a giant, angry *BON-JOUR*, like a battle cry. And the room would reply in one voice, *BON-JOUR*, at the same time that he slammed shut his door.

But then there were the *bises*, which were conditional.

In French class, I did well in spoken tests, but my written French was appalling. The conditional tense confused me, and the French loved the conditional tense, French conversation practically being founded on relativity—*perhaps, maybe, I don't know.* In kissing, some people were ripe, others were not. Whole groups could be off-limits. It definitely wasn't appropriate to kiss your boss, except when it was, though it *was* correct to kiss your underlings, except when it wasn't. Young men generally didn't kiss other young men, unless they were friends outside work. But older men did, sometimes. You never knew. Also, these kisses were intended not to touch the cheek but to glance it. People kept their eyes locked on the middle distance and seemed, while kissing or being kissed, very bored.

Honestly, I had no idea how it worked. There was one woman, an Italian down the hall, who visited us at ten-fifteen each morning, making loud smooching sounds even before she entered the room; then she'd deliver long-drawn, suction-fueled *bises* all around: on Julie's cheeks, Françoise's cheeks, Tomaso's cheeks, Olivier's cheeks. Even my cheeks, once we were introduced. But it wasn't always done. Maybe four days out of five, but that fifth day . . .

September found me frequently *bise*ing inappropriately. Male clients, IT support workers, freelance temps. Any female who came within ten feet. They'd return my weird kisses reluctantly, or else back away and attempt to ignore the gaffe. I asked Pierre how he knew whom to kiss, whom not. Pierre said there was no way of knowing this unless you'd grown up in France, then you just knew. He himself preferred to shake hands.

André overheard Pierre saying this and suggested, in that case, Pierre should move "the fuck" back to New York.

Gradually I learned to *bise* in the local mode. There weren't any guidelines, just intuition. It required months of calibration. I mimicked Pierre and Chloe, the way other young people around Paris went into kissing each other: regretfully, with a forced, resigned air, as if playing out an obsolete ritual. The procedure by which teenage atheletes in America lined up to shake hands: nice game, kiss kiss, whatever.

8

Tactics to learn French via shock immersion: Accept and make telephone calls. Do this despite a crippling fear of conducting phone calls in French, terror so real you begin to experience it in nightmares about speaking French on the phone—your daily life repeated at night with no embellishment. Still, do it, call strangers. Answer telemarketing calls and delay the person on the line. Or book your wife, as she requests, *un shampooing avec une styliste qui parle anglais*. Which is not easy to find in Paris. Nor easy to explain to hairstylists who do not speak English why they should desire to do so for your wife's sake.

Keep a notebook in your pocket for words or phrases you don't recognize, so later you can ask your boss or other friendly Parisians to define them for you. For example, *Ça m'énerve.* (That annoys me.) *C'est classe.* (That's classy.) *Dégueulasse!* (Vomit!)

At the coffee machine, entrance coworkers with descriptions of your apartment when you say things like, "There is a kitchen," or "There is a table for the time to eat," or "There is a bedroom." You can also try rendering American idioms into French. Coworkers will stand flamingo-still when you so casually drop *Moi, je ne donne pas une merde* (I don't give a shit). Because other people might pass along feces as gifts, but never you, cool you.

Finally, when you are unable to indicate what you want, explain what you do not. For example, say you desire a Coke. Specifically a can of Coke, because the can version is colder than the bottle, in your opinion. But the vendor, from his booth near the Luxembourg Gardens, is selling Coke by the bottle *and* the can. And you don't know the French word for "can." So, request *un Coca*, but specifically *un Coca qui n'est pas dans une bouteille*. Or not the sandwich that is made of ham, nor its neighbor of tuna, but *oui*, that one, what? Ah, you call it *dinde*, which means turkey? *Super.*

Soon I hoped I could express what I wanted, not merely its negation. Until then I had migraines. The sun rose and I woke up feeling raw. Living in Paris while barely speaking French was like drinking coffee through a veil. Within a month, I blew three projects' deadlines due to miscommunication. Account supervisors frowned at me with their whole bodies, leaning forward while exhaling poofs of air. What had they done to deserve this American?

One morning during my commute, a squad of police officers blocked the exit when I got off the Métro. Two cops in blue uniforms waved me over. Behind them, in the sky, clouds with gray snouts were materializing like an armada.

"Where is your identity?" the first cop said.

I showed her my New York driver's license. At that point, Rachel and I were still waiting for our residency papers to arrive.

"No," cop number two chided, "your identity for the Métro."

The first one said, "If you buy a monthly pass, you must also construct an identity. It is the rule." Then she said something I couldn't follow—*"Père framboise, Day-Glo glass, Narragansett Bay."*

I interrupted, "What? Why?"

"It is the law," the second cop said, with exhaustion. I said,

What law? *Quelle loi?* Though, really, who knows what I said? All of us were aware that, in French, we belonged to different armies, perhaps weren't even engaged in the same battle.

"You're getting a ticket," the first cop said.

"But the machine, the machine that sold me the ticket," I said, "the machine did not tell me about my identity to construct."

I believe I was saying "car" in lieu of "machine." It probably didn't make a difference.

"There was an office in the station," said cop number one, staring me down. "There you would have received an identity card after the completion of your dossier. This you must have in order to use a monthly Métro pass."

"A dossier?" I said.

She didn't even reply to that, as if I'd said, The sky is blue?

"But me," I said, "how do I know to ask about an identity card and a dossier I do not know to construct, when there are not directions that say I should construct the card and dossier?"

"You will pay forty euros," the first cop said, and handed me a summons.

At the office, Bruno and I had a meeting with our infant-nutrition project managers. Afterward, he translated my Métro ticket during his second morning smoke break. We stood in a sunny patch on the Champs-Elysées. The long *allées* of chestnut trees reverberated in the breeze. Bruno said I would need to give the Métropolitan Police my checking account number and routing codes, and afterward they'd siphon off my fine.

I said it sounded like Big Brother. Couldn't I just write them a check?

That's how it's done, Bruno said. But why hadn't I assembled an identity in the first place?

I said in French, "I try forever to construct my Parisian identity."

It was the first time I'd made Bruno laugh. Which was nice, but a little sad, actually, considering how lame the joke was.

Same evening I got my transit fine, there was *un pot*, an office party, organized for an employee who was leaving us, a tall man named Guy who wore flip-flops. Around seven p.m., about forty people assembled in the canteen around the cube of toilets. There were towers of salmon sandwiches, and terrines, and small cakes. Plus champagne from the office champagne refrigerator. I hadn't seen it yet, but a refrigerator just for champagne was kept upstairs, in a small room off the agency's *terrasse*. Anyway, André was standing at a counter, grinning at me while he squeezed a lime wedge into a cocktail, his smile a bank robber's bandanna. I saw Keith, a Scottish copywriter I'd come to know, across the room and started threading my way toward him. Then I slipped in a puddle and went down in a split, and knocked a small cake off a bench while my drink shot out of my hand and exploded rum on the feet of Guy, the guy in whose honor we'd gathered, the one in flip-flops.

I picked myself up and shrugged. I knew just what to say to him, because nothing else fit: "*C'est la vie.*" There you have it, that's life in Paris for us bumblers, what could we do?

No reply from Guy.

For months, I'd feel like an infant wandering into rooms that filled with tension the moment I appeared: *What is the giant baby doing here?*

That weekend, I purchased a cell phone. I followed the instructions to set up voice mail. A computer voice, in French, implored me to *taper dièse*. I was confused. *Taper* sounded like "to tap," but what should I tap? I knew the names for numbers 0–9. Star was *étoile*. Perhaps *dièse* meant pound? I tapped pound. There were more commands. A question this time? *What do you want from me?* I pressed another button, and the voice said something about voice mail, something about *cinq*. So I pressed five, *cinq*. The voice said, "*Jacques Cousteau château trois, en flâneur, mettez deux*."

I pressed *deux*, two. Nothing happened. I pressed two again, another time—and that turned out to confirm that yes, I did want to operate my cell phone solely by voice command, no buttons, in fluent French.

The next day I needed Pierre to unlock it.

9

The joke began with Claude—account supervisor, of the orange arms—and his main client, a London-based Internet portal. Basically, Claude's account was in trouble. Europe wasn't satisfied with his client's product, and his client wasn't satisfied with us, so the client had asked Claude to create a "revolutionary brand-awareness campaign." Should it not move them, they threatened to move elsewhere.

Somehow Claude convinced André to pull a third of the creative department off other jobs for a one-week effort. The total group was me and two other copywriters; two senior art directors; three graphic designers; a business strategist; an information architect; several programmers; and a battery of project managers to shepherd us and refill easel paper.

Bruno wasn't invited for some reason, and didn't like it. Our infant-nutrition project would be further delayed, he complained to me by e-mail, and it wasn't fair—another setback in a line of many.

Once again, Bruno had been left to feed the babies by himself.

For the rest of the week, morning to night, we were locked away in conference rooms while Claude tried to inspire us to greatness. On the first morning, Claude made a big speech, flanked by his project managers. This campaign would be our legacy, Claude said. A world changer. The next "Just Do It." Our mission, he said, was to "think outside the box"—English-language business jargon being universal—and produce an advertising campaign "that makes them say, like, fucking *wow*, guys!"

But each day his eyes had plumper bags. Claude was running out of time. None of our ideas were satisfactory, never mind avant-garde. By Thursday, Claude was exhorting, "You guys, don't you realize you have a chance to make history? Do you want to be fucking famous or not?"

The client's business was a website where people sought answers to general questions, about plumbing or computer maintenance. Fame through the ages seemed a long shot here. To Claude's credit, the client's brief did demand something both "totally out there" and "outside the box," to address their drop in business: people asking fewer questions on their website.

So my slogan was "Ask More."

Genius, *oui*.

To promote it, my idea was to install a forty-foot-tall translucent plastic chicken in Trafalgar Square filled with thousands of green eggs. *Un poulet énorme*. Surely, I explained, using my French-English scramble, people would wonder, "How did that get there, that giant chicken and all those eggs?" After all, I said, was there *une question* more fundamental to mankind than *l'œuf et le poulet*, and *en quel ordre* they originated? I explained that we'd host a contest: the client would award an obscenely large amount of money to whichever passerby got closest to guessing how many eggs were inside *le gros poulet*; and there'd be experts on hand to answer questions about how to measure a giant chicken's volume; and we'd film it all, and stick it on YouTube; and what the fuck.

"Okay, but why not rugby-sized eggs?" someone asked. "To pick up World Cup spirit?"

"Yes," I said. "Absolutely."

"But wait, why a chicken?" Claude asked, clutching his chin.

"That is exactly the question," I said, in an effort to buy time.

Claude snapped, "No, exactly what question?"

In fact, I had no idea. My chicken had appeared to me that morning on the Métro, somewhere beneath the Louvre-Rivoli station. The rest I was inventing on the spot. At what point I should cease and apologize for stringing bullshit streamers around the room, I figured they would let me know.

"*Oui, exactement*," I said, and paced beside the conference table. "*Donc, vous voyez . . .*" A few more seconds. Then it came to me. "Indeed, Claude, this is the type of question, *c'est la type de question*, that people will be asking. 'Why a chicken? *Pourquoi un poulet?*' 'Hey, a giant chicken in London, what is that doing there, *qu'est-ce qu'il se passe?*' But this is the chicken's raison d'être, just like our client's: to inspire questions. Because how are questions formed? From provocation—the very raison d'être of advertising itself. Thus, it is our job, *notre obligation*, to provoke and inspire, *faire l'inspiration*. We make people 'ask more,' and thus the chicken becomes this slogan embodied."

Claude had been frowning. Now he switched to cautiously eager. "Okay," Claude said, "whatever, go do it," and he ordered Jean-Luc, a young designer, to develop some drawings of my chicken.

Jean-Luc, who spoke very little English, looked confused.

The next day, we gathered in a boardroom on the agency's top floor. The pitch would be done by conference call, addressed to a telephone shaped like a starfish. A few directors were attending, as well as Bernard, the main boss, who stood against a wall, chewing gum and reading his BlackBerry.

Of our three ideas to present, my chicken went last. I'd say I was nervous, but in fact I was semicalm. I'd never pitched anything before, so what could they expect of me? The previous evening, Pierre had said, "Just tell a little story."

Luckily, the clients were English speaking.

I began by explaining what it had been like for me to arrive in

Paris. To leave behind the accustomed and be thrust into moments where the only solution was to inquire, to request help. I talked about my passions for the Place des Vosges and *croque-Monsieur*, and how little they'd helped me so far. I explained about locking myself out of my cell phone. I described how Paris itself was becoming *my* catalyst, my provocation, and how it made me ask more.

So, rather than Paris, a giant chicken.

Ten minutes after that, once I'd finished, the client's marketing team requested a five-minute break. Their team was a Eurozone trio: Spaniard, German, Brit. On return, they said they disliked all of our ideas. "These were big disappointments, guys." The main problem with mine, the Spaniard said, was that one of their Israeli competitors already had a slogan, "Ask Me," that was too similar to "Ask More." The giant chicken, they said, was okay. The Spaniard said, "It was good, and totally out there, as per our request."

"But maybe too much," the German said.

The Brit chimed in, "At the moment, terrorism makes promotions a bit difficult to orchestrate in London. A giant chicken appearing overnight, it could be perceived as a threat."

A minute later, the Spaniard admonished me in particular. "Believe me, it is the very last thing we would like to be associated with, terrorism."

After the call, Claude led the team out to the terrace. In a haze of afternoon cloud, almond-colored, the Eiffel Tower was fuzzy in the near distance, its bodice and skirt obscured. Domes of churches below us were like brown mushroom caps. Smokers smoked. Everyone made sarcastic comments that the wind took away. The clients were lambasted as philistines and dickless nerds.

Bernard came up next to me. "Hey, that was a nice presentation."

"They thought my slogan was stupid," I said.

"Yeah, well, it's how you sold it. You did a good job, actually."

"But they didn't buy it," I said.

Bernard looked up from his BlackBerry and shrugged. His long hair, loose to his shoulders, was about two-thirds black, one-third silver.

"Anyway, how about pitching a motel chain tomorrow?" he said.

Thus, the joke: Two French advertising bosses, a Texan marketing executive, and a novice American copywriter walk into a bar . . .

The next morning, Bernard explained, our agency would be pitching a giant French motel chain. The chain had recently been purchased by American investors, who were prepared to spend a big chunk of money on advertising. So far, Bernard said, the agency had pitched the chain's marketing director once and been rejected. But he was granting us a second chance. Ever since the first pitch, a creative team had been reworking the material around the clock. A lot of money was at stake. The agency would be going into the pitch with its biggest Parisian guns: Bernard's boss's boss, Nicole, who was the president of our holding company's Europe operations; a guy named Paul, known as the agency's "branding czar"; and me.

Why me? I said.

"Just do the same as today," Bernard said, dodging the question.

That evening, Paul the branding czar was not happy. His creative director, Céline, who would *not* be at the presentation, was said to be livid. Paul and Céline had been reworking their pitch with a big group, Paul explained, but there was one intractable problem: the motel chain's marketing boss, an American, specifically a Texan, was believed to personally dislike Céline and her team.

"And that is why," Paul wearily explained, "you will play the

American creative director brought in specially from New York to replace Céline and save the job, okay?"

I said something like, Yeah?

Paul handed me the presentation to memorize.

The next morning, Friday of my third week at the agency, I wore my one suit to meet the branding czar in the president's penthouse office. Handshakes all around, but no kisses. Nicole, the big big boss, gave me a compressed smile from behind her desk.

"So," Nicole said, "I hear you are good at presenting. You are new?"

Nicole was small but commanding, a slender older Parisian wearing an expensive-looking suit. Her head rested on a cloud of gold scarf. Nicole appeared to have two assistants, who fluttered when she moved. She radiated something—prestige? Perfume? In the taxi to the presentation, Nicole told me the Texan would most likely say no to whatever we presented, but perhaps not, perhaps my accent would win the day.

The motel chain's office was located nearby on an imperial, leafy boulevard in the eighth arrondissement, not far from the Arc de Triomphe, surrounded by embassies. Their building was a traditional Haussmann wedge, *très beau*, six stories tall plus an attic the color of ripe blueberries. We were shown into a conference room on the third floor. When the Texan arrived, he didn't look American. He wore a sleek, trim suit, and he and Nicole immediately swapped *bises*; he knew whom to kiss. The Texan's assistant brought us coffees. She was a brooding French girl with black glasses and a faraway look, and she bid us to sit at a massive table.

The Texan set the mandate in English: "Now, you are aware I've already said no to you guys before. But we're here, my mind's open, let's see what you've got."

Paul told the Texan not to worry. "We really have something to knock your socks off." Nicole introduced me, saying I'd been flown in specially from New York for a fresh perspective, and that I and my crack team of *créatifs* had been working in seclusion nonstop.

Nicole nodded at me to begin. The Texan's assistant dimmed the lights.

I guess the feeling was like I wasn't wholly in my body.

The previous evening, before going home, Paul the czar had given me pointers on how to present, like Sell the Slogan First, and Make Him Believe We Know His Business Better Than He Does. So I explained to the Texan that our new slogan was guaranteed to be remembered. As soon as people heard it, his motels would be perceived as higher-class, cooler than at present, "more Hollywood." All of this had been prepared for me, about Hollywood and perception, the new galaxy of *hôteliers* that his revamped motels would rule. But I tried to make it mine. I clicked through PowerPoint slides and showed pictures of French celebrities I didn't recognize, stars I said would be his "brand ambassadors." I was really building it up; it was time for the kill. I told him to get ready. I clicked the remote. The slogan for his motels would be "A New Fourth Star Is Born."

The Texan asked me to pause.

"I don't get it," he said. "Hotels are rated on a five-star system. You're saying my hotels are subpar?"

Actually, Pierre and I had noticed the same thing the night before, when Pierre had helped me run through the pitch before going home. But we'd figured we lacked the caffeine to read it correctly.

Paul snapped to high alert. "No," Paul said, "it is three. Three stars, the Michelin Guide? This is why, your hotels, they create *a fourth star*. They're so good, it is *a new level*."

"Trust me," the Texan said, "you're talking to a hotel man. It's a five-star system. Please do not tell me my business. In fact, please do not tell me your whole pitch is geared around, what, taking us down a peg?"

Nicole said smoothly, "No, of course not. It could be changed.

For example, 'A New Fifth Star Is Born.' 'A New *Sixth* Star.' It is the concept that is important. Why don't we look at the rest of the creative?"

Nicole nodded at me, and I resumed talking my way through slides of mocked-up magazine and television advertisements, where young women lounged in rooms that looked like bedchambers in a Danish space station. When I'd finished, the assistant relumed the lights with a remote control, which also raised the blinds.

"Listen to me." Nicole addressed the Texan. "We can rework the slogan, of course." She placed both of her hands flat on the table. "Five stars, six stars, this is math. But the concept is very sexy. Extremely compelling, don't you find?"

The Texan also put forth his hands.

"Nicole, you know I appreciate all the work you do." He took an extra moment to nod at me and Paul. "Look. Yesterday I threw away our mattresses. Every hotel in the country, every mattress, thousands of mattresses headed for the dump. You know why? Because we're going to replace them with these wonderful new beds—hypoallergenic, state of the art. So let me assure you, we are committed to this overhaul. What I mean is, our new residences will by no means be inferior products."

Nicole fenced charmingly for a minute, but the Texan was reluctant to engage. He was tired but smug; he'd been planning to turn us down no matter what. The Texan stood up and dallied beside the conference table.

"You know what I like?" he said a moment later. "I like that BMW slogan. Do you know that slogan? 'The ultimate driving machine.' Now, you know why I like it?"

According to the Texan's posture, there was a podium in the room that was invisible to the rest of us.

Paul said dryly, "Because you can't go above 'ultimate'?"

"That's it," the Texan said. "It's better than the best, the best you can get. And I just don't think—well, if you had an option between a five-star hotel . . ." His hands weighed the decision. "Even if we're the *new* fourth star? I don't think it's a tough decision."

"But let's be honest," Nicole said, smiling, "your hotels are not BMWs."

The Texan chuckled. "Maybe so. But that's why we hire people like you."

Olivier whistled at me when I got back to the office. "Ooh, the man in black, but you look so serious today!" He touched the right sleeve of my jacket and sang in French, "So beautiful, my little choo-choo!"

Françoise muffled her laughter with her hands. Julie frowned at both of them while I hung my jacket off the back of my chair. My shirt was soaked from armpits to hem. My pulse was just beginning to slow.

Julie said in English, "But why today are you wearing a funeral suit?"

Then Nicole and the czar appeared in the door. The room went quiet. Nicole crossed the room and spoke to Pierre and André for a moment, then she motioned for me to join her in the hallway.

Nicole told me she'd just received an e-mail: the Texan said no.

"Forget it," Nicole said in English, patting my arm. "Today the stars were not in our favor." She laughed. "But we may use you again, would that be okay?"

When I'd returned to my desk, everyone had heard the news. Françoise said, "Now see, I don't understand why they ask you to do this in your first month?"

"Ah, but he has the advantage," Olivier said. He knotted his hands behind his head. A number of people gathered around to listen. "He is American. You think, in all my years, have I ever talked to that woman?" Olivier pointed at me with a ruler. "And him, already they're good friends!"

Olivier switched to English and asked me, "Hey, mister, how say this, *fwacking crazy*."

"Fucking crazy," I said.

"This business?" Olivier said. "IS FUCKING CRAZY."

Olivier walked out. Not only was he pissed, but he seemed injured. For a minute, lots of people stood around not saying anything, then they went away to resume their work.

10

Parisians love Paris more than anybody does. I heard it all the time from Parisian coworkers, how much they loved their city's charms. Leaves on the grand boulevards changing color, window displays adjusting to the season. In late September, somehow all of Paris seemed more French for being in flux.

Pierre had two sisters. One of them, Monique, an economics lecturer at the Sorbonne, invited Rachel and me to a party. "I have a marvelous view this time of year, you must come see." Monique and her husband lived close to us, four floors above the Canal Saint-Martin, in a trendy district on the Right Bank, north of Place de la République.

We walked over from our apartment, going up along the canal. At nine p.m., hundreds of twentysomethings were having picnics along the banks, throwing tiny impromptu dinner parties under a purpling sky. Normally the canal is a working waterway, but at that hour no boats were moving. Fishermen lined the banks, homeless and otherwise. At Monique's apartment overlooking the canal, sixty people, young and old, were dancing to a remix of "Toxic" by Britney Spears. We met Monique's husband, Jérôme, a mathematician, at the door. He was tan, sharp, all eyes. Jérôme had appeal off the charts, yet an aura of no bullshit. He had a way of talking while smoothing back his hair that said he'd obtain your secrets.

"You're the writer," Jérôme told me in French, after he fetched us champagne. "The guy working with Pierre. You speak French?"

"Not a lot," I said, in French, *pas beaucoup*.

"Okay," he said, "but I won't speak English with you!"

"No problem," I said.

"Fuck English," Jérôme yelled at me in English.

"Fuck English," I repeated.

Jérôme had plump lips. He licked them a lot. Jérôme pulled me in close to say in French, "I love this, this word 'fuck.' But I agree, it's not good for you to stay protected inside English."

He said something else in French that I didn't follow. At the end of the room, behind the dancers and through the hanging smoke, was an enormous plate window. There you could see the depth of western Paris in blues and grays, its Gothic buildings staggered like rows of folding chairs. Finally I heard Jérôme say, "This city, you must embrace it. Learn something, or you're lost."

"*Oui*," I said. "*C'est ma stratégie*."

"Ha! Good, be strategic," Jérôme said, laughing. He added in English, "You will make an army."

By midnight, the air was speared with cold. I told Rachel during our walk home that I was pleased to have snuck *stratégie* into conversation. It was a new word I'd learned that week from Olivier. I'd also learned the French for "stapler"—*agrafeuse*—because Olivier hadn't understood me when I'd asked to borrow "la stapler," so he taught me its gorgeous name, which sounded to me more like an expensive motorcycle.

Later, I'd have trouble remembering *agrafeuse*. I never figured out why. Even as my fluency increased, I couldn't latch on to it. At the office, I'd say, "*Pardon, Olivier, est-ce que je peux emprunter . . .*" and when I couldn't remember *agrafeuse*, I'd mimic clenching my hand, as if squeezing a stapler, or a hand exerciser. Which confused Olivier. The first time it happened, he pulled out a hand exerciser from his bottom-left drawer and told me to keep it.

•

Our weekday routine quickly fell into place. At night, I'd leave the office around seven or seven-thirty, then have dinner with Rachel before putting in an hour or two on the online magazine that I helped edit. Around eleven, we'd unwind with some TV. In New York, Rachel had worked for nonprofits while writing on the side, but she wasn't allowed to work in Paris without a visa, so she was taking French classes five days a week and working on a screenplay. She also did all the household shopping, cooking, and cleaning—playing the part of *femme au foyer* (housewife).

Our budget allowed for two dinners out each month. I heard from a journalist friend in the States about a "secret" restaurant located near our apartment, where two young Americans served gourmet food in their dining room, without permits. We obtained reservations via e-mail and set out for dinner on a Saturday night. The sun was setting. Dusk bloomed on otherwise plain streets. The shadows were oblong, bowing into Place de la République, and the wind blowing north from the Seine came in gusts, scattering dust and leaves. I took Rachel's hand, we zigzagged through alleys, and our evening seemed terrifically Parisian: going down Rue Turbigo at that hour with the smells of autumn, out for a dinner party like the rest of Paris.

So we didn't want anything to spoil the mood.

Rachel and I were seated in the chefs' dining room with six American investment bankers who mostly knew one another from Dartmouth; two retired college professors from Lewiston, Maine; and a young Polish woman who was visiting Paris with her mother, who'd never left Poland before and spoke neither French nor English. Aside from one of the bankers' girlfriends, who was Canadian, there wasn't a single French-speaker in the room. For several hours we ate a menu of American gourmet comfort food—courses like miniature grilled cheese sandwiches floating in tomato soup—while the bankers talked about working too hard to have any time to spend all their money.

"The thing about the French is, they're death eaters for hours worked. I mean, go home, be French already."

"It's true, Parisians work crazy hard."

"My boss is a monster."

"It's not like I don't try to speak French? But, you know, screw *you* very much."

"Parisians don't like English-speakers."

"So I had, like, my mother visiting? And we went to Boulevard Saint-Germain? I mean, she didn't recognize anything."

"Paris is a morgue, architecturally, they all say it."

"The food's in San Francisco now."

"I don't know. I kind of like Paris. The bread."

"Well, yeah, the *bread*."

"So did you go undergrad, or business school?"

"We should picnic this weekend."

"There's a Small World picnic on Saturday, I think."

"You hear Berlin, but everyone I know's in London."

"The money in London is incredible right now."

"Well, you should see the Arabs they have."

To give them credit, the professors were nice, but I didn't talk to them much. Sitting across from the Polish girl, Lilli, I was constantly needed. Lilli wore a red cotton dress and had flat blond hair. Frequently, she'd grab my wrist and stare at me, as if she had state secrets she needed me to smuggle out of the country.

Her mother looked like a pile of gym towels.

Early on, Lilli began by proposing three toasts: to Paris; to her new business; and to Eli and "the beautiful Jessie," our chefs. Then she took my hand and taught me a Polish tongue twister: *W Szczebrzeszynie chrząszcz brzmi w trzcinie*. It meant, she said, "In the town of Szczebrzeszyn, a beetle buzzes in the reeds."

Lilli got tipsy fast, too fast. There were a lot of sudden declarations, whispered or shouted. She confided in me, "Mama is a farmer's bride; my father is a pig farmer. To make more money, you see, I have convinced them to turn the farm into a hotel. In Warsaw, I am a travel *agent*. The bed-and-breakfast, it's *the* trend now, you know, people staying to work on the farm and eat from the land."

Lilli shouted at me, "*Attention!* This is why we are in Paris. To study."

To study hotels? I said.

"Perfectly," she said. She beat my arm with a fork. One bottle of wine down, another opened. "To *exhaust* Paris," Lilli said, refilling our glasses. "Café de Flore we did yesterday. You know this: amazing. L'Opéra, Printemps, Le Louvre, *amazing*. Le Lipp, you know it? Of course."

At one point, the bankers got loud, and Lilli glowered down the table. "TO THE CITY OF LIGHTS," she yelled, pointing her empty wineglass at them like a flashlight.

"We are also here to eat," Lilli confided in me. "My mother, she loves French food. But in my opinion? It is mostly terrible. Like this tacos. This is hell!"

We'd just been served fish tacos. Personally, I thought they'd do San Diego proud.

Next, Lilli's mother said something in Polish, which were her first words of the evening. One of the professors asked Lilli what her mother had said, and Lilli frowned. Lilli said, "I shouldn't tell you. It is stupid." She snapped at her mother in Polish, and her mother went back to eating. "Well, okay," Lilli said, in the tone of a guilty five-year-old, "Mama says she likes the tacos very much."

She laughed: "Whatever!"

By course four, Lilli had finished all the wine. She shouted for Eli—"that bastard Eli"—to bring us more. The other chef, Jessie, appeared. Jessie said quietly to Lilli, "Eli is plating the next course. Is there anything I can do to help?"

"We need wine," Lilli said, pouting. "But I want Eli to do it!"

"Well, like I said, he's busy right now." Jessie tried to escape. Lilli snatched her arm. "It's not fair," Lilli said, pulling Jessie, "him being chef all night when you play servant. What happened to us, what happened about women having *power*?"

A minute later, Eli appeared in the doorway to introduce the final course: "So here we've got a small portion—"

"Eli," Lilli interrupted loudly, "stop talking, please. We would like to hear from Jessie now." Lilli tried grabbing Eli by the belt and fell out of her chair. "Why do you," she stammered, getting up, "get all the credit, because Jessie is your slave? Women are *not* slaves. Women are chefs, too, didn't you know this?"

We walked home in a daze, down a quiet street of shuttered chain stores, Métro stations, and cafés closing for the night. Somewhere, surely, I thought, French people in Paris were doing French things, but how to find them? At home, Rachel propped up my laptop on the bottom of the bed while I threw open the windows. We watched a DVD we'd started the night before, from the Ric Burns documentary *New York*, a history of New York City. Since our move, we'd gone through the whole series twice, Rachel pointed out.

I said, "We have?"

Rachel said, with a kind of sadness I hadn't heard in her voice since we'd moved, "I miss knowing what people are saying. Being part of what's going on around me."

"Oh, the bankers?"

"No no," Rachel said. "I'm not superinterested in knowing what's new at Goldman Sachs. But people at the grocery store, on the street. I really wish my French classes were better, for what we're spending."

Rachel had said before that her teacher was good, but the class was a struggle. Students cycled in and out so frequently, it was hard for the instructor to make headway. Plus, since few of Rachel's classmates shared a language—her classes were truly global: students from Japan, Russia, Saudi Arabia—the only common tongue in class was French, which none of them spoke. But Rachel did her homework, practiced conversation. And when she wasn't being *une femme au foyer*, she loved her time at home writing and saw progress in her creative work.

Outside, inside, the night was us alone, with zero noise. Nothing but a chill. We were amateurs at everything.

II

Carlos, a Parisian senior Web developer at the agency, took to calling me his nigger. Sometimes his Negro, but mostly his nigger. Shouting me out in a corridor, thumping me on the back, "What's up, my nigger?"

The second time it happened, I told him it could not continue. Carlos was crestfallen. He'd thought it was okay; he said he thought it was our little thing. After all, it was what I'd called him the first time we met.

That is impossible, I said.

"You don't remember? I don't believe you," Carlos said in English. Then, raising his eyebrows, ". . . my nigger?"

Evidently my French was so bad, it produced slurs.

At work, my desk was papered with breasts. I didn't think anyone would mind, cleavage in Paris being everywhere—décolletage on the street and in the office revealing a lot more than found in the States. There were sexy girls on the sides of newspaper huts and buses, and on TV channels during lingerie advertisements (*ba bum bum bum ba ba . . .*). Only a few years earlier in France, busts of the Victoria's Secret model Laetitia Casta had been installed—busts of her bust—in municipal buildings across the country after Casta had been elected by France's mayors to embody Marianne, symbol of the French Republic. Each statue's bra, of course, covered just one breast.

On my desk, though, these were not Victoria's Secret breasts.

These were breasts busy feeding. Breasts like soda fountains. I'd never associated breasts with nutrition before. In fact, *not* doing so was one of my favorite parts about being married without children. But for Bruno's and my infant-nutrition work, my desk had become a slush pile of topless pics that coworkers found unpleasant for their lack of sexiness. Olivier even made a tower of books to block them from his view.

One day after lunch, I found André fiddling with my laptop.

"You left your music on," André said. "You made the office sound like a sushi restaurant."

I pointed out that Air was a French band, in fact. André shrugged. He was wearing a magenta Lacoste, showing wooly cleavage.

In eighteen months, there would be, at most, ten instances when I'd see André in a non-Lacoste shirt. He owned them in two dozen hues and fades—André the office crocodile, grinning or snapping, pooped or hungry.

"So, please explain this . . . cleavage," André said doubtfully, picking up a book from around my desk. "Look, it's okay to have pictures of naked girls at work, but this—"

He lifted up an illustration showing a nipple in cross-section.

André said, sighing, "You've ruined it."

Bruno, my morose art director, was lurking behind André's shoulder, clutching his laptop. That week, he was working in a room upstairs; for some reason, André and Pierre couldn't settle on where to seat him permanently. He burst out laughing, *huk huk huk*. André ignored him and went back to his office, and Bruno resumed his permanent frown.

Bruno's and my work together involved me writing, and Bruno designing, a series of booklets to be distributed in third-world hospitals to teach new mothers how to feed their babies. It was something I knew nothing about, yet our first booklet was due in two weeks.

I'd asked during my first meeting, Where does the information come from on how to feed babies? No, the managers said, the important question is, how will you "message" the information? Okay, I said, but where do I obtain the information to message? Ah, they said, but you can use the information that has already been created by previous writers on this account. (Which I'd reviewed and found to be wrong.) Or you can make up more. (Which terrified me.) Or use the Internet. (Which made me start laughing.)

The style of the thing is the challenge, one manager said; less what is said than how.

They wanted to know how would We, the royal We that was our team, the editorial We that was the client's brand, how would We convince new mothers that We were their most valuable resource? I said, "Well, aren't We a little worried about Me from a Legal Standpoint?"

"You see, you can't talk to them," Bruno told me afterward, chain-smoking on the street. "It is a war, the difference between managers and artists. They really are different people."

Similar meetings went on for a week. I told our managers I would figure out their style problem once they'd figured out my information problem. Seeking détente, they offered to hire two experts, a British nutritionist and an Austrian pediatrician, who would provide the factual information I could "craft" into proper "brand messages." To facilitate the job, I was advised to read a number of maternity guides: the French and British equivalents of *What to Expect When You're Expecting*.

Doing my homework on the Métro, I found Frenchwomen giving me friendly, flirty looks.

An e-mail came from a friend in the States, asking how I was holding up. I told him that after two months in France, I had breast fatigue. Oh, I can imagine, he said. I said, No, you can't.

•

Everyone in the office took an hour's lunch. It was the midday reflex, but it was also required: professionals in France were docked lunch money from their salaries, then reimbursed through little booklets of meal tickets they were expected to use in nearby restaurants.

Typically, coworkers preferred to get takeout, bringing food back to the canteen, where they ate in groups. Almost no one ate alone. The only people I saw eat at their desks besides me were Pierre, who'd worked in New York, and Keith, the Scottish copywriter, who liked to watch Jon Stewart clips on his computer while he ate his *jambon beurre*.

But eating at your desk was not cool. The third time I tried it was my last. Olivier complained: Why couldn't I eat in the canteen like a normal person?

"I am sorry," Olivier said, his voice rising, "I am *sorry*, but this is not the United States." Olivier turned and said to Françoise, "This is an office, a *communal* office!"

Julie whispered to me in English from the corner of her mouth, "You should go."

Olivier's face was reddening.

"And now it smells terrible!" Olivier shouted. He walloped his desk with his fist. I made my exit while he raged, "How am I supposed to work when it smells in here like a burger shop? Do we all work in a burger shop now that the American is here?"

In fact, we did work in a burger shop most days. At least in the canteen. Two-thirds of people's takeout food came from the McDonald's next door. My fellow advertising employees, including Olivier, loved McDonald's. After lunch, the trash cans would be full of bags with golden arches.

There were plenty of fast-food outlets on the Champs-Elysées, but McDonald's was considered by my coworkers to be classier, more delicious. "It's for families," a guy named François told me. He said, surprised, "You don't go to McDonald's in the States?"

The McDonald's next door was thoroughly French: spacious, handsome, clean. It featured a McCafé up front, which sold McDonald's espresso and McDonald's croissants and McDonald's *macarons*, and in the back were the registers that sold burgers, fries, and also beer. Some coworkers, I learned, would walk all the way to a McDonald's on Rue Troyon, ten minutes away, "because the sandwiches are better." But either way, most people stuck to what I found a very French way of enjoying McDonald's: in multiple courses. Chicken nuggets first, then fries and a burger (a Royale Deluxe, or a Big Tasty), frequently two burgers for the men, followed by a salad, and finished with a chocolate muffin or a shake or a hot-fudge sundae. No matter if the ice cream melted by the time they'd finished courses one through three over a span of forty-five minutes.

According to *The New York Times*, an average visitor to McDonald's in France spent fifteen dollars, versus four in the United States.

Bruno, on the other hand, never ate at McDonald's. Bruno was a gourmand. He spent thirty euros on lunch, dining in nice brasseries or at a sushi restaurant if he could rope someone into joining him. Most days I refused, and he'd drive his scooter back to his neighborhood for a steak and some wine with friends. Like everyone else, Bruno did not eat alone. The fact that I *preferred* to eat alone was considered weird.

Bruno would say, "Fine, go ahead, go do work even at lunchtime."

Lunch, however, was how I stayed on track, I could have explained to Bruno—but I didn't know the French for "on track." Advertising did weird things to writers, I would have told him. In New York, I'd seen it water down friends' ambitions and force them to collect mid-century furniture. So I'd flee the office at noon, buy some Italian takeout, and walk to a park on Rue Balzac. There I'd grab a bench and employ a red pen on whatever progress I'd made that morning on my novel, and afterward take a nap and daydream my muddled fantasies, smelling Paris, hearing the universe remind me that it didn't owe me crap.

Early autumn in Paris was temperate and dry. My lunch park, a rolling grassy lawn in the eighth arrondissement, was about an acre in size, engraved by gravel paths. Paris was dotted with tiny parks such as that one, and lunchtimes were crowded with office workers picnicking, students smoking and chatting, and college girls who would undress down to bikinis and sunbathe on the lawn while men gazed from their benches, eating their sandwiches with two hands.

Not me, though. I was married. Plus I was fed up with breasts. I'd think, Oh, cover up your functionality already.

But I spent a lot of time in the park thinking about Bruno, not my novel. Bruno was mentally difficult to resist. I'd decided Bruno was a lover, not a fighter. As a lover, he was never satisfied. Especially at work. Bruno felt neglected. He was abused by middle managers and overlooked by higher-ups. We talked about it a lot: how Bruno fought daily against the idea of quitting, even leaving Paris, his hometown.

Bruno was one of the least theoretical people I'd ever met. Maybe it was specific only to Bruno, not all Parisians, the way his eyes dipped, how his spirit battled with the status quo. Perhaps the chip on his shoulder was in some ways a cushion. Or maybe it was a leftover trait from thousands of years of Parisian evolution.

Anyway, happy or threatened, Bruno laughed like a puppet, unblinking, alert to whichever disappointing thing would come next. I got all of this from conversation, that Bruno had the perfect life all figured out, a basic French model, but it seemed increasingly beyond his reach. History had screwed his generation, and no striking would restore a dying way of life. Basically, Bruno was fucked on all sides, by bosses, coworkers, and society at large. During his smoke-break confessions, Bruno acknowledged irony, but he did not employ it; instead he was earnest, vexed, and his motives were fathomable, his emotions intense—he was STUCK in Paris, in a job where he was GOING NOWHERE, indeed his life was GOING NOWHERE and this was a SERIOUS PROBLEM, after all he ONLY HAD ONE LIFE and it was FROZEN, which was HOW THINGS ARE IN FRANCE for most people at the moment, and yet, and yet, Bruno remained Parisian, surrounded by SO MUCH BEAUTY, and anyway IT DOESN'T PAY TO BE BITTER, he knew—after all it was QUITE PARISIAN to bear luck in mind and also remember WE ALL MAY DIE TOMORROW—thus he needed to LIVE IN THE MOMENT and RIDE HIS SCOOTER and BE HAPPY with his lot. All of this to explain why Bruno sounded SAD when he LAUGHED.

If Bruno was a pure strain of Frenchman, that strain was in touch with the depth of its feelings. Bruno ventured bravely across a sierra of emotions every day. So did most Parisian men, in my experience. They were constantly self-justifying. Only no one had told Bruno he wore the wrong sneakers. No one told Bruno he could be cloying, too familiar. Bruno did not know the bourgeoisie's discreet charms.

One cold day in late September, Bruno wore a new coat to the office. It was a black bomber jacket, trim at the waist. It had a fur collar. Not a fuzzy collar, but something svelte. Givenchy might have designed it to match a pillbox hat. By the way Bruno delicately hung up his new jacket, I could tell he loved it. At ten a.m., however, he left it behind when he went downstairs for a cigarette, and two *bobos*—French for hipster + yuppie—took the opportunity to mock Bruno's jacket behind his back. They rubbed the fur between their fingers like it was cash.

I said I thought it was beautiful.

Around that time, President Sarkozy was attacked in the newspapers for wearing stacked heels. Bruno was taller than Sarkozy, but not by much. In the morning, my eye would linger that extra second at the newsstand when I bought my papers, where, each day, Sarkozy turned browner, as if tanning on the front page, his family around him bunched together like a clutch of toffee lollipops. Sarkozy's *bronzage* was the armor of confidence. It gave the Paris newspapers their radiance—his smugness their hydrogen, his expressions their helioscope.

Chalk it up to a blindness for all things French, but I found Sarkozy beguiling. Whereas my coworkers told me he was a pig, *un vrai con*.

12

Pierre needed me to work one Saturday, so Rachel spent the day with Lindsay, a new friend. Lindsay and Rachel had recently become acquainted through a mutual friend in the States. Lindsay was new to Paris, too, and she had what we had: the big France love.

Lindsay was a pretty, snappy Wisconsin blonde who stood six-three or six-four. She'd played Division One basketball in college and then moved to Chicago, where she'd worked as a paralegal. Now Lindsay was in Paris for adventures. "I got to that stage where I'm wondering, what the hell am I doing?" she told Rachel. "And why Chicago while I'm working it out? Why *not* Paris?" Now in Paris, Lindsay freelanced from an attic room she was subletting in the eleventh arrondissement, doing research online for Chicago defense attornies.

Rachel called that evening from a bar near the Louvre, Le Fumoir. She and Lindsay had just arrived for a cocktail event, for something called A Small World—an invitation-only social network for the world's wealthy and/or connected classes. Thirty minutes after I got there, a man wearing a hunting cap told me he was the Left Bank's only gardener for hire, and its best, *absolument*. Also, he liked my head.

Since arriving at the bar, I'd talked to a number of strangers, but none had been so complimentary; I wondered if this was some type of Small World initiation. The guy's business card said "Thierry le Jardinier." Thierry was substantial in the glow. A handsome dude, hyper*bistre*, mustached with a shag beard that bulled down into his shirt. He had freckles across his nose and a green scarf around his neck. His French had a ducky twang, a Provençal accent.

I asked him what kind of gardening he did.

"Private clients," Thierry said dismissively. "The rich, the bastards. Look, seriously, your head. There are a lot of good heads in here—" He took another look at mine, all the way around. "Honestly, your head is very good. What form, this head," he added quietly. Then he whistled at it. By that point it was the fifth way he'd complimented my head: stroking it, circling it, eyeballing it, chatting it up.

Rachel was sitting behind me with Lindsay and a girl named Dana, an acquaintance of Lindsay's, a young woman from Melbourne, Australia. Dana had an expectant air—a real fun girl in the wool. Dana was in Paris, she'd said when we were introduced, "for the hell of it. To meet men. Find a man. Whatever."

"Oh, she found one. An aristocrat," Lindsay said. "With any luck, he'll be the king of England someday."

Dana explained that if two hundred people died in the correct order, her boyfriend would inherit the British throne. "But he's very bashful about it," Dana said.

Thierry the gardener now had his eye on Dana. He played his wineglass left and right. He said to me, "You also have a good nose. I study noses. The size to me says a lot. Now, hey, look at that—" The gardener turned me around by the shoulder and pointed at Dana, and said loudly in French, "Regard her nose. Excuse me, miss, but your nose is incredible. It has character. It's beautiful. Please?"

Dana shook her head. She meant it. She was a good-looking girl, but her nose was a dorsal fin.

"I insist," the gardener said, switching to English, tilting toward Dana from the hips, "that you accept your beautiful nose. For me. Please."

And it looked like Thierry wanted to impregnate her by leaning. It reminded me how, at work that week, there'd been a meeting when a client visited, a woman, and after she'd left the conference room, the first task had been to evaluate her aesthetically, to weigh in on her breasts and legs, the make and quality of her handbag. Sabine, one of the project managers, had said to me, "Don't be a prude, what did you think? You don't like breasts, is that what it is?"

"Tell me," the gardener said softly to the Australian, "you hate your nose?"

"It's okay," Dana said. She was uncomfortable. Thierry began staring at her funny. Something was wrong.

"Wait," the gardener said. "This nose—we know each other!"

Dana laughed nervously. "I don't think so."

"Please, I'm sure." Thierry pushed up his hat. "I don't forget a nose. What is your name? I must have your telephone number."

"Honey," Rachel said to me, leaning in to cut off the gardener's path to Dana, "excuse me, but would you mind getting us the check?"

Tons more people were pressing in. At a table near the front, I recognized several Dartmouth bankers from the secret restaurant; sometimes Paris was about as big as a sandwich bag. The event's organizer turned up. Her name was Georgie—a little over five feet of sequins, a Hungarian-Parisian of twenty-six. She was escorted by a redheaded American boy wearing a fluffy fur collar. The two of them arrived with ceremony, kissing everyone. The guy's name was Richard. Wealthy from a trust fund, someone said. He looked twelve, with hair a mother had brushed. Richard told me he was studying at the Sorbonne "for, like, forever, whatever, I should get a job, I *know*." I asked Richard about the city. Oh, absolutely *sick* of Paris, he said, sipping a Perrier. Then

Richard dropped his pen. I stooped to pick it up and he patted my head, giggling. Georgie, watching from a stool, squished my fingers between her hands and *vowed* to make me a Small World member. "Now, darling," she said in a grand-dame voice, "don't make me regret it."

On our way out, Rachel was approached by a Frenchman the size of an Oscar statue. He wore a blue T-shirt with a penis on it jutting from a banana peel.

"You're exactly my type!" he shouted at Rachel over the noise.

"I'm married!" Rachel said.

He said, "This is it! My type exactly!"

At that hour, downtown Paris was deserted. We all shrugged on our coats. Across the street was the Louvre. I'd forgotten it was there. It was massive in the dark—the Pentagon of Western Civilization. At that moment, a security guard was probably shimmying toward the Poussins. Meanwhile, for the past hour I'd been drinking beer with rich assholes across the street.

The cobblestones were glimmering with rain. Lindsay pointed out a dead bird in the gutter. We all walked to the Métro station, hungry for dinner and completely smoked out.

"What's creepy is, I did know him," Dana said.

"The gardener? How?" Lindsay said.

"From the street," Dana said. "He came up to me last week. I was sitting at a café on Saint-Germain. Honestly, he used that same line on me, about my nose?" She laughed. "You know, I think he's famous for it. He cruises the Left Bank for expat girls and hands out his little business cards."

"Seriously, though?" Dana said a moment later. "Of all the things to compliment me on? He told me I had the most beautiful nose in the world."

Asif threw a party in our courtyard in the middle of the week. I went downstairs. He pulled me into a big embrace and poured shots of whiskey for the two of us, calling me his American brother, demanding to know when he and his daughter should visit New York, which dates exactly.

The next morning, our oven baked our dishwasher. They were both the size of VCRs, stacked on top of each other, mysteriously connected in the manner of a television and a cable box: turning on one device might shut down the other. While Asif tried to repair our dishwasher—he said it was a wiring problem—I asked him about all the construction noise in the building, *la bruit de toute la construction*, when would it cease?

Lying on the floor, Asif snorted and assured me the noise would be over soon. I wasn't so sure. Every day, from nine until six, with a one-hour break for lunch, construction noise rang from three sides of our apartment. When I'd signed the lease, our landlord somehow failed to mention that the apartments below, above, *and* next to ours would be undergoing renovation.

Rachel began to experience visions of drills going into her head.

A Small World opened Paris a crack. They seemed to hold events every night: parties in Left Bank clubs; parties near Colette, the fashion boutique; parties *in* Colette. We went to a few and met consultants and tech-sector moguls, artists and aspiring artists, copywriters and aspiring copywriters; an American author my age living off a trust fund, who, among other Americans, spoke only French, despite having a Parisian accent by way of Seattle.

But mostly it was Parisians and expats speaking the universal language of hedge fund. We met American financial types who cultivated saying what was passé—"Well, first off, La Prune, and Chateaubriand"—being masters of Le Fooding and Cityvox, websites for tracking the new. We saw fashion models attached to Small World members, and models who were members themselves—girls who were shoddy just-so, their hair teased to nests, while playing a game of how audaciously, how open-shirted they could dress and not care what men saw.

Where for most of the guys in attendance, the rich Parisian *dragueurs* in tight jeans and popped Lacostes, style was meant to demonstrate an interest in sex. *Dig my undershirt, which I fashion to be a shirt.* Or white Repetto shoes worn for dancing, to honor Serge.

At our third Small World event, Rachel saw the penis-banana guy again. We were attending the opening of a new restaurant, which wasn't unlike other new restaurants around Paris—there was a cheeseburger on the menu—and the guy had on a shirt this time that said "This Thing Isn't Going To Suck Itself."

"Rachel, don't you love it?" he said, grasping both her hands. "Oh, Rachel, I was so *afraid* of you the night we met. You hated me!"

He said he collected shirts with English messages to help him strike up conversation with American girls. "I get them on Bleecker Street. You know Greenwich Village?"

At that moment, I was talking to a young British banker. He said he hated Paris. He was desperate to return to "the real wild," Southeast Asia, and resume his life there where downtime was marvelously complicated by bonuses, drugs, and pussy. Paris was a museum, he said. Whereas doing finance in "the East" still proffered fresh adventures and clean whores, and had I read Alex Garland's *The Beach*?

I hated everyone in the room—myself most of all. Rachel said afterward, "That guy with the T-shirt? When we were leaving, I saw him with a very hot chick. They were *aggressively* making out."

13

On the weekends, we went to the farmer's market on Rue Bretagne to admire produce. We gazed on rotisserie birds that butchers displayed on the sidewalk, and sniffed melons like we saw old women do, at the stem. We admired men walking around with bags on their shoulders, like enormous straw purses, with leeks poking out of their armpits.

Unfortunately, those leeks were out of our price range. Like many in Paris, we did the majority of our shopping at chain grocery stores.

Then we discovered Picard. *Shazam!* Picard was a French chain that had only freezers, that sold only frozen food, though it was frozen food of very high quality. Lovely meats, vegetables, fish. Tagliatelle with white truffles, or lamb confit. Rabbit in olive sauce.

Once you knew what to look for, Picard was everywhere; no Paris dinner party was complete without a tray of Picard hors d'oeuvres.

"Oh, Picard is extremely popular," Chloe told us. "It is the family's cook." Everyone in Paris used it, she said, and not ashamedly, especially families where both parents worked.

Other friends, both expats and natives, suggested that Paris had become a city of home cooks who specialized in reheating, thanks to Picard.

A few weeks after Le Fumoir, Lindsay was sitting at our

kitchen table on a chilly Saturday evening. I'd just warmed up a tray of frozen mushroom tartelettes (from Picard) in case Lindsay wanted a snack. Rachel was changing in the bedroom. That evening, Lindsay had been invited to a party nearby, and she'd asked us along.

The sun was still out, and the air was cold but floral. There was sort of a permanent good mood, weatherwise, during a Paris October.

Lindsay was watching Asif take a piss in the courtyard.

Lindsay had on a black leather jacket over a dress; the rest of her was icicle white. Frenchmen found her an exotic plant, so tall and pale. "American guys, I freak out," Lindsay had said before. "Anyway, they only want skeletons with big boobs." In Paris, Lindsay was frequently harangued by men on the street, but it wasn't such an awful problem: "I'm like a mountain they want to summit, so that I'll give them tall sons."

We set out walking. "Now, Dmitri won't be there," Lindsay said. "The party's at Pascal's apartment, Dmitri's friend. But Dmitri is sick of him. Pascal's sort of an iceberg—Dmitri doesn't think he's right for me at all."

Lindsay had had her first adventure: the previous week, she'd met a fat, rich Parisian named Dmitri. Dmitri dressed like a drug lord and knew everyone in town. They met at a dinner party. Afterward, he'd shown Lindsay Paris from the back of his Vespa until two a.m. Then he proposed marriage under the Eiffel Tower. When Lindsay said no, he proposed sleeping with her. When Lindsay said no to that, Dmitri vowed to be her best friend in Paris, so long as Lindsay kept open the concept of the two of them having sex one day.

"So Dmitri has a crush on Lindsay," Rachel said. "But so does Pascal."

"Whatever, Pascal wants to scale my heights—get in line," Lindsay said. "I wouldn't do anything with Pascal. Dmitri already introduced the two of us; he's super-bourgeois. This is hilarious: I told Dmitri we were going out tonight, and Dmitri was like, 'Baby, you are forbidden from sleeping with Pascal. He is boring and he is fat.' I said, 'Dmitri, one, you're an incredible snob; two, you're not one to talk. Besides, you said fat men make better lovers.' Dmitri's like, 'This is true—fat men know what to do. But, baby, Pascal would crush you during sex. You can't sleep with him, or I will never talk to you again, ever, you're killing me with the idea alone.'

"So who knows," Lindsay added, "maybe I'll have sex with Pascal just to torture Dmitri."

Lindsay had figured out Paris pretty quickly.

We skirted Place de la Bastille and followed the houseboats down Port de l'Arsenal. But it wasn't easy: Bastille was swarming with five thousand kids. A techno parade had begun that morning and was still going strong: where once had stood the guillotine, people were doing their best Tecktonik, a dance craze that summer all across France.

To do the Tecktonik was a solo act: arms twirling while the knees clapped together. Mostly it was popular with teenage boys, whose hips didn't move anyway. I knew about the Tecktonik from an art director at work named Franck. I'd asked Franck to recommend a good hip-hop club in Paris, and he laughed, saying rap was "children's music"—music for *les ados*, adolescents, immigrant black kids. According to Franck, in Paris techno was king. But even Franck drew the line at the Tecktonik.

The signature move in the Tecktonik was to brush the side of your face coquettishly while simultaneously whipping your arms. To me, it looked like boys who were trying to imitate an actress from the movies—Bernadette Lafont imagining herself seduced, eyes closed while she stroked her face to simulate a lover.

But that's probably not what the kids intended.

Pascal's apartment, down the block from Bastille, was a Paris bachelor pad as if unpacked from a carton: green poker table, dartboard, stereo with matte components. Sitting on a couch was Richard, the young redheaded American from A Small World. Richard had on a V-neck T-shirt and an *ushanka*, a fur hat with earflaps. "Thank you, thank you," he gushed as we entered and everyone kissed, "we were extremely bored until now, and how are we?"

The music was loud: songs by Pulp. Lindsay and Rachel started dancing by themselves, though not the Tecktonik. The Australian girl from the bar, Dana, was there, too, sitting with her boyfriend, a tan blond Parisian named Michel. He was fondling her thigh, smoking with the other hand.

"But how do you not know Michel?" Richard asked me while playing with his hat. Richard turned to Michel and said in French, with an extremely good Parisian accent, "Michel, you must tell him."

"Tell him what?" Michel said.

"About becoming king."

"*Please*, Richard," Michel groaned.

Michel's hair seemed constructed from two waves of yellow ice.

Dana said, "Michel is royal, like to the Bourbons? He'll be king of England if two hundred people die in the correct sequence."

"I'd heard that," I said, and thought, Logistics suck.

"Two hundred and seventy-one," Michel said a moment later. He rotated toward me, his open shirt puckering like lips. "You're from New York. You know Café Gitane? I have an apartment near there. So cool. Except for all the French, of course."

I knew Café Gitane; I'd gone there once on a date. Café Gitane was New York's Le Fumoir, where rich people from other countries had meetings to discuss their leisure careers—fashion consulting, cupcake stores.

He aspired, Michel said, to become an entrepreneur. But in the American mode. "Funny, it's a French word, *entrepreneur*, but the concept does not exist in France today." He dreamed, Michel said, of opening a chain of gourmet cheeseburger franchises in Paris, like what he'd seen in New York. But taxes and bureaucracy made it difficult to start a business in France. So far, his first outlet was mired in red tape, and it hadn't even opened yet. He wanted to kill himself!

I found Pascal in the kitchen warming platters from Picard—this would be our fifth party in Paris that featured Picard hors d'oeuvres. Pascal asked if I wanted to examine his cheese plate, using the same tone as an American hostess offering a tour of her house. Then Pascal told me in English about his *macarons*: "From my mother's favorite patisserie. Better than Ladurée. No wait in the queue, and much better taste. It is fundamental to have the best taste."

Pascal preferred to speak English with me so that he could practice. "I do not have people here, mostly. You come anytime," Pascal said. "Just call, we take a dinner. I do not have lots of friends," he added.

It made me a little uncomfortable, Pascal's English. Did my French come across so bald and vulnerable?

"Pascal," Lindsay asked in the living room, "why do Frenchmen always call me baby?"

Pascal said, "Because you *are* babies. American girls, they are the most—"

"Stupid?" Michel said.

"Immature," Pascal announced, with good cheer. "They are the most immature women in the world. They come to Paris, you meet, and they take off their pants. Like Sarah Jessica Parker."

"As soon as those cheese straws have cooled," Lindsay said, "I am out of here."

Half an hour later, we left. The night was full of house music. Dana, Michel, and Richard said they were tired and decamped to find the Métro. Lindsay said she'd heard about a party in the Bois de Boulogne, in a château, so we caught a taxi. The cabdriver was mute, listening to jazz on the radio. We go? Nod nod, hurry hurry. Normally, Bois de Boulogne would be a thirty-minute drive, but with the techno parade and Saturday-evening traffic . . . Pascal figured it would take an hour. The Eiffel Tower was all lit up. We rocketed along a highway that seemed level with the Seine. In the distance, La Défense, the outlying skyscraper district, was our lighthouse, atop the edge of the Bois. Twenty minutes later, we entered the forest's perimeter.

In total, the Bois was more than twice the size of Central Park. Trees hung over the road: black, globular, frozen. The woods seemed to go on forever.

At the palace gates, cars approaching were twenty deep. Two hundred bodies were queued around the shrubbery. People standing near the street rushed over to obtain our taxi.

"We won't get in," Rachel said.

"I'm more worried about getting home, actually," I said.

It was already two a.m. It would be an hour before we got inside. To get home would take another hour and fifty euros, assuming we found a cab.

Lindsay sank in her seat. Fine, she said, let's go home.

A dozen people were jostling outside our taxi.

"We go back? Okay, turn around, we go back," Pascal commanded the driver. A second later, he said to the driver in French, "They're like children," referring to us.

Living in another language and speaking defectively, I could not be clever. At best, I was genuine. Accidentally funny, but never funny on purpose. Earnest, not savvy. I'd worked this out, that it was difficult for me to influence other people's impressions of me favorably when I didn't speak the language well, and apparently this was something I needed, people having favorable impressions of me based on what I'd said.

So moving abroad was not unlike psychoanalysis.

But it was round-the-clock therapy, most of the time unwanted. Where every minute I needed to make myself understood, and was at the mercy of others.

That sandwich is what?

Which immigration form exactly?

I am lost.

Of course, lots of people in the office were semiadept at multiple languages. English, German, Italian, Chinese. But when they spoke poorly, they seemed comfortable in the floating state, hovering between full comprehension and zero. Meanwhile, I found myself reflected in Pascal—feelings from the mouth of a giant baby.

For example, I'd be in a meeting with Bruno and our project managers, and flash! something would occur to me. Well, how'd it go in French? Two minutes later, when I produced my idea out loud, inevitably Bruno had already said it better, only I hadn't heard him say it because I'd been too busy in my head.

But I learned from Tomaso that he and my non-Anglo coworkers were required to take a telephone exam each year that measured their English fluency and influenced their pay. It would be idiotic not to recognize that globalization was on my side. I also developed more respect for non-English-speakers back home, anyone crossing the border to clean toilets, and also Hiro Take, a friend from sixth grade who'd learned English rapidly after moving to the States from Japan and had made doing it seem cool. I looked him up on the Internet, but he wasn't there.

Each day, I brainstormed, I presented, I butchered the French language bloody.

It was petrifying.

14

Semibig announcement on the newsstands: Cécilia Sarkozy wanted a divorce. President Sarkozy and his wife married in 1996, and Sarkozy was on record as being head over heels in love with her, but no one was shocked. Cécilia had fallen in love elsewhere. Besides, Cécilia had said on TV that the idea of being First Lady bored her.

Now the president faced *catastrophe*. Many times, Sarkozy had said how besotted he was with Cécilia. He'd promised voters they would love her, too, assuming they loved that other great French heroine, Jackie Kennedy—born, let's remember, Jacqueline Lee Bouvier. No, a divorced president was not a symbol France needed, the papers said, not when France traditionally desired stability, a father figure, even a grandfather figure. If French leaders kept girls to see at lunch, fine, men were men. But they should not be left alone at night to whimper and second-guess their decisions.

At the office, I asked my deskmates what they thought about Sarkozy, the bachelor. Summing up for the majority, Julie explained that France desired a macho man, not a president who was unsure of himself, especially this one who was already prone to *nombrilisme*, navel gazing, she believed.

Pierre suggested I e-mail the Palais de l'Elysée and give them the address of that Notre Dame apartment I'd seen. Perhaps, he said, Sarkozy needed a room with a view.

•

A letter arrived requiring me to take a day off work and attend a *formation civique*, a "civic education" class. The day's purpose would be to provide "a day of civic training to present the fundamental rights, principles, and values of the French Republic." If I blew it off, "the *préfet* could terminate your contract or refuse to renew your residence permit."

Bruno didn't believe me until I showed him the letter. He said it was a stupid Sarkozy initiative, to entrench France against Muslim/Polish/Roma hordes.

"But what about lunch?" Bruno said. "You could come back, maybe we could go out and grab a pizza?"

I showed Bruno where, toward the bottom of the letter, the class promised lunch.

"Whatever this is," Bruno said, flicking the letter away, "I would fail it. So would anyone who's French." Then Bruno started laughing. "Hey, so today you're Steve Jobs?" It seemed that morning I'd worn a black turtleneck, blue jeans, and New Balance sneakers—the trademark uniform of the king of Apple Computer. In good American English, I told *mon cher compatriote* to go screw himself.

Bruno replied, "*Je ne comprend pas.*"

My class was held in a quiet neighborhood, in northern Paris, that I'd never seen before. We might have been in a French surburb on the moon—so many buildings reflecting 1970s futurism. My fellow immigrants and I arrived and took our seats around a conference table. There were about twenty of us. The instructor was a thirtysomething guy wearing red wire-frame glasses and a brown, long-sleeve T-shirt with a star on the chest. He commenced by asking us our names, countries of origin, and why we'd come to Paris. I was the only American. The rest of the class were mainly African, mostly from Morocco and Senegal.

Two women arrived late and tried to sit in the back.

"Excuse me," the teacher said. "You're in the wrong classroom."

The women apologized. The instructor said, "No, you do not understand me. This is not your classroom. If it were your classroom, you would have arrived fifteen minutes ago. Please, go find the right room, we are working here."

One of the women said that her babysitter had not shown up.

"Excuse me, this is not my problem," the teacher said, laughing. His teeth were brown and uneven. He looked around at us in mock wonder—did we hear ourselves challenged? The teacher said, "None of us were late, none of us decided we would take advantage of the group. My class commences at nine. You must belong in a class that begins at nine-fifteen. Hello, are you deaf? You're stupid?"

Some guys, student-age, urged the teacher to go easy, but that only made him shout louder. Once the women had left, he turned on us. Was this a problem? Did someone have a problem? After a moment, the teacher explained that here was a good example of democracy in action. To be equal under the law, everyone obeyed the same rules.

"Then how come we couldn't vote if the women could stay?" one boy said.

Murmurs of agreement.

The teacher said, "What is your name?"

"Hasan," the boy said. Hasan looked sixteen. He had a wispy beard and wore green track pants and a black motorcycle jacket with Kevlar shoulder pads.

"Hasan," the teacher said, "do you think if I came over and punched you right now, the class should be able to vote whether or not I am punished?"

"No, because you can't hit me."

"That is correct," the instructor said. "That is exactly the law."

"Actually, I'm an Arab," Hasan said, "so you probably can hit me. Maybe it depends *where* you hit me."

Everyone laughed. The teacher raised his hands for calm, though he was smiling. "The answer is that no matter what you are, I can't hit you. That would be a crime. In France, laws and rules are applied the same to everyone—whites, blacks, Arabs, even Martians. This way, we ensure equality."

Hasan said, "Hey, we know the laws are not the same for everyone. Not truly. Not even in the United States," he said, gesturing to me.

"Maybe this is true. Let's talk about it," the instructor said. He turned to me. "What do you think?"

"It depends," I said, "how the rules are applied."

I'd learned the verb *appliquer* the previous week.

"Anyway, Hasan," the teacher said, "this is your opinion. Another right of the Republic: you are free to have your opinion. But please, everyone, open your pamphlets now. Do you know *liberté, fraternité, égalité*? Today we begin with the second aspect. Now, introduce yourself to your neighbors."

By that point, my French was good enough to follow most of the conversation. After we met our classmates, the morning was devoted to French history and cigarette breaks, the instructor calling for a seven-minute pause every thirty minutes, which he spent smoking and texting in the courtyard. Mostly we nodded off. My neighbors were an old woman from Tunisia and an attractive girl from Russia. At one point, my eyes jerked open and I noticed that the old man sitting across from me had a wooden leg, a prosthesis stuck into a white sneaker.

At noon, we broke for lunch, and the instructor escorted us to a bistro. There we were served three courses: pork terrine or potato soup; *entrecôte* and fries or *croque-Monsieur* and salad; for dessert, a rice pudding, two types of cheese, and coffee or tea.

The instructor requested the Russian girl sit with him. He ordered them wine. I sat with a girl my age from Senegal who loved film. "Tarantino, *vous connaissez* Quentin Tarantino?" She'd come to Paris to study nursing. After I told her what I did, she said she hadn't realized that advertising required writers. *"Donc, cette pub-là"*—she pointed at an Orangina poster—*"un auteur a écrit ça?"*

It showed a cheetah in pinup pose wearing high heels and a bra. I answered affirmatively: a writer had been responsible, if not for the idea, then its promise of *Naturellement Pulpeuse.* Back in class, our instructor introduced an oral quiz. "In France," he asked, "can a husband beat his wife?"

Responses from around the room: *"Non," "Jamais," "Ça dépend," "Chez moi, chaque semaine."* (No; never; it depends; every week at my house.)

"The answer is no," the teacher said. "In France, a husband and wife are equal. This is important. In France, men and women are the same."

"Man and woman are never the same," a woman said. She was sitting across from me, an older woman from Nigeria. "Not husband and wife."

"In the eyes of the government, you are wrong," the instructor told her, now sitting beside her on the table. "Tell me, you think a man and a woman, if they are husband and wife, they have different rights?"

"Of course," the woman said.

People voiced agreement.

The instructor got up and said, "Okay, say a man meets a woman at a café. They are not married, but they become friendly. Later, he wants to go to bed, but she does not. Can he make her go to bed with him?"

At this, the class agreed no. An old man in the back with a beard said, "Actually, sometimes, if you're quick." Some young guys shouted him down, but he yelled at them that in France, as we'd learned, he was entitled to his opinion, so they could go fuck themselves.

What if, the teacher said, the people are married, then can a husband force his wife to go to bed?

"In a marriage, things are different," another woman said.

"Not true," said the instructor. "The law says it is *always* forbidden to force sex. In all cases, rape is illegal. This is very important. Now, what if a woman wants to get divorced, does she need to ask permission from her husband?"

The Nigerian woman said, "Of course!"

"Not of course—why of course?"

The Nigerian locked eyes with the instructor. She said slowly, "A wife must obey her husband. This is a rule of marriage, without a doubt."

"In fact, the answer is no," the instructor said. "Under French law, the wife does not need to ask permission. Okay? Does everyone follow?"

"Well, in *my* culture," the Nigerian woman said, glaring, "this is the law."

A young guy shouted at her, "But we're in France now, not Nigeria!" Several people clapped and whooped.

"Actually, this is an interesting question," the instructor said. "What is the difference between culture and law? In France, we say we are French before we are anything else."

"What about if you're religious?" asked Hassan.

"Religion, good. A French Muslim, is he Muslim or is he French?"

Hasan said, laughing, "But it's forbidden to be Muslim in France."

"Okay, good joke," the teacher said. "In France we say he is French *before* he is Muslim. Same for the French Jew, the French Catholic, the French atheist. Good? Now," the instructor said, looking at the clock, "let's take a break."

On return, he asked who was allowed to purchase condoms in France. The young Russian woman said anyone, which was correct, though it stunned the Nigerian woman, who wanted to know if this meant children could purchase condoms, too. Then we discussed polygamy. By class's end, we'd learned a lot. For example, how genital mutilation was *not* allowed in France, but this didn't include genital piercing or shaving, assuming the genitals' owner wanted them pierced or shaved; it took ten minutes to work out that distinction. Hasan spent five minutes speculating that if a man came from a country where polygamy *was* allowed—like South Africa, or "Utah" (*ew-tah*)—and he emigrated to France with multiple wives, then died, under French law would all of his children inherit his property? Or only the children from the wife that France recognized? What if he'd had an affair outside of his marriages, what would his bastard children receive?

At four p.m., our instructor congratulated us on our efforts and gave us certificates from l'Office français de l'immigration et de l'intégration. We all shook hands. In the courtyard, the Senegalese nursing student and I wished each other good luck in our professions, *bon courage*, and parted ways.

On the sidewalk, the workday was over. People streamed home. At a nearby Métro station, a man played accordion on the crowded platform, but we couldn't hear him because we all wore headphones. People waiting stood four ranks deep. The cars were packed. When a train arrived, filled to capacity, desperate commuters would throw themselves at the fleshy spots, and either they fell back stunned or they stuck for a moment and used the closing doors to pinch their asses and squeeze them in.

Finally I got a spot. Everyone was pressed together, but no one spoke. At night, Paris swayed home in silence, all of us leaning on one another. At worst, people got hooked on each other's earbud cables, and they'd apologize while they helped one another unwind.

The big book on the Métro that season was *Millénium*, a trio of crime novels by the Swedish author Stieg Larsson. At that point, the books were still unknown in America, but they were everywhere in France. Coworkers lugged their copies to the office each morning, walking through the front door with their noses buried deep.

I wasn't feeling very hopeful about the future of books. The novel I was writing appeared to be going unhurriedly backward, sliding toward the trash. I'd sit at the kitchen table in the morning, stare at the laptop screen, and think, Maybe I should do a sidebar in the second booklet about mother-child bonding at feeding time.

Everyone knew Paris was where artists moved to pursue art. But I was only writing in stitches, having journeyed to Paris to pursue ad sales. And meanwhile some people, the trust-funders we met through A Small World, had all the time in the world to write the shittiest novels imaginable.

These were my thoughts on the Métro.

Autumn arrived in wools, cool and gray. At dusk, the Grand Palais looked just as golden-orange as the surrounding trees, and every Parisian man wore a scarf. Some even wore coats. The benches at my park, where I ate lunch, were often empty. Our crowd thinned to a few regulars, whom I nicknamed:

Stephen King, late fifties, every day reading a Stephen King book, wearing a shapeless jacket, black glasses, and a mustache that defined his face.

The Puzzlers, a man and a woman about the same age as Stephen King, who'd curl up on a bench, him with a cigar and her with cigarettes, smoking together while they did a puzzle in the newspaper.

Two crazies: ATC and Louis XIV. ATC was Air Traffic Controller, because he wore plastic shopping bags over his hands to conduct park visitors in through the gate. When there weren't visitors to conduct, he conducted birds. When there weren't birds, he talked loudly to himself.

Louis XIV was the sun king, lord of *bronzage*, a fat brown man who wore orange surf trunks even in cold weather. No shirt, no shoes. By the time I arrived for lunch, he'd be in position, depending on whichever part of him needed to improve its color.

One afternoon, we had the park to ourselves. A dark sky swirled above us like a wind-blown lake. Rain started to fall. I ran for cover. Louis XIV was lying facedown on the lawn and didn't stir. Then, after a minute in the rain, he got up slowly, staring angrily at the sky. He treaded slowly toward me across the lawn, and we stood there a good ten minutes while I ate my pasta and he watched the clouds. We didn't exchange a word.

15

La grève crippled Paris: a strike. To protest Sarkozy's new reform plans, transit workers walked off the job—meaning no trains ran in Paris, no buses and no Métro—and other unions soon followed suit.

Paris became a throng of vehicles, all the boulevards jammed.

The agency instructed us to bicycle, skate, or walk. Cyclists wore reflective vests and carried knapsacks, bringing changes of clothes to work. Some of my coworkers faced two-hour hikes each way, up and down Montmartre. But few complained. Paris for the most part was on the strikers' side, at least in the beginning.

Some mornings, Pierre gave me a ride on his scooter. I'd resist holding on to him while we threaded our way between trucks and cars, with a half-inch of clearance on either side. I expected to have my fingers rubbed off. Some days, if Pierre couldn't pick me up, I walked the hour to work through the highlights of Paris—along the Seine to the Tuileries, past the fountains and windblown chairs; past chauffeurs idling outside the Ritz; up the Champs-Elysées to my desk—and it was the world's most pleasant commute.

And some days, if I left home early enough and found one available, I rented a Vélib. Vélibs were hot commodities during the strike. Rumors circulated that people were hoarding them, storing them at home rather than returning them to their stations. When I was lucky enough to nab one, I'd bike along

Rue de Rivoli, Paris's equator, and fly past the Louvre's arcades, where scooters zipped out like birds from a birdhouse. Next came Place de la Concorde, an enormous, bewildering traffic circle where I almost died several times. There weren't any marked lanes for traffic—there wouldn't have been in the eighteenth century, when Concorde was constructed—yet there were four or five lanes full of speeding vehicles that I was expected to enter. One time, my coat got stuck in the back wheel and I flipped over in front of a truck. Twice I cut off cars and made them stop. Why couldn't everybody cooperate to avoid my slaughter? Later, André explained why I hadn't had the right-of-way, and he suggested that visitors who came from countries where people preferred four wheels to two shouldn't be allowed to rent bicycles.

But I continued cycling, and I also learned from Tomaso some proper French insults, like *Enculé de ta mère!* (Goddamn motherfucker!).

Anyway, I switched to riding on the sidewalk around Concorde. It was illegal, but much less dangerous—for me and for France. I'd ring my bell and pedal up the long rise of the Champs-Elysées until I reached the office, hung up my coat, *bonjour*ed the room and chose a few people to kiss, and got to work.

Julie, my desk neighbor, invited me out for pizza. She'd never invited me anywhere before. She said, whispering, while Françoise and Olivier discussed some layout problems with a project manager, that she needed someone to talk to who wasn't French.

On the sidewalk Julie explained why: she didn't want to stir up trouble, but she was sick of the strikers—she drew a finger across her neck—as well as those coworkers who couldn't stop talking about sympathizing with them.

"Françoise wanted to get lunch, that's why I asked you instead," Julie said in English at the restaurant. "Françoise is one of them," she added darkly.

"It is not very cool to be my age and prefer Sarkozy," Julie said, after we'd ordered pizzas. "Françoise, for example, hates Sarkozy. She's traditional, a socialist—she's like all French people who drive me crazy, who live in dreamworlds. Dreams are fine for poets, and I am a poet, you know, but come on, this is not reality."

Julie started getting worked up, gaining volume: "Françoise looks at society and says it should be this particular way—traditional France, what she's known. Why? Because that's how life *should* be, she says. The French mode. Then I explain to her that with globalization and the EU, with world trade, we cannot expect to preserve our 'beautiful way' and not pay for it. And she returns to, Oh, but you see, it *should* be this way. If we just wait, the rest of the world will adapt to us."

I was going to say something, but Julie wasn't done: "Look, it would be nice to live in Françoise's dream. Believe me. But that is not the world today. Ancient Europe . . . it's corrupt. But you can't tell that to Françoise. The Left in France—which is all of Paris, mostly—they say they're liberal, but in fact they are extremely conservative. They want to cut us off from other countries, from sharing, trading. And then what?"

After ten minutes of this, our lunches arrived. Julie ripped open a packet of red-pepper oil and squirted it all over her pizza, as the French do. Julie said in English, "We need to live in the world and look after our interests—that is my position. But, come on, you need to look at reality once in a while to come to this opinion."

I was about to tell her that I appreciated her sharing her perspective with me, but at that moment Françoise and Olivier, and some other people—François, Scottish Keith—came up the stairs, and Julie gripped my arm and swore me to keep her capitalist confession.

•

Back in the summer, a story had appeared in my morning papers that the president was in really good shape. Sarkozy, already known as a jogger, one so badass he wore NYPD T-shirts and state-trooper glasses to look tough when he exercised, had come under suspicion for being *too* fit.

Now that he was no longer running for president, the papers wondered, wasn't there something despotic about his desire to run more?

A trainer told *L'Equipe*, the sports newspaper, that Sarkozy was, in fact, running wrong. His stride was off. His feet hit the ground with inefficient strokes. During a television program that ran on the subject, which I didn't catch but read about later in the London *Times*, a French philosopher said, "Western civilization, in its best sense, was born with the promenade. Walking is a sensitive, spiritual act. Jogging is management of the body. The jogger says I am in control. It has nothing to do with meditation."

A French media critic also told the *Times* that images of Sarkozy going running were "a major weapon" of "manipulation."

Perhaps all of that was true and made some media-academic types feel better about their lack of fitness. But it didn't account for the thousands of joggers in Paris. During the worst week of the strike, Rachel and I attended an art gallery opening in the Marais with Pierre and Chloe, and Pierre's sister Monique, the economics professor. Sipping champagne, Monique told me all this worrying about *le jogging* was out of date. Running was chic these days; the media were simply stirring up old clichés. You'd see Parisians running everywhere now, she said; it was simply another form of sport.

And it's true, we had seen them. At Buttes-Chaumont or the Tuileries Gardens, the parks where Rachel and I jogged, there were plenty of Parisian runners, and many much more serious than we: timing laps, interval training, wearing Lycra tights and ventilated shirts. Their enthusiasm wasn't just for conditioning or weight loss, but running-as-sport, which was Monique's point and which seemed to be the distinction the Sarkozy watchers were worried about. In France, sport was considered good—soccer, rugby, tennis, martial arts—but running for running's sake? Pure body management.

Being trim today was important for appearances, Parisians confirmed, but probably best achieved—if you didn't play a sport—through means other than huffing and puffing. My co-workers said the best thing to do if you wanted to lose weight was catch *une gastro*, an intestinal bug. They were only half joking. *Une gastro* was a mysterious wind that sporadically blew through Paris, attacking half the city. Locals knew a *gastro* was circulating when the streets were painted with vomit.

During one week in November, almost one-third of the office called in sick with a *gastro*. I would swear all of them had lost ten kilos by the time they returned, beaming with a glow.

As the weather cooled, Rachel decided to join a gym in our neighborhood. It belonged to the Club Med corporation, which operated more than twenty gyms in Paris; it had taken a company known for islands of pleasure to succeed in selling the gym concept to France. Rachel took a tour before she signed up. The manager was proud to show her his new pool. It was about the size of a large aquarium, Rachel said. "I would guess a lap requires two kicks." A woman in a black bikini had been floating in the pool under purple lights, listening to ambient techno music.

The gym offered two levels of membership. The basic package included use of the facility, but for an additional thirty euros a month, Rachel would receive a towel, plus a comprehensive accident-insurance package in case she was harmed by a Nautilus machine. *For a little extra cash each month, you, too, can wipe away any signs of body management, and rest assured you will not be injured by exercising*. Rachel told the manager she'd take the basic level. Excellent, he replied, now all he needed was for Rachel to fill out an application and supply two photographs; a photocopy of her passport; a photocopy of a recent bill; a photocopy of our apartment's lease; a photocopy of our residency application; a notarized document translated into French that proved Rachel had internationally covered health insurance, since our residency papers still hadn't come through; et cetera.

Bureaucracy being France's first sport.

Bruno and I had our first fight at work. We were sitting in the canteen when he slammed down his espresso cup. His shoulders tilted toward me. I began to stare out the window.

We were at odds over my productivity. According to Bruno, I'd churned out the first drafts of our baby books too quickly. He insisted I slow down. "You can't let them do this to you." He was disgusted. Obviously I hadn't learned anything about business in Paris, at least not from Bruno. "What are you, a slave? This schedule is bullshit. I thought we were agreed."

My argument was that the faster we finished, the sooner we'd be done. Wiser to play monkey among the monkeys. But Bruno said I didn't have the right perspective, I was being too American again.

Behind us, coworkers were battling at Tekken 5 on PlayStation.

"This is hell," Bruno said, stabbing some printouts with his finger, "you agree?"

"*Comme-çi, comme-ça,*" I said. I stared at the scar on Bruno's ear. I said, We're wasting our lives on work, yes, but no, this wasn't exactly *hell*—typing, chatting, having coffee, and when there was leisure time we played video games in a converted ballroom under frescoes?

"It *is* hell, listen to me," Bruno said sharply. "You do not understand hell. You think hell is something that stops. You pass through hell and at the end you think there is something new.

This is what I'm saying: there is no end to this project. Only more hell. We must stop together, you and me."

I realized: he was asking me to go on strike.

Bruno quavered, "Sometimes you forget we are a team."

I said I'd think about it, and left him sitting there on a red vinyl couch.

Truthfully, after hearing many opinions floated around the office, I found the public-sector strikes in Paris a little ridiculous—more pantomime than struggle—never mind a pain in the ass. And I didn't agree with Bruno's logic. But I had a secret. Pierre had told me he was going to switch me off infant nutrition to another account in January, "something more 'luxe,'" he said, meaning Louis Vuitton, the firm's big fashion/luggage client, one of France's most storied brands. Pierre's plan was that I'd train Keith, the Scottish copywriter, to take over my breast-feeding work, then switch. But Pierre didn't want Bruno knowing any of this yet, because he didn't plan to bring Bruno onto fashion/luggage, too.

Traditionally, art directors and copywriters moved within agencies as couples, never splitting. But Pierre wanted me and Bruno divorced. For the moment, I needed to keep the plan secret.

I walked away and Bruno called in English after me, "Hey, don't forget, when you go speed, I forced to go speed, too."

By early November, I understood more than half of what I heard. I no longer returned home each night with headaches. I still needed to squint at my coworkers to read their lips; telephone calls remained misery. But my life in French was improving.

Rachel had it harder. Because our budget was tight, she'd quit her French classes that month when we couldn't afford them anymore. Now she was trying to learn on her own from her old schoolbooks, if not osmosis.

"The stupidest things will drive you crazy," she said. "Like I went to the grocery store yesterday, I didn't tell you this, that

Franprix on Bretagne? So I filled up a cart of groceries and brought it to the cashier. She'd rung up almost everything when I reached into my purse and realized I'd left my wallet at home. But what could I say? There's a line of people behind me. I tried to communicate, but I didn't even know how to say 'wallet.' It was awful. I'm miming, *I'll be right back*. So I sprinted home, grabbed my wallet, and ran back to the store. Of course they were very pleasant about it, they'd kept my bags for me to the side. They even seemed surprised to see me back so quickly. Like, *Madame, it's okay, no big rush*."

Living in a country that had been loaned to you, there were plenty of moments when you were grateful. Bridges sparkled. Cashiers smiled. The girl at the pâtisserie took an extra minute to wrap up your éclair like it was a present for the king. But when you didn't know the words for "Shit, I forgot my wallet," any moment could implode.

16

In the media dustup around Sarkozy's running habit, a journalist in *Libération* commented, "Jogging is, of course, about performance and individualism, values that are traditionally ascribed to the Right."

Observed during one morning's run in Buttes-Chaumont:

A man in a white collared shirt, khaki trousers, loafers, no socks, with the cuffs of his pants rolled to mid-calf. His running companion wore black tights, a black cashmere sweater, ballet flats, enormous black Chanel sunglasses, makeup, and a gold pendant necklace. Both of them were chatting while jogging a ten-minute mile.

An elderly man running in sweatpants, T-shirt, headband, sneakers, and a green houndstooth blazer.

A beautiful woman jogging in jeans and suede loafers, while swinging an oversize handbag.

Buttes-Chaumont is located in the nineteenth arrondissement, a mixed neighborhood of whites and blacks and Arabs. The *Herald Tribune* reported gang fights occurring in Buttes-Chaumont, but I only saw groups keeping to themselves: teenage boys chasing teenage girls; teenage girls glomming together. On Saturdays, Orthodox Jews strolled around the lake. Above the lake, a Greek temple sits atop a crag, surrounded by cliffs. On sunny days, the hills would be dotted with picnickers, women tanning in bikinis. Firemen, *les pompiers*, staged rappelling exercises down a waterfall.

One Sunday, for variety, we went running in the Luxembourg Gardens. The whole city was out, including dozens of people running in fancy workout gear. But how they'd gotten to the park was a mystery. No one outside the gates wore exercise clothes, not a single person. Did the runners change into their Lycra in a phone booth? Did they arrive by pneumatic tube?

Walking home across the Seine, feeling conspicuous in our sweatpants and T-shirts, we passed a group of teenagers lounging around the Saint-Jacques Tower dressed like punk mimes, in black cargo pants and striped shirts. One shouted at me, "Hey, here come the athletes!"

I shouted back, "Yeah!"

That made them laugh. The guy yelled, "Keep going! You're winning!"

Only in Paris did Goths bully the jocks.

According to my computer, the song I listened to most while running that fall was "North American Scum," by LCD Soundsystem. I didn't realize the irony until about the fourth time I heard it, while running around the lake at Buttes-Chaumont:

I hate the feeling when you're looking at me that way 'cause we're North Americans . . .
But if we act all shy, it'll make it okay, makes it go away.

Among the *créatifs*, the only other native English-speaker was Scottish Keith. Keith was my age, tall and shaggy, very outgoing and kind. He'd lived in Paris for several years and had worked as a copywriter for multiple French ad agencies. He was an autodidact—Keith spoke fluent French, Italian, and German, some Swedish and a little Japanese, almost all of it self-taught—and had a fund of quotations, particularly from works by French authors whom even the French overlooked. Keith also collected fluorescent sneakers. Prior to working in advertising, he'd been a professional skateboarder. He'd once skated in Tehran, for the ayatollah.

One lunchtime, I showed Keith a 2006 article from *The Guardian* about Japanese tourists in Paris suffering a condition called "Paris syndrome." It occured when a Japanese visitor was so disappointed by Paris—by the city not living up to her romantic expectations—that she suffered a psychological breakdown. The Japanese embassy in Paris said it reported a dozen cases each year. Most patients were women in their thirties, with extremely tender ideas about Paris and France, who collapsed at a waiter's first bark and were repatriated to Japan, accompanied by a doctor. A psychologist was quoted saying, "Fragile travelers can lose their bearings. When the idea they have of the country meets the reality of what they discover, it can provoke a crisis."

Imagine, Keith said, what those fantasy Parises must look like, if the disappointment of the real thing—because surely Paris was still pretty great—put women in the hospital.

One afternoon, Keith visited my desk to tell a joke. "What do you call someone who speaks three languages?"

"Trilingual," I said.

"Right," he said, "and what do you call someone who speaks two languages?"

"Bilingual."

"And what," Keith said, relishing it, "do you call someone who only speaks one language?"

I said I gave up.

"American!" Keith said, and laughed. At which point Olivier pulled off his headphones and asked Keith to translate the joke into French. It became Olivier's favorite joke for a month.

No French person could resist a good joke about Americans, especially an easy joke. And vice versa. Witness: freedom fries.

But I never heard a joke in Paris about the Brits. Londoners and Parisians were too comingled by history and business. Whole strips of northwest France were occupied by Britons' summer homes, and French kids learned their English with London accents. America and France, however, were separated by an ocean, not a channel. Only the most hardened jokes could survive a transatlantic journey.

One coworker after another told me how much he or she longed to see New York or San Francisco. To drive west across the plains—several had done it—to Arizona, California, "the big sky" of Montana. One guy, who'd watched *Badlands* too many times, talked about the Dakotas like they were Tahiti. Another, Yassine, asked me for travel tips for Detroit. Detroit? I said. Yassine longed to photograph the auto factories and hard streets—"The 'grit,' you say in English?" He told me he was planning a family vacation there soon, he'd take his wife and children. I said I'd never been to Detroit. Yassine only had pity for me. He looked past me the way addicts do, with far-seeing eyes, as though I couldn't appreciate what he sought.

A letter from the government arrived. Rachel's and my *cartes de séjour* were ready, our residency papers. We'd officially been made Parisians.

I met Rachel at lunch under the awning of the Brasserie Les Deux Palais on the Ile de la Cité, under Gothic spires and charming steeples. It was a bright gray morning, with wind blowing from all directions, leaves spun in twisters or magnetized to building corners. Both of us were thrilled. Chestnut roasters had begun appearing around Paris, and there was a charred smell citywide. We entered a municipal building, a colossal fortress of heavy stone—formerly a garrison, it now protected bureaucrats—and waited ten minutes on a bench. Summoned, we handed over our paperwork and received laminated permits from a filing cabinet.

We examined each other's photo: two hard-faced Parisians, properly unsmiling.

"I can't believe it," I said when we were outside again, standing on the riverbank next to the *quai*.

"We're Parisian," Rachel said.

"But look, it's going to pour." Clouds were flexing above us, as usual. Paris wasn't the city of light—it was the city of clouds. But beautiful clouds normally, clouds colored and shaped like almond cakes. Clouds at arm's length, thin as ribbons, detailed as monuments. Leonine clouds with shoulders and tails.

At that moment, they were black, rippling with purple and yellow veins.

"Let's go celebrate," I said. There was a café downstream, tucked under a wall of ancient homes. The sky opened up and we fled the rain. I knew what I'd order: two *coupes* of champagne to celebrate, plus a *café* for me and a *citron pressé* for Rachel, and with the proper words not only to demand those items, but to do so breezily, to demonstrate my Parisianness.

We reached the café. A man held open the door and smiled. He grabbed two menus, with gargantuan Union Jacks on the covers, and announced in English, "Hello! Today will we be drinking or eating?"

17

Before we enjoyed a late Thanksgiving in Italy—more on that in a moment—I took a train with Pierre and Marcel, an account director, to Belgium. For several weeks, we'd been working nights and weekends, Pierre the hardest, for a chance to redo the Levi's website. Pierre wasn't sleeping. His smoking had doubled. To reduce nerves on the train, I made a bet: How many times could I insert the word "boom" into my presentation, like Steve Jobs did during his Apple speeches, in order for them to buy me dinner at Taillevent?

Taillevent was a famous Paris restaurant where dinner was about three hundred euros a head.

"How many times do you think you can do?" Marcel asked.

"Maybe five," I said.

"Do six," he said, "and if we win the account, I'll buy dinner. *Bon courage*," Marcel added, which meant "good luck," though it also meant "be bold, do not fear."

Levi's European operations were based in Brussels, a mournful city. To me, it looked like Boston if Boston had lived through the Dark Ages. The sky wore a gray armband where the sun was obscured by clouds. A cab took us to an office park outside the city, past marshes of faceless blocks. Was the city always swamplike? For a panel of businessmen dressed like Lou Reed, we presented our designs, and during the presentation I said four "booms." They loved it. They offered us free jeans. We left in high spirits and got drunk in the bar car on the train ride home, and Marcel told me four "booms" were good enough for dinner, assuming we won.

Except we didn't win. The Levi's chief reported that they'd liked our ideas, just not the IT infrastructure our technical director had proposed afterward. I must have shown disappointment. Well, I was pissed. The next day, Pierre told me not to be depressed. I said, Of course not, don't be ridiculous, depressed? Depressed about advertising?

"It's only one pitch," Pierre said, seeing through me. Or perhaps it wasn't him saying it, it was André, showing me his teeth. The two of them had looked up simultaneously from their computers when I'd interrupted them, barging into their office, to hear what I'd assumed would be good news.

Riding home on the Métro, I had visions of working in French advertising until death. I heard myself pitching diaper campaigns at ninety—myself in a pair of Ça Dépend undergarments to demonstrate their pliancy.

Since August, I'd told myself not to care about work; only my fiction mattered, and the job sufficed to provide our *cartes de séjour*, that was it.

But I've never been as hard as I'd like.

Some lunches in the park, sitting next to Stephen King, I'd be finishing my pasta when memories would pass by in a convoy. Faces from New York, or smells I knew. I'd find myself crazy homesick—tasting bitterness. I was constantly an inch off normal.

More lessons from work: a traditional Thanksgiving dinner was not well understood, never mind easy to assemble in Europe. This Tomaso said smoothly, with authority. He asked me, How would I transport my *dinde* to Venice, by train?

"Yes," Olivier wondered, "in a *dinde*-shaped attaché?"

Ohohoho, ahahaha, they both laughed.

My father had a business meeting coming up in Venice, over the Thanksgiving holiday. My family, including several aunts and uncles and cousins, had decided to join him. It would be a Thanksgiving overseas, a destination Thanksgiving.

An American invasion! Olivier said.

My mother, I explained to Tomaso, said that she'd found a Venetian restaurant that could roast us a turkey; it was a restaurant that was known for not even serving fish. Tomaso, who was Venetian, laughed, then he looked offended and alarmed.

"In Venice?" Tomaso said. "This is impossible. Seriously, my friend, be careful with your digestion. Venice is *not* about having turkeys."

We flew to Venice on a Friday evening, *nous avons voyagé de nuit*, and from the airport we took a vaporetto, a public transport boat, across the lagoon, toward buildings ahead of us wavering in the dark. There were bleak harbor sounds, and a wind that smelled of moss and gasoline. No foghorns, though there was plenty of fog. The boat docked. We tried to get our sea legs and carried our luggage down a path beside a canal, and found our hotel set into a blackened stone wall. Inside, past the empty front desk, in a sitting room decorated with Greek statues, my parents were eating bar snacks and reading newspapers. It was fun to see them, and we all caught up.

The next morning, emergency sirens struck at breakfast to announce *acqua alta*, high water due to the lagoon's rising. Venice was flooded. Outside, Venetians knew what to do and wore knee-high rubber boots, while the rest of us explored in our sneakers from trembling wooden planks that had been laid out across the piazzas. The talk at lunch among my dad's Venetian colleagues, who all wore rubber boots, was of a cruise ship docking that afternoon that would squeeze thousands of tourists "out from the bowels," disgorge them into the city "with their plastic water bottles."

For Thanksgiving, our restaurant was in the Dorsoduro, a

residential neighborhood distant from most tourist spots. The chef had indeed roasted a turkey, even prepared mashed sweet potatoes and pumpkin pie. Our family tradition required each person at the table to name something they were thankful for. Rachel and I said we were thankful to live in Paris and to see everyone at the holiday. We also toasted Jeremy Irons—the owner of the restaurant had confided that Irons had eaten in her restaurant most evenings during the recent filming of *Casanova*.

At night, Paris was quiet, but Venice was a tomb. Deserted, but magical. Late the previous evening, after we'd checked into our hotel, one of my dad's coworkers had taken us for a boat ride. He'd poled us across the Grand Canal, into a system of narrow waterways. It was like a night canoe ride across a lake. Only here a thousand-year-old city had been pushed up through the water's surface, and its homes were also islands, so a person paddling around was level with his front door. People in their apartments were washing dishes, watching TV—oblivious to us as if they had no idea other cities weren't also submerged.

After twenty minutes, we arrived at a bend where our gondolier stopped poling and turned on his flashlight. On the wall beside us was a shimmering painting, a fresco of a woman praying. We didn't say anything.

On the way to Venice, at Charles de Gaulle, we had seen several Parisians in tooled boots, Wrangler jeans, and white Stetson hats—way more cowboy than cowboys—getting on a plane bound for Dallas. I was flabbergasted, though I shouldn't have been. Earlier that fall, we'd joined Pierre and Chloe for a picnic in Parc Saint-Cloud, a massive forest on the outskirts of Paris. In the parking lot, there'd been a man and woman in full cowboy gear. Pierre had explained that in France there was still a wide affection for the myth of cowboys and Indians.

Parisians and cowboys, of course, having many common interests, like tight blue jeans and cocaine.

After lunch, Chloe had disappeared into the forest, then returned after twenty minutes with a plastic tray of espressos. No big deal. In Europe, the normal wasn't abnormal, just differently fashioned. The accoutrements changed. Espresso oozed like sap if you knew which trees to spike.

18

One December morning, two gorgeous girls in lingerie opened the door for me at work. Their high heels were aeronautical. I could almost hear them shivering. Was this normal in Paris? Did a branch of the government send underwear models outdoors during the holidays, to promote spending on lingerie?

Turns out a newspaper had hired them to stand outside our building's entrance, to open the door and pass out Christmas flyers. In the lobby, Doo-Doo the intern was erecting our office Christmas tree. It was a red metal fir tree, fifteen feet tall. It creaked.

Olivier walked in behind me. "Not bad," he said. "Last year's tree was much worse. Good job, Doo-Doo."

"Thanks, Olivier!" Doo-Doo shouted from under the tree.

"Why was it worse?" I said.

"Well, it was black," Olivier said. He unwound his scarf. "A black metal tree, with black balls. Huge balls. For décor. Very chic, of course, quite beautiful. But not for me."

December in Paris was gorgeous but there wasn't much sunlight. Even midday light seemed thinner, as though the sun was retreating. On the weekends, the boulevards were madcap with visitors and locals out shopping, to get the most from their daylight hours. Since we'd be spending the holidays in Paris, we decided to send home wine—Gallic *and* affordable.

I called the post office to confirm we could ship wine to the

States, and the woman answering had a laugh like a shovel hitting cement.

"Sir," she said, "this is France."

Paris had plenty of Christmas spirit. The city was draped with electric bulbs. Inside Galeries Lafayette, a department store equivalent to Saks Fifth Avenue, there was a mammoth Christmas tree that climbed to a stained-glass dome. In Montmartre, on a Saturday morning, with the wind snapping our coats, we saw a green fir tree hung with black stilettos, in tribute, a sign said, to Karl Lagerfeld—*Joyeux Nöel!* Tourists filled the sidewalks. Women shopped together holding hands. On the walls of the Métro stations, advertising posters were hung for toys, Disneyland Paris vacations, trips to Zermatt, and lots of lingerie, too.

Pierre said he needed me on Louis Vuitton sooner than expected. The other writers on the account were French, and there'd been complaints about their English copy sounding wrong. First, though, Pierre said, I needed to meet the account's creative director for TV and print advertising, Jean-Paul, who worked across the street in the agency's other building.

"You must see the account from the big picture," Pierre said as we darted across the Champs-Elysées. That morning, Paris was gray and frigid. We could see our breath as we puffed our way down France's Rodeo Drive, its Avenida Presidente Masaryk—the Champs-Elysées being both a red carpet of French pride and an escalator ride through globalization's shopping mall, Adidas to Zara. Pierre said, "This account is a big deal, a very big deal. You need to understand what the brand means to the agency's reputation. And to France's identity. To French people, in effect."

Pierre was more tense than normal. For many years, he'd worked late, but Chloe had become worried about his hours and stress level. Normally, Pierre was in the mood for liking everything, but his face had grown darker recently, his beard longer.

"Don't worry, you can count on me," I told Pierre. "You'll remember, I did luxury humor."

"No," Pierre said sharply. He lit another cigarette. "Look," Pierre said, "this is about celebrities. It's big-time. 'Funny' is the wrong attribute. You need to do 'emotional' now. 'Inspiring,' okay?

"They do not do funny," he said.

The account revolved around celebrities posing with luggage, and Annie Leibovitz taking their picture. Andre Agassi, Steffi Graf, Catherine Deneuve, Mikhail Gorbachev. The idea, Pierre had told me, was to evoke travel and well-lived lives. *Judge a man by his duffel, a woman by her clutch.* Pierre handled the Web, Jean-Paul the print and TV. For his part, Pierre had convinced Louis Vuitton to let him interview each celebrity about his or her favorite city, specifically their attached emotions. Then Pierre would dispatch a movie crew, a director and a composer, to make short films about the chosen city, and he turned the results into little treasure chests of websites, memoirs made from film. Visitors would see the city portrayed in dreamlike sequences and narrated fragments, drawn from the famous person reminiscing about his or her own experiences.

Jean-Paul's office was huge, walled by glass. Light shot through it. Behind Jean-Paul's desk hung a large abstract painting, and around the room were awards, more art, mid-century furniture, art books in vertical piles. Against one wall were several video-game systems that looked dusty and unused.

Jean-Paul was in his sixties. He was cheerfully patrician. He had fleecy eyebrows that protruded winglike—either he grew them purposefully or they were long ago forgotten. Pierre told me Jean-Paul had worked at the firm for thirty years. He sat us down on tufted, cube-shaped leather chairs. He wore a brown suit, white shirt, and dark blue scarf, as if a breeze had flung it around his neck. An assistant served us sandwiches from a wicker basket.

It reminded me of the scene in *Charade* when Audrey Hepburn visits Walter Matthau at the American embassy, and he likewise serves her sandwiches from a basket—"liverwurst, liverwurst, chicken and liverwurst."

Jean-Paul was offering chicken, liverwurst, or grilled vegetables on ciabatta.

"Pierre tells me you are new to Paris, to advertising," Jean-Paul said in French. He had a friendly smile. "You're from New York, which neighborhood again?"

"Brooklyn," I said.

"Of course," Jean-Paul said. "I've heard that all the artists live in Brooklyn. I've been meaning to visit Brooklyn, specifically one neighborhood, where you find the painters now, how do you call it?"

"Williamsburg," Pierre said.

Jean-Paul relished the word: "*Williamsburg . . . fantastique.*" He turned to me. "So, do you like advertising? Living here in France?"

I suppose I decided to test my French a little. Truthfully, I never really knew what I was going to say in those interviewish moments; I tended to find my head after the fact. "So, this weekend," I said, "in the Métro, I saw an advertisement for a video game. For girls. It was interesting. An electronic game, but for a girl. You see?"

"Really?" Jean-Paul said.

"Yes, yes," I said. "This was my first advertisement that I see for a video game. For girls. About horses."

"Ah . . . ," Jean-Paul said. He looked at Pierre. Pierre shrugged. Jean-Paul said, "Perhaps I don't understand. Do girls not play video games?"

"So, in the Métro, on a poster," I continued, "I thought it was very good. Also, very French. So, in a good fashion."

To be clear, the reason I said "so" a lot was because I loved the way the word sounded in French, *donc*, and how the French used it. *Donc* was pronounced with a hard "c." It sounded like a rock being chucked into a creek. Parisians were always using it to begin a sentence, *Donc . . .* , and they'd pause afterward, and let the ripples flow.

"Please explain," Jean-Paul said.

"Because it was egalitarian," I said. "So, in the United States, you do not see advertisements that offer technology for girls. It is progressive, and I like that. So, I like the promise of the advertisement. You must understand the game," I said, leaning forward toward Jean-Paul. "Imagine you are a girl. You have a horse in your pocket. Not a true horse, a digital horse. But this is the dream of a girl, to have a horse. So she is happy. And because she adores her horse, the game gives her a way to care for it. To give her horse something to eat. Carrots, I believe."

"Yes, but what is the promise on the poster?" Jean-Paul asked. "What is the ad?"

"So, on the poster," I said slowly, "the promise is: *Your horse. Your boyfriend. Your mushroom.*"

Jean-Paul waited for me to explain further. He said after a moment, "Your mushroom?"

I conferred with Pierre. The difference, it seemed, between *champignon* and *champion* was too much for my embouchure. Pierre said, "He means your champion. And *friend*, not *boyfriend*. 'Your horse, your friend, your champion.'"

"Ah," Jean-Paul said, and Pierre and Jean-Paul both laughed. Pierre added, "Yeah, he was confused. Look, I promise, he will be good for this account."

After that, Pierre and Jean-Paul did most of the talking, telling me things about luxury. I sank in my chair and listened to the differences between *une marque de luxe*, a luxury brand, and a plain old *marque*, a brand like the kind that sold infant formula. Infant formula was not *luxe*, Pierre said, and Jean-Paul gasped and nodded in horror. That someone might think such a thing!

I ate my pâté sandwich. I tried to remember the scene I'd struggled with in my novel that morning, but couldn't recall a thing. My brain was a moth. And outside the windows, Paris was a unicorn. Old-hat magic, a mythological creature. Beautiful, but not exactly real. And its image was bought and sold like a mass-market toy. I jotted in my notebook, "Paris = My Little Pony."

On our way out, Jean-Paul said in English, "It was nice to meet you. And I like your mushroom, this was funny."

The evening after I met Jean-Paul, Rachel called to say she was going out with Lindsay, some party they'd heard about, she wouldn't be too late. By ten p.m. at my desk, I was dead tired, but I decided to walk home to kill time.

Men had draped the trees on the Champs-Elysées with twinkling purple lights that blinked in sequence. Like two rows of neon saline drips, as if the avenue were a hospital ward.

A Ferris wheel had been erected in Place de la Concorde, *une grande roue*, spinning with lights. Very beautiful in the cold black, like a setting moon. I considered riding it. I didn't, though I couldn't say why.

A line from Camus: *There were but few people on the quays . . .*

On my walk home, each streetlamp had its own heavens, thanks to the dark and the fog. By day, the coloring in Paris was all contrast—as compared, say, with Rome's haze—but wet nights in Paris were simply black and tinsel.

Rain started to fall. Les Halles was closed; a Starbucks was lit.

Walking beneath the Pompidou Center's white foghorns, I got an itch for company, so I stopped in a bar on the Boulevard Sébastopol and watched snippets of a dog race while drinking two beers and reading from *Exit Ghost*, by Philip Roth. How did he create such fathomable worlds? Why, tonight, when Paris normally consoled me, did the city make me feel so empty? In the front of the bar, a man was bitching out a woman. She said she hadn't done it: cheated on him. Her makeup was sliding down tectonically. She said through tears that she was true. The guy shouted, How can you lie? The bartender turned off the TV. Everyone watched the woman go out. After a few seconds, the bartender switched the TV back on, then the guy threw his beer bottle through a window, shattering the glass, which fell all at once, like a sheet whisked off a prize. He ran. The bartender and two men gave chase, and many of the rest of us left, presumably, like me, to go home to an empty house.

But it wasn't empty. When I walked through the door, Rachel had just arrived. She was hanging up her umbrella. She smiled. I grabbed her. She pinched the lapel of my coat and laughed, saying I'd need to replace it soon, it had lost its water repellency. I know, I know, I said.

19

The first time I was bum-rushed, I was in the Place de la République Métro station. It was during my normal morning commute. I'd just waved my Navigo pass over the turnstile when a small woman humped me from behind. She shushed in my ear, "*S'il vous plaît, monsieur*," then jimmied us through the gate.

On the other side, she waved at me and jogged away.

Second time it happened, a guy shoved me at eight a.m., with zero politeness. And he looked affronted once we were through, when I showed my surprise. The prick. After that, approaching a Métro turnstile, I'd watch out for assault, because I knew what to expect. A Parisian bum-rusher was easy to spot. He stood near the ticket machines looking for marks, ready to move forward.

One afternoon, after a cold day's jog, I spotted a shabby bald guy idling near a map. He set himself in motion once he saw me pull out my Métro pass.

Four feet from the turnstile, he was behind me.

Three feet, I could hear the whisking of his windbreaker.

Two feet, I stopped, and his momentum shoved him into me. I turned around and said nothing. The guy swore; maybe he was expecting a scene. But I was happy to step aside. Confused, he made to go through the turnstile and came up short, slapping his pockets as if he'd forgotten his ticket. He rode the escalator back up to street level while eyeing me hatefully.

At the office, I told this story to deaf ears.

"Perhaps he *did* forget his pass," Olivier said. "It happens to everyone."

"You know, this is not an easy city if you are not rich," Françoise said, chastising me. She said I needed to learn to be more sympathetic—people should make sacrifices to improve society's lot, and let us not forget, she said, the Christmas spirit.

Of course, Françoise was right: Paris wasn't easy without money. Paris wasn't easy in the first place. People were always cutting lines at the *épicerie*. And for every good-looking girl, there were a hundred old Frenchwomen shouting at people on the bus. But modern forces had long ago shoveled out the poor beyond *le périphérique*, the highway that surrounded Paris like a moat, beyond which were *les banlieues*, "the suburbs." Around Paris, the *banlieues* ranged from poor to rich, but its poor towns made "the surburbs" a far more sinister term in the public imagination than America's bland commuting towns. The suburbs to the north and east of Paris were its anguished Bronx tenements. If you read the newspapers or listened to Sarkozy, they were bleak zones of neglect, full of immigrant scum, where society's ills reproduced on the city's doormat . . . Sarkozy tending not to mention, in my opinion, that central, decadent Paris was dead as fluff, and it took immigrants to give a city life, never mind friction—some tread as Paris tried to move its bulk forward into the twenty-first century.

The bigger world so valued by Julie, my colleague who'd endorsed Sarkozy's policies over lunch, was a lot more likely to sleep five to a room in Clichy-sous-Bois than in a studio overlooking Montparnasse.

But in central Paris, the most visibly poor were street people. Drunks and punks with neck tattoos and dogs. Or Algerian and Moroccan beggars, and the Gypsies who pleaded for coins from the foot of ATMs. Olivier hated the drunks and punks the most;

he railed against how they occupied the sidewalks in camps. Coworkers alleged the police couldn't jail them because in Paris if a person had a dog he or she was considered a caretaker, and it was illegal to separate a caretaker overnight from his or her ward.

I never found out if that was true. For two weeks in December, though, an encampment of street kids took over Rue Béranger. I'd pass them on the way to and from work, and sometimes be jeered at. They were always drunk or high, on the brink of survival, but they kept their dogs in beautiful shape, and fed them bones passed along by employees at Monoprix, the fancy supermarket around the corner.

Third week in December, I risked my life and rented a Vélib to ride to work. Face-smacking loveliness of a day, and while I navigated around Place de la Concorde and began climbing up the Champs-Elysées, I heard a loud rushing *RRRrrriiiiiipppppppp*. Whence cometh hell.

It had sounded like a scooter revving its engine. In fact, my crotch was gone. I'd pedaled too hard, and the seat had been ripped out from my jeans. So I made a diaper of my trench coat, attended a meeting, and rode the Métro home to change my pants.

Around the same time, the president became enviable. "Bling-bling" Sarkozy had a new squeeze: Carla Bruni, ex-model, successful musician. And where did Sarko l'Américain take his new girlfriend for the weekend? Disneyland Paris. Sarkozy was in love—same for the newspapers, with the spectacle. Especially because Bruni was the ex of Donald Trump and Mick Jagger, and she confirmed the papers' worst suspicions about Sarkozy's lust for celebrity, especially non-French celebrity (never mind Bruni's thing for powerful men).

"Power crazy, this girl," Julie said, confirming much of what Paris thought, "but it's true, she can sing."

According to reports, also attending the Disneyland Paris weekend were Bruni's mother, a concert pianist, and Bruni's son, whom she'd had with Raphaël Enthoven, a philosopher whom *The New York Times* reported Ms. Bruni had stolen away from an author named Justine Levy, who was the daughter of the philosopher Bernard Henri-Levy, and who'd gone on to write a novel about Bruni's romantic poaching.

Sometimes the French were so incredibly French—so cultured, so reliably contradictory—it thrilled me. There was nothing else to say. What a wonderful place.

I tried, but no, I could not articulate my frustration at discovering that our Christmas presents to America had been quarantined in a hangar near Brest, in western France.

I said, "I was told I could put wine into the mail."

The postal clerk said, nodding, "I understand. But you see, it is illegal to send wine to the United States."

"But you told us we could send wine to the United States," I said. "A woman from the postal service, by telephone. I wrote 'wine' on the form, before I sent it," I said, pointing it out on the page.

"You wrote it clearly, I see. I don't know what happened," the clerk said. He was sympathetic to my problems, but everyone had problems. "I don't know why they told you that you could ship wine to the States; it is absolutely forbidden."

I said, "Can we try calling the office where the boxes are resting?"

The clerk glared at me, waiting in case I should dissolve. He got up with a sigh and went back to a room full of boxes. A long line of people waited behind me. After two minutes, he returned to his seat. "I have tried to call them," he said, "but they are not answering."

"Do you have a system on the Internet to look at the box?"

"I have tried this also," he said. "Our system is down."

I wanted to say, Of course, because, let me guess, we're powerless in the face of bureaucracy, and you feel my pain but there's nothing you can do, after all France in 2007 is the equivalent of Russia in 1981, isn't that right?

Instead I said, "What else can we do?"

He considered it for a moment. "So, the recipient could try calling immigration."

"Immigration," I said. "In the States?"

"Immigration in Europe, for the States. Please, sir," the clerk said, looking over my shoulder, "it is out of our control."

"But you are *La Poste*," I said.

He apologized again. He said, "I do not know why they said you could mail wine to the United States. It is truly bizarre."

"So what happens now?"

"They will send the box to the return address you inscribed on the form, your home. You will receive it in four to six weeks."

"I am superangry," I said.

"I am sorry," the clerk said. "Have a good day."

He motioned to the next person in line.

The director of the infant-nutrition account threw us a holiday *fête* on Rue de Lappe near Place de la Bastille, in a Mexican restaurant/dance club. Technically, I was still on the account while Keith, the Scottish copywriter, got up to speed. Technically, according to our project managers' deadlines, we should have completed all six booklets by that evening. Instead we were celebrating the fact that we'd nearly finished one.

That's France for you, an Italian project manager said.

Every day I learned fourteen new things about France.

Over a dinner that was Mexican by way of Toulouse, with crêpes for tortillas and lots of crème fraîche, I tried explaining to Keith what to expect from the account, now that he'd be assuming my role. For example, why the first booklet still wasn't done: our colleagues in Malaysia, rather than translating, had decided to replace the booklet's words with pictures, like an airplane safety pamphlet. But the club was too loud for that sort of talk, and we decided to get drunk and watch Bruno dance with every woman.

"He's fucking great," Keith said in my ear.

"I *know*," I said.

Now it made functional sense why Bruno's shirt always needed to be unbuttoned: to dump heat. Women were slayed. I was proud of him, mostly envious. During a break, Bruno slung around my chair and pointed out a beautiful woman illuminated on the other side of the room, dancing alone.

"She's gorgeous," I said. "But you don't have a chance."

Meaning, were I single again and to approach that woman with the extremely long legs, I wouldn't have a chance. Bruno laughed in my ear, frowned, then stood up. In fact, Bruno did have a chance. There were always chances. The Way of Bruno was often cynical, but never despairing. Bruno fetched champagne and did his walk—he had a walk. He held his head obliquely and snuck across invisible borders, smiling and laughing with his eyes half closed. One second, he was whispering in her ear, then he was laughing, she was laughing. Soon he had her whipped to castanets.

I asked Bruno the next morning if he'd gotten laid. Bruno shrugged a combination of "who cares?" and "*pas mal.*" He'd arrived at seven, beating me by two hours, to finish up our work for the Malaysians. He looked miserable from a hangover. We did a conference call together; afterward we fist-bumped.

I still hadn't told Bruno about leaving infant nutrition for Louis Vuitton. I knew how betrayed he'd feel.

That evening, we were revising our Malaysian brochure on Bruno's monitor for perhaps the forty-fifth time. Bruno's concept of hell had expanded to include me reading him copy edits and telling him where to click. Around nine, we decided to drink some champagne left over from another office party, and for a second, I swear I almost told him. Instead I refilled our cups and asked Bruno if there was any food a Parisian wouldn't pair with champagne.

Looking back, I think, Oh, the sum of small acts . . .

"Cheeseburger?" I said.

Bruno turned away from his computer. "Cheeseburger, why do you always talk about cheeseburger? But it's not bad, sure."

"How about sushi?"

"Sushi, beer is better," Bruno said, "but sure, champagne."

"That works?" I said. *Ça marche?*

"That works," Bruno said. *Ça marche.*

Ça marche was my phrase of the month.

"What about cheese?" I said. "A platter of cheeses?"

Bruno said, "Now this is tricky." He explained that it depended on the cheeses served and the type of champagne. Perhaps a rosé? He'd have to think about it. Next I asked him what was required for a proper French Christmas dinner.

"Shellfish," Bruno said. "Parisians eat shellfish."

"This is also not bad with champagne," he added.

Several times in those eighteen months, over coffee, at lunch, Bruno explained to me that native Parisians were disappointed by default. "We say *pas mal* before we say *très bien*. Look where we live. If you have Paris, what lives up to it? The strikes—you know, the fathers went on strike, so the sons follow. But it's theater now. Everything changes."

At the office, Bruno put in enormous effort. Despite his

dissatisfactions, he was never late that I saw. He was good at his job whether or not it went recognized. Creative, sensible, Bruno worked hard, the same way he smoked and tracked photography exhibits. He had imagination. There were features of dreams thick on the ground, and Bruno absorbed what Paris had to inspire him. But he seemed aware to the bone that he was stuck, and that hell was relative to where you stood.

20

The office closed for two weeks for the holidays. Seafood merchants occupied street corners, men in yellow bibs with ice chests full of *fruits de mer*—oysters, clams, shrimp that were two feet long, with orange eyeballs big as marbles. At Monoprix, sections of the floorplan were devoted to holiday gluttony, with items arranged like displays in sporting goods stores. Mountains of champagne. Pyramids of foie gras. Some crawfish with tails fourteen inches long.

One cold Saturday afternoon, the doorbell rang. It was our *poissonnière*'s teenage driver, one of those delivery guys with a cell phone tucked inside his helmet. He had a platter for "Monsieur Bald-ween?" A present from Pierre and Chloe, enough shellfish for twelve, including a pile of giant shrimp to be guillotined.

The next night, we went with Lindsay to an expat Christmas party in an apartment above the Luxembourg Gardens. Slippery roads, glowering clouds, cold gales. Streets around the park were deserted, flower boxes were empty. Rachel's purse strap caught on a scooter mirror and was whipped off her arm. We wandered past a Christmas fair. There was a merchant, bundled up, filling bread bowls from a cauldron of melted cheese.

At the party, no one was smoking. No one smoking at a Paris party, even in 2007, meant no one there was French. It turned out to be true. The hostess said, "I don't think I even know a Parisian, isn't that appalling?"

The rooms were filled with people with very shampooed hair—Americans like us nibbling on topics of specific relevance to expats: dentists, taxes, and weren't we dying to move to Berlin, or San Francisco?

The Picard puff pastry was delicious.

In expat conversations, the lingo tended to be from endurance sports—what could she stand; what tested her limits; how much longer could she take it before the exertion was too great. The same story played on repeat: how, when an American girl arrived in Paris, she went to Place de Furstenberg in the moonlight and kissed the stones. But when summer nights became online photo albums, and Europe's darkness fell, she wasn't a tourist anymore. Why were all the people she met at parties just like everyone back home? She couldn't admit to feeling bored, but she was. Buying dessert for one: depressing. And she felt her loneliness like stomach rolls, forming over who she'd been.

I was talking to a guy from San Francisco, and we were talking about how each of us had come to Paris, and I stopped midsentence, realizing I'd told the same story forty times by that point, and each time *the exact same way*. Extremely depressing. I begged off, found Rachel and Lindsay in the kitchen, and said, We're leaving. We thanked our hostess and ran.

"In the future," Lindsay said, walking up the street, pulling Nicorette from inside her raincoat, "I would like a sign around my neck that says, 'I am not interested in your complaints about employment at UNESCO.' "

The following morning, we found a skinny fir tree for sale on Rue Bretagne. We named him Pyotr, figuring he was from Ukraine. I brought him home on my shoulder, dressed him with ornaments from a Monoprix Christmas kit, then we went out again and bought a bottle of scotch for Asif, and left it for him with a ribbon and a note, "*Bonne année, de tes Américains préférés.*"

On Christmas morning, Paris was a quiet mountain village, with electric lights strung between houses. We went for a walk. The slogan could have been "Paris—It's manageable." At Notre Dame, tourists got off a bus wearing matching holiday sweaters.

That same week, my sister, Leslie, came for a visit. She was an ideal guest, adventuresome and eager to try new things. We took her to Bofinger for dinner—I wanted to show her French traditional, and got it: the service was atrocious—and Le Bar du Caveau for lunch, which was much cheaper, and more delicious. "Doesn't Paris just make you feel young?" Leslie said at one point, and the way she said it—as if to no one—hit a lovely, sad note, like striking a wooden bell. Occasionally, Rachel and Leslie went out for tea, or Leslie explored the city on her own, and I stayed home and worked on my novel. Then it was done. On the second-to-last day of the year, I finished my draft, and we celebrated with a twelve-euro bottle of champagne that was probably better for degreasing a lawnmower.

On New Year's Eve, I put on a tie and roasted a bass and heated up hors d'oeuvres from Picard. Leslie contributed *macarons* from Ladurée. Lindsay arrived for dinner, then a few minutes later Georgie appeared, the Small World madame, with champagne and forced cheer. She'd texted earlier, asking if we had an extra seat.

Apologizing that she might need to leave at any minute, Georgie spent the first half of the evening checking her *textos*. Then Rachel's friend Olivia stopped by with a guy called Gonzalo. Olivia was lovely, a former lead at the dance company where Rachel had worked as a fund-raiser in New York. Olivia had left the company and moved to Paris to try living abroad. She was from Tennessee originally, petite, with a quiet voice, though determined: Olivia had landed in Paris with no job and no visa, but within a month she'd landed a position with a dance company, plus benefits. She introduced Gonzalo to the group. Gonzalo was twenty, handsome, a model with an afro and a gap in his teeth. He knew he was beautiful—the IPO was available to any girl who didn't mind sharing.

Suddenly Georgie came alive. Turned out Gonzalo and Georgie knew each other, sort of, through A Small World. She sat next to him at the table and practically signaled to land a plane. At midnight, we watched a revue with cancan dancers. Around one, Olivia said she and Gonzalo had another party to visit, and Georgie said, Oh good, she'd share their cab.

The next morning, the Interior Ministry reported 144 cars torched in the suburbs—a smaller number than in previous years, but still troubling; a distress signal, reports said; a protest that was seen and heard by almost nobody in the city center.

The morning Leslie departed, taking a train to the airport, we hugged and wished each other good luck in the new year. "Not like you need it," Leslie said. "You live in Paris, remember?"

I said, "It's not quite like that." Then again . . . the following weekend, Rachel came home on Sunday afternoon with her cheeks burning, tears on her face. I jumped up. "What happened?" Rachel said she'd been returning from the Left Bank. She'd been walking along the Seine, listening to her iPod, Renée Fleming singing Strauss; she'd stared at the golden dome of Invalides; she crossed the Alexandre III bridge with its black lampposts and gold statues; she passed a million tiny parks in the Marais. "I walked and walked," Rachel said. "I couldn't get over how beautiful it was. Sometimes I just really love it here." Then she laughed at herself, wiping away tears, and put down her purse.

EGO TOURISM

WINTER

—Young people in the twenty-first century are confused—Rachel and a plumber share a moment—Political correctness still kills—What Parisians desire in a mate—Mikhail Gorbachev packs his own shirts—Sarkozy gets married—Vertigo is not "a thing forever"—We drink champagne with Karl Lagerfeld—In Paris, an aristocrat eats chocolate only in bed—The women of Keef Richards prove difficult to capture—

21

On a cold day in January, Claudia Schiffer was sitting outside our office wearing only her bra and underpants. She didn't look cold; she looked expensive. Ten assistants surrounded her, squeezing radios or holding up silver shields to reflect the sun's light toward her face.

I watched an assistant pass Claudia Schiffer a cup of tea. Some agency, not ours, was shooting a lingerie ad, and they'd convinced Claudia Schiffer to pose seminaked below our balcony.

"Dude, imagine her day rate," a designer said.

Paris winters were freezing cold and fragged with wind. What light there was was ice-gray. But the cold was bearable if a person was braced with tea or coffee, or a coffee with calvados, the French apple brandy. I took to buying rounds of espresso for my tablemates. I wanted to show not only goodwill, but participation in culture. At *un pot*, an office party, one evening late that month, Doo-Doo and Gabriel were drinking pastis by a massive empty fireplace, and Doo-Doo said to me, nodding at the pastis bottle, "You want one?"

Absolutely, I said. I added, "But no water."

"No water?" Gabriel said. He looked like I'd ordered beef broth. No water with pastis?

But I never drank scotch with water, so why start here?

"Never," I said. "No water."

Gabriel laughed nervously. "Seriously, are you sure?"

"No water!" I ordered, gulped it down, and asked for another. I said, *Donnes-moi la France*. At least that got a laugh. Later, I'd learn that Doo-Doo had told one of the project managers from upstairs that "the American" drank pastis neat. He'd never seen it before. (For good reason; it tasted like licorice crossed with sap.) The manager agreed, the American was strange in multiple ways.

After the holidays, a lot of conversation took place about foie gras. How much foie gras people had consumed during break, and in what varieties. There were arguments about proper preparation. Olivier, Doo-Doo, François, and Nico fought over who knew foie gras best—eaten cold, or sautéed in a pan, or stuffed in tiny ravioli. François won by saying he'd eaten not only numerous special preparations, but also multiple types of foie gras, from several regions, while he'd driven around France visiting different sects of his wife's family.

François rolled his eyes at the memory, clucking his tongue, and clutched Olivier's shoulder, with Olivier cooing and hooting, "*Oh, mais François, mon pauvre François* . . ."

Our first day back, Keith and I met for coffee. He'd just returned from holidays in Scotland, wearing a sweater his mother had knitted for him, thick as a sandwich board. He also had on new patent-leather, Day-Glo Reeboks. I shared my observation with him about the popularity of foie gras talk, and Keith nodded emphatically.

"But they're contrarian by nature, that's why they're fighting over it," Keith said. "When it comes to foie gras, each Frenchman knows it best." Keith fiddled with his glasses, polishing them. "It's not just that every man is entitled to his opinion, it's that every man believes he is *right*, is what it is."

Keith said a minute later, "Listen, here's why working in France *dans la pub*, in advertising, blows. You do the pitch *avec ton idée*, yeah? And they say no automatically. They say, *absolument fucking pas*. Because they say 'no' all the fucking time, it's become a natural response. The *national* response. The French are on a team, see: the bloody team of refusal. Only they don't know they've signed up en masse. So each Frenchman thinks he's unique in refusing to ride on the conformity train. He just doesn't realize he's one of millions on the even bigger train of 'No.' "

Keith's theory held that since Parisians maintained convictions passionately, they ran the risk—even the requirement—of being misunderstood, and so had evolved the French mastery of repartée, the kitchen-drawer bottom lip, and dinner parties that lasted eight hours.

Keith nipped my sleeve. "Hey, so have you read much John Fante then?"

That afternoon, Bruno bragged about his own goose-liver consumption. He pulled up his sweater to show me where his belly had become engorged from too much paté. He invited me to slap it. Bruno laughed and laughed, with his eyes semiclosed, and I knew something was wrong.

Bruno always liked to preface confrontation with bonhomie. He suggested a coffee, his treat. We sat down in the canteen, and Bruno's jaw and mouth drooped. What was this, he said in a whisper, about me leaving infant nutrition, leaving him behind? He'd just been told, Bruno said, but he hadn't been told much. Where was I going? Would he be going, too? And why hadn't I told him before?

To Louis Vuitton, I said. Going alone. Very soon. Pierre's decision.

Bruno stared over my shoulder. "That's not how it is supposed to work," Bruno said.

We talked about breast-feeding for a little bit, then Bruno said, "Are you sure there's no room for me on the team?" Bruno raked my arm with two fingers. "I've done plenty of luxury, you can show them my portfolio." Another minute, when I tried to change the conversation, Bruno said loudly, "This is bullshit. You know this is bullshit. Will you at least ask Pierre?"

I said I would ask Pierre. I didn't know if I'd ever seen Bruno more dejected.

Three brief Paris stories that, to me, seemed connected by bigger trends. One: I was assigned a new neighbor at the office, a young designer named Sébastien. Sébastien took Julie's spot. Julie had been moved to the agency's other building after a blowup occurred in December between her and André. One day Julie was shouting and crying, her cheeks swollen. The next day she was morose, like she'd been medicated. A week later she was gone, transferred across the street.

We weren't told why, and no one discussed it out loud, not even Olivier or Françoise.

Sébastien, her replacement, was oily, maybe twenty-two. His default mode was louche. He wore a leather jacket and black jeans that were tight and unwashed. He needed to sweep his hair from his eyes on the two-minute mark if he wasn't wearing headphones, but mostly Sébastien wore headphones, big ones shaped like fist-size flowers.

The day we met, Sébastien showed me how his iPod rang an alarm whenever his girlfriend had her period, so he'd know when not to initiate a fuck. Then he brushed the hair out of his eyes and resumed Web surfing.

Sébastien was an expert Web surfer. It appeared to be what he did in lieu of working. It was simple, Sébastien's approach to work, even audacious: he did not work. Did not meet deadlines. Didn't acknowledge being assigned accounts. Gradually, he refused to read his business e-mail or attend meetings, and he'd arrive at noon and leave at three, after an hour's lunch. Occasionally he'd work for a week, and work hard. But then he'd disappear for several days, whereabouts unknown. Sébastien's project managers vented their frustration to us because they were reluctant to confront him. Instead, they stopped assigning him work. Then Pierre found out. He summoned Sébastien to his office. After that, Sébastien worked hard for a couple of weeks, but then he stopped again and went back to his position of *Je refuse*.

One day when Sébastien was at lunch, I asked everyone why he still had a desk.

You can't fire someone in France, Olivier explained.

It's too difficult, Tomaso said.

"You simply stop giving them things to do," Françoise said, "and they sit in a corner for a few years, and you hope they quit. That's how it works."

Story number two: Around the same time Sébastien arrived, I received an espresso machine as a belated Christmas gift from my parents, a great big machine from Nespresso. I was ecstatic about it; I became emotionally involved with a kitchen appliance. The truth was, Paris was a fantastic place to drink coffee, but the coffee in Paris was mostly awful. Anyone but the French would tell you. Tomaso and other Italian coworkers would get in arguments about Parisians even calling their coffee espresso, when it was too watery and tasted like mulch. Perhaps that explained why Nespresso's home systems were so popular in France. The coffee quality was better than what was served in most Paris cafés. People in the hallways at work discussed the "latest seasonal blend" from Nespresso like it was a new Beaujolais.

What set Nespresso apart for me, though, wasn't how good the espresso was—there were plenty of decent home espresso systems—but its value as a symbol of *bobo* ranking and elitism. Nespresso machines made coffee from Nespresso pods only, tiny capsules that cost thirty cents each and were available only online or from Nespresso stores. No other coffee company had a two-floor boutique on the Champs-Elysées; few stores on the Champs-Elysées were so crowded. And to purchase those pods a person was required to join the Nespresso Club.

Membership included a black identity card embedded with a personalized smart chip. I was reminded of writing luxury humor in New York, for the magazine published for American Express black-card holders. With this coffeemaker, had I crossed over? Pierre told me he'd been a Nespresso member for several years. His father had been a member for much longer. In fact, due to how much espresso he bought—"he drinks a lot of espresso," Pierre said—his dad had achieved some kind of elite status within Nespresso. The more coffee he drank, the more frequently he received special treatment and gifts in the mail.

Story number three: In early January, one of the Louis Vuitton account managers, Marc, invited me out to lunch. Marc was dorky, smart, ambitious. He was a Nespresso member, plus he owned a Mont Blanc pen. At the start of meetings, he'd withdraw his pen and lay its felt case next to his cell phone on the table. At lunch on a sunny day, sitting outside on Rue de Valois across from the Louvre's glass pyramid, Marc wanted to know what it was like to work in New York. He explained that he felt locked into his career in Paris, no way out. Marc was on track to be an account director, but at heart he longed to be a creative. During *un brainstorm*, Marc would often contribute ideas that were more creative than what some "creatives" suggested, but they went ignored, and Marc's superiors would mock him for breaking rank.

I said I knew many people in New York who were stuck in the rat race, too, but also many people who had switched careers. Marc said this was impossible in France. "Stability is the most important thing," Marc said, his fingers trembling; he'd been *stressé* for months. "It's the Great French Dream: save money, get a good watch, find a partner, have babies, buy a country house, then retire."

Well, I said, the Great French Dream didn't sound much different from the Great American Dream, only with More Vacation Days.

"No, seriously," Marc said, "the French dream? It's dead."

And Marc was cuckolded by that death. Because Marc wanted all of those things he'd named, only he didn't see how he could obtain them and still be happy. These days, wasn't "happiness" a hollow word? The dream was cheating Marc; behind every grin, he was dispirited. By early winter he'd developed a fluttering-eye tic. And when Pierre fired Sébastien, my neighbor, not only for not doing shit but for personally insulting another employee in front of Pierre (Pierre was extremely loyal to his employees), Sébastien was confounded. He was furious, distraught. *Fâché, morose.* He knew he'd done wrong; now he felt he'd been *done* wrong. Why would Pierre go for maximum punishment? Fired, as in fired-fired?

About half the office, who had despised working with Sébastien and had said so out loud while Sébastien listened to electroclash in his peony headphones, still didn't see why Pierre had needed to purge him. André never would have fired Sébastien, people said. Perhaps he would have relocated Sébastien like he did Julie, but never fired him, no. In gossip at the coffee machine, fetching macchiatos or *double-cafés*, people made Pierre out to be the villain. He'd broken an unspoken trust. The same people attributed Pierre's firing Sébastien to the influence of Pierre's years working in New York.

22

At the end of January, our shower basin leaked. Asif turned up at eight a.m. because our downstairs neighbor had knocked on his door, Asif said, after the guy's ceiling began raining when I showered.

Asif lit a cigarette and squeezed into our bathroom. He tapped on the drain. He took a breather from contemplating the situation to brush his shag in the mirror.

The previous week, drunk one night, Asif had told me about his women problems. "*Ach*, it's difficult, man, but what can I do?" Those words summed up his whole regime. Asif said he was keeping several chicks on the line. One was a widow who lived near Versailles. She was wealthy, she called him "pet," and while he slept she stuffed euros into his jeans, rolls of bills in rubber bands. None of which he minded. "I love her, you know? And not just for the money." Recently, though, he'd begun seeing a new girl, and the widow was upset. She'd said to Asif, it was her or nothing, and if nothing then no more fat money rolls.

"I don't know yet," he said. "But my new girl, *waouh*. From Marseille, you know Marseille? The real France."

Unable to repair the bathroom, Asif dropped his cigarette in the toilet and said he'd telephone for a plumber. I left for work with an apologetic look while Rachel reorganized her plans.

The doorbell rang at eleven. Plumber: handsome, young,

big-armed. He said quietly, *Bonjour*, and Rachel said back to him, *Bonjour.*

I had to interrupt at that point: "Give me a break." Rachel was telling me the story later that evening over dinner. "Hey," she said, "when do you know me to exaggerate?" Anyway, Rachel said, the plumber didn't speak English, so they'd relied on her French.

The plumber brought in his tool bag. She showed him the bathroom. He removed his jacket. Rachel returned to the dining table to resume writing. Twenty minutes later, the plumber came back out—he was down to his undershirt by that point—and began speaking in French.

"I'm sorry, excuse me," Rachel interrupted him, also in French. "I telephone my husband? He speaks French, please wait."

But when she called, I was in a meeting. It would be hours before I got her voice mail saying she needed help translating Le Colin Farrell.

Rachel had hung up the phone and returned to the bathroom.

"My husband is not there," Rachel told the plumber. "But, okay, you explain to me. I'm sorry, but my French is bad."

The plumber nodded. He added bashfully, "I will go slow." The plumber explained there was a leak behind the tub, beneath the outer layer of molding, and he needed to make a hole—

"Make a hole in the wall of tiles?" Rachel asked in French.

"Yes," the plumber said.

"But not big?"

"No, a small one. But first I need to turn off the electricity."

"Why the electricity?" Rachel said.

"Well, I do not want to be injured," he said.

"Oh no," my wife said. "No, of course not."

Soon they were crouching on their knees, shoulder to shoulder in our cramped, hot bathroom with only a flashlight between them, while the shy, sexy plumber explained what was happening in front of their noses.

I said, Do I want to know how this story ends?

"He fixed the tub," Rachel said.

Due to the number of hours I was working, Rachel and I didn't see much of each other after the holidays. One Saturday we took a field trip to Père Lachaise, the graveyard established by Napoleon, where Oscar Wilde and Jim Morrison were buried. At noon, the sun was low. There was ice on the roads, frost on the walls where buildings were in shadow. The cemetery had a pleasantly countryish landscape, rolling with crypts. We sat on a bench in the sun while Rachel explained that her writing was going well; she enjoyed working on it. The only trouble was that construction now had expanded to include four sides of our apartment. From three to four sides in a few short weeks: all-day racket that penetrated two-thirds of our apartment's planar surfaces. Rachel hadn't wanted to complain, but it was becoming unbearable. Drill sounds, hammering, beams being cut. To the point that Rachel now heard the sounds inside her head when they weren't occurring. Not just intolerable noise, but interior.

"You could try working in a café," I said. Didn't everyone in Paris work in cafés? Wasn't that the expat thing to do?

"You know that's not me," Rachel said.

"What about that library we found?"

"You mean in the children's room?"

Libraries in Paris tended to be reserved for licensed students, or they charged admission. We'd found a free branch near our apartment, but the study carrels turned out to be part of a day-care zone.

Across the street from Père Lachaise, we found a café for lunch, and sat by a glass wall. Outside, Parisians went about their Saturday business, pushing carts of groceries home. In the afternoon we went down to the Seine, where the river was chopped up white and blue. We huddled on Pont de Sully in the wind, in view of Notre Dame, and absorbed the cathedral and island buildings at dusk, then ran to a café to drink.

That night, Lindsay and Olivia visited for dinner. Olivia told us she'd gone on two dates with Gonzalo, the model-boy from New Year's, but she'd called things off after she found out he was seeing other women. In fact, he liked to see them all at once.

"I swear," Olivia said, "this boy believes he is God's gift. Do you know what he does? We went out for lunch last weekend, and he invited another girl to join us. He had two dates in one, me and this skinny little . . ."

"Maybe he's a multitasker," Lindsay said.

Olivia said after a minute, "He thinks every girl wants to kiss on him. He's like, 'Baby, I am in love with you, but by the way, I'm in love with her, too, and that one over there, and that one.' "

Olivia explained that she'd recently gone on a date with a different guy, this time an air-traffic controller. They'd met through the French equivalent of Match.com. He didn't speak English, so they'd subsisted on her French. When they ran out of words, they ate sorbet.

"That's sweet," Rachel said.

"You know, it was," Olivia said. "And at least I was the only girl on the date. He drove me home, and I thought, okay, this is nice. We parked on my street. And you know what? If he wants to kiss me, I was thinking, I'll kiss him. So we're sitting in the car. We sat some more. In silence. Like we're meditating together. Finally I said, *Uh, ciao, à bientôt*, and that was it. Me getting out of the car, end of date. I was like, aren't you supposed to be French?

"Oh, and by the way? He has a kid," Olivia said.

"Well, that's how you know he's French," Lindsay said.

The rule held that if a contemporary Parisian man was single after thirty, it meant either he had a child somewhere or he was gay. But since no Parisian men were gay, at least not openly, most likely there was a kid somewhere, plus an ex-partner with great legs to whom the man eventually would return. And the ex-partner usually was that killer combo that Parisian men found irresistible, of Certified Lunatic and Really Good Cook.

At the agency, among men, references to sex as a form of punishment were part of business. It was a daily aspect of conversation, ten times more frequently invoked than I'd heard in American offices. Either the women rolled their eyes, or they didn't notice; mostly they didn't notice. How our clients were fucking us in the ass. Ramming it down our throats. Bending us over, or fucking us in the face. I heard it from coworkers, bosses, consultants. Whenever there were two or more Parisian men in a room, someone would likely invoke something done to an ass or penis. Maybe the agency's collective ass, our team's penis. It would be phrased in a way that seemed humdrum and mildly annoying, like waiting in line. Such as sucking dick. We sucked our clients' dicks a lot. Which wasn't terrible. Because the guy making the joke could imply, *Hey, sucking this dick isn't so bad. I could suck it one more financial quarter if necessary, sure. Let's all try and meet our deadlines, okay, guys? Just suck this dick a little bit longer and we'll be great.*

But when we were doing well? If a manager got his client to approve a big new budget, or, better still, if we won a new account? Then they were sucking *our* dicks, and that was *super*.

Less frequently told were black jokes, though they weren't uncommon. Maybe two or three a month. Mostly they concerned the size of black men's penises. *What's the problem? Hey, I'm saying a good thing about blacks. I wish I had a black dick!* Though guys were careful not to tell those sorts of jokes in front of our black colleagues. Then there were the Jew jokes. It wasn't a big deal if you let one fly in front of a Jewish coworker; frequently it was your Jewish coworker telling the joke. For example, about clients being stingy like Jews. Or when someone, being generous, boasted he wasn't "acting like a Jew." In fact,

Jew jokes were looked down upon as cliché. Bad form: they weren't good enough as comedy. Because though all of the joking was performed lightly as farce—white boys making noise—it symbolized a serious purpose: taking a stand against the grand evil that was political correctness.

Tolerance was high for sucking black dicks like a Jew, but there was no room in the office for political correctness. Never. None. It needed to be fought actively, and if that required telling anti-Semitic jokes while pretending to gag on a client's cock . . . However, should you seem uncomfortable, or protest the appearance in conversation of a black dick, a stingy Jew, or a thump on fags, well, watch out. By doing so, you were curtailing that joke teller's personal freedom to be open-minded about causing offense, and the freedom to offend needed protection.

Either *Murphy Brown* never aired in France, or Paris was stuck in the early nineties. I hadn't heard the term used in maybe ten years, but in our office *politically correct* came up twice a week. In meetings, if someone called your idea P.C., *pay-say*, there was no possible recovery. The label was nuclear. Anyone accused of *pay-say* during *un brainstorming* would be shouted down—*Don't be so American!*—to sit shamefaced in his seat, excluded from the rest of the session.

23

There was a lot to observe in Paris about seduction, about the Parisian manner of seduction. If only because seduction was the base syrup of most exchanges, business or otherwise, along with confrontation.

I found more lessons in my coworkers' social-media updates than in watching lovers make out along the Seine—most of those lovers being tourists. Of course, plenty of French people still made out along the Seine; they simply had more company these days, Paris having so many goldfish in the privacy of their bowls . . . Anyway, my French coworkers used the Web pretty much the same as Americans did, but with greater respect for individual privacy—I never saw photos of any coworkers shotgunning beers, though perhaps shotgunning beers wasn't the best test case—and, in almost all exchanges, with flirtation.

There was also greater tolerance for sexy material. Men, and plenty of women, would get up from their desks to cluster around whatever nude flesh was trending on the Web. Of course, it was excused as a business exercise; we worked in an ad agency, and we required inspiration. And French advertising didn't lack for nudity. Like one condom TV spot that got passed around. Six of us clustered around Josette's computer. The video showed a woman's face and bare breasts responding to something being done to her offscreen—a lot of tickling, perhaps, during an earthquake.

"What I like is the music," Josette said. The sound track had a young Wayne Newton saying thanks in German. "That and the joy that is presented by the contrast, rather than anything nasty."

The men chimed in, *Ah oui, la musique . . .*

Josette was a designer. She had pestered me for weeks about wanting dinner at our house, to meet Rachel and enjoy some girl chat. Finally, we booked a date. The promised evening, I arrived home early with champagne and flowers, and found Rachel just cooking dinner, wearing a blue apron over her dress.

I said I'd noticed in the courtyard there were cones and machinery that hadn't been there in the morning.

Rachel said, "Well, as of today we now have construction on five sides of the apartment. Five. That's five of six surfaces now." She explained: "They have to tear out the water main in the courtyard and install a new pipe—anyway, I think that's what the guy said. It should take two months." She paused. "I almost threw a can of soup through the window today."

When Josette arrived in a thick winter coat, we were halfway done with the champagne, cursing our landlord. Luckily, Josette had brought more champagne, plus a plant.

Josette spoke perfect English from living in Los Angeles for two years. Over dinner, Rachel quizzed her about the men in the office—who was hot, who was charming, who interested Josette?

"How about that guy you work with, what's his name, Bruno?" Rachel said.

"Oh, Bruno did chat me up once," Josette said, "for a pull."

"Get *out*," I said.

"Sorry?" she said.

"It's an expression. I mean, when?"

"Oh, during a *fête*," Josette said. "We were having a dance, and Bruno asked if I wanted to go off with him. He said there were lots of empty rooms. I mean, he was rather direct. He was pissed, too—drunk, I mean," she said, laughing.

Like a lot of Parisians, Josette learned her initial English from a British instructor, so she was always going on about getting pissed and feeling knackered afterward.

"And did you?" Rachel said.

"Well, no. For a second, part of me thought, Why not? He's attractive, you know. But the rest of me thought, Hey, look, I'm not just some tart who has sex on the copy machine."

Josette went on to say that Parisian women, by and large, were unfortunately tempted by their Frenchness to be weak. To give in. To let men do whatever they wanted. Herself included, Josette said. At the office one coworker frequently grabbed a breast when he gave her her morning *bises*, but she didn't complain; she probably never would. What Parisian men ultimately wanted, Josette explained, was the *coquette*, the brainless cutie who plays at being a little girl until gradually she yields to his wolfishness, then bears him sons. Josette named several women in the office who fit this archetype. Ah, I said.

Rachel asked, "So what do Parisian women want?"

"Oh, romance, of course," Josette said. "Power, charm. And force, it's true." She continued that Parisian women rarely desired a visitor or expat. Definitely no visitors who didn't have their own apartments—too unstable. Parisian women were like Parisian men; they wanted the big love, and for the right guy they'd do anything. But unlike male Parisians, Josette said, the girls didn't spread it around. We wouldn't find many prudes among Parisian girls, nor many sluts.

"And please," Josette added, "don't give me your artists in love with Paris. These are the worst, the guys who go all *franco-français*. You keep your poets," she said, laughing. "I hate the poets. Put him in a leather jacket. Give me a rough chap. You know, French women *love* a criminal."

After midnight, when we were past drunk and I was making coffee, Josette said sadly, "You know, French men can be difficult to bear. If you're the one breaking up with them? It's impossible. God, they're emotional." She was playing with the foil wrapper on the plant she'd brought. "They're womanish, you know? French women, I don't think we fall in love so easily as the men. Not just like that."

The next day, at work, Scottish Keith confirmed Josette's findings.

"I tell friends coming over, do *not* attempt to date proper Parisian girls," Keith said. "Big mistake. First, there's no sex in it, am I right?"

Tomaso nodded that Keith was right.

"Second, Parisian girls want to see a lease on the first date," Keith said. "You don't stand a chance if you're not French. Being rich helps, if you have a banana-colored Ferrari or what the fuck."

"Or if you are a sexy motherfucker," Tomaso added.

"*Or* that," Keith said.

The newspapers showed President Sarkozy and Carla Bruni sightseeing during a trip to Egypt. The president wore jeans and a black turtleneck, and stood hunched against the wind. Bruni was beside him in jeans and a purple top, with a sweater around her shoulders. Two pyramids for background symbolized their pasts; perhaps they contained the mummies of previous lovers. Anyway, no matter that France knew its president to be several inches shorter than his girlfriend, in the Egypt pictures he appeared her equal. And the two of them looked happy. They were in love.

From reading the news and hearing stories from office friends—from female colleagues, and from male colleagues—an indubitable truth emerged about Parisians, that when they fell in love, they really fell in love. No aspiration was more important, profound, or dangerous. They didn't go into it with reluctance or self-consciousness. They respected love like they did beauty: among life's highest states.

•

The last Friday morning in January, Paris was a melancholy bubble. Dribbling rain, infernal cold. On the Champs-Elysées, as I exited the Métro and began my march up the hill, drivers sat in traffic, huddling inside their cars with the windows closed, or cracked open with a cigarette protruding like a snorkel.

I could picture the tables crammed at Café de Flore, with guests warming their hands over *café crèmes*—tourists downstairs, locals upstairs on the ugly but oddly charming brown vinyl seats. And in some Montparnasse garret, more likely a couch swap, a young woman who'd traveled all the way from Montana, or Vermont, was sitting down to write the Great American (in Paris) novel.

Meanwhile, I was going to the movies. Which could have been great. That morning, Pierre had asked me and a coworker named Arnaud to meet him at a theater at the bottom of the boulevard. A new film, *Whatever Lola Wants*, was being released soon in France, and the producers had asked for a "viral ad campaign" to bring in audiences. Well, worst movie I'd ever seen. Perhaps someday it would be a cult favorite—but I doubted it. The story had a blond American moron deciding she badly wanted to become a belly dancer after her Arab friend showed her footage of a master performer. The American, named Lola, then unleashed her gullibility and bodacious flesh (she *was* bodacious) upon Egypt in order to learn the Orient's ways while sleeping around, offending local customs, and by hook or crook becoming an icon of gyration.

According to the publicity packet, *Whatever Lola Wants* intended to bridge East and West. Sure, on the back of every French cliché about Americans.

"You know," Arnaud said as we walked back to the office, in the rain, "that was actually pretty good."

"That was the worst movie I've ever seen," I said.

"Come on," Pierre said, "the worst?"

"Well, maybe the girl," Arnaud snorted. "She was bad. *And* annoying."

Pierre chided me, "It's a popcorn movie. It's for fun."

For a while, we climbed the Champs-Elysées in silence. Then I was forced—*forced*—to explain how the movie had been an exercise of stereotypes: Americans as childish, naive, brutal, vulgar, thoughtless, selfish, domineering idiots—

"Don't forget hot," Arnaud said. "Her body? *Waouh*."

"All we're seeing," I continued, "is what France already knows: dumb Americans and backward Arabs."

"Well," said Arnaud, "it *is* for a French audience."

We reached the office, and the rain slowed. Pierre plunked down his shoulder bag and lit a cigarette. "Remember," he said, "there was a gay Arab in the beginning. Isn't that progressive? You don't see many gay Arabs in movies."

"I don't know," Arnaud said. "It was kind of P.C. Hey, I have an idea. Okay, what if we made belly dancing the new thing for women in Paris? We organize classes, start Facebook groups, throw an expo. You could do it in gyms, you know?" He turned to me: "It's popular in the States, right? Rich women learn how to be strippers? Maybe we make that the new fashion in France."

"Maybe this could work," Pierre mused.

Across the street there was a hubbub outside Fouquet's, the storied restaurant. A passerby said Sarkozy was inside having breakfast. At the same time, Carlos the programmer came outside to smoke. He laughed when he saw me, and pulled me close by the shoulder: "What's up, my Negro?"

Then he noticed the publicity packet in our hands.

"Dude, what?" He shouted in English, "You guys going to the movies? Man, this is bullshit." He turned to me: "Yo, dog, why you so hooked up?"

24

One evening commute, I made a list of what's typically seen on Paris streets: People coolly bumping into each other. Posters for expos about beekeeping or cheese. Comics stores and hobby shops. Motorcycles equipped with fleece mittens and lap blankets, to shield their drivers during winter. Clothing boutiques for two-year-olds that sell exquisite cashmere sweaters so small, so unlikely to suit a toddler for more than five weeks, that their obscenely high prices make sense: to wear such a thing was a privilege, even for a day.

I made another list, of what there wasn't in Paris: No berets anymore, except on tourists. No more mustached *bistrotiers*. No Yale dropouts in khakis. No one loitering on Rue de Tournon. No bistros worth their price on the Boulevard Saint-Germain.

Bien sûr, there were still plenty of three-star restaurants. Beautiful parks to visit, and booksellers operating on the Seine. Fashion boutiques and *épiceries*, and *boîtes libertines* for politicians who wanted to let down their pants. Books penned by intellectuals about sex, yes, of course—which, I'll point out, always seemed to be discussed in newspapers and magazines with an academic, detached familiarity, like your next-door neighbor had just shared with you his poems.

But no, Parisians were not rude, I told Americans who asked—it's what everyone asked—at least no ruder than typical employees at Disney World. A single *s'il vous plaît* on your part went a long way. I said, *You* try being asked for directions every day in seven languages.

And yes, there was an expat store in the Marais that charged twenty-four euros for a bagel sandwich. Yes, most everyone in Paris spoke a little English, but speaking English in Paris remained a dead horse. Yes, *poivrotes* wore American Apparel leggings to flaunt their Parisian asses, which remained flawless, *absolument*.

Something new I learned: Mikhail Gorbachev had ideas about luggage. His face was the latest emblem of Louis Vuitton. For our digital campaign, he'd chosen Moscow as his city to remember, though during the interview we arranged, Gorbachev basically suggested that Moscow was a shitty convention center with bad traffic.

But when asked about luggage, specifically how he packed for traveling, Mikhail Gorbachev got excited. He packed his own bags, he said, and had a special method for stowing his shirts. He could imagine how his ideal suitcase would be designed. And so on.

Up next would be Keith Richards, Keef to the French. I begged Pierre to let me interview Keef. Pierre said no, the photo shoot and interview were being done in New York, and he couldn't afford to fly me over. However . . . "The plan is for Keef to talk about London," Pierre said. "So we will make the movies about London. I thought you could go do that instead of me. Chloe is upset about me taking so much time working."

I said yes, of course, happily.

It sounded a long way away from infant nutrition.

At that point, I was taking time off from working on my novel to let it sit, and reading a lot of Henry Miller. He'd been pressed on me by Scottish Keith. Nothing highbrow, Keith insisted, only the good stuff, the sex that frightened Americans. *Under the Roofs of Paris*, for example. I started it one morning on the Métro. I was on page two when I started worrying about people reading over my shoulder: *Marcelle wants us to look at her. She's bending over her father with his prick in one hand, gesticulating with the other, and calling loudly for an audience.*

Living abroad pierces your skin until one day you prevent it. You make yourself unshockable. The buildings on Rue de Rivoli give no new light, and you cease to see things fresh.

Same day, it was a chilly Wednesday, during my park time at lunch I thought how I didn't want to reach that point, but it seemed bound to happen, Henry Miller or not. If I inspected myself honestly, the Paris I knew best was from my commuting hours, before sunrise or during the dark blue winter twilight, and it was difficult not to think of Paris, my Paris, as a hallway in a shopping mall.

But Henry Miller nagged me for thoughts like that, for being so pedestrian.

A note from the government arrived at the beginning of February: our health-care cards would be further delayed until proof of my employment was supplied.

Of course, proof had been supplied. But this letter was from a different ministry; they needed the proof supplied to *them*. Dossiers not being shared between ministries, I guessed.

Plus they'd need copies of our birth certificates, certified French translations, et cetera.

Thankfully, our physical well-being was fine. But the problem of our health cards had become arduous. The prescriptions we needed we purchased at full cost, from our pocket. Health department officials assured me over the phone that as long as we saved our receipts, we'd be reimbursed down the line, once our cards arrived. But that day appeared to be far away. Until then, our monthly budget would stay tight, and get tighter.

Lindsay texted to say she'd found a new boyfriend, Christian. We'd meet him that night, Lindsay said, at some party of

Georgie's at a new club in the Latin Quarter, above a block of art galleries.

The cold became penetrating after dark—it got into the bones—but the Left Bank that evening was alive with people carousing, eating *daube niçoise*, drinking wine in cafés behind plastic walls erected for winter.

The club, a new construction, had a peculiar fusion: white leather, loud house music, and a sushi menu with fish priced as high as cars. When we arrived, Richard the redheaded cupid was just leaving. He looked miserable. He told us the party was *extremely* dead. Ten minutes later, Lindsay showed up alone—tall, blond, and pissed. Her new boyfriend would not be surfacing, she said. He'd promised to come, then he broke his promise, and they'd had their first fight. Rachel suggested she bring him by for dinner the next weekend. Lindsay said okay, but we shouldn't get our hopes up.

"Holy mother does he have issues with eating," she said. "Meaning, he doesn't eat. He smokes four packs a day and drinks Coca Light, but that's it."

Informed she'd just missed Richard, Lindsay said, "Well, you know he's got money troubles." Apparently Richard was depressed, Skypeing everyone he knew for consolation. Either money from his father wasn't being doled out anymore, or Richard was expected to start adding to his own pocket. Richard had even begun busing tables in the Marais, Lindsay said, at the restaurant that served diner food to American backpackers—his Parisian nightmare.

After ten more minutes, the club was full. We mingled. Georgie was chatting up several stockbroker types, their hair oil looking *très* Société Générale. But again, who was I to judge? Wasn't I standing there, too? Hadn't I become a mingler with expats?

My portrait's title was easy enough: *Schmuck with Heineken*.

And then we'd had enough.

A minute later, we were out on the street, and Rachel and I decided it would be our last event with A Small World, and Lindsay said yeah, hers, too.

End of the first week in February, I finally read my novel. Five a.m., the hour was black and icy. In the newspaper office across the courtyard, SORTIE signs were backlit in the dark, and Paris was a submarine.

But in the kitchen, as the baseboard heaters clicked on and smelled of flint, my book seemed to hum with life. At least for the first hundred pages, every turn of the plot was a surprise, even to me, and I was thrilled.

Fifty pages after that, I was ready to throw it out the window.

The book was DOA.

Oh, I knew enough to be able to say that, I swallowed whole careers. Carved up classics that never lost their power while I marveled at Greene, Austen, and Roth, never mind the regional specialists—never mind the global spymasters, island voices, and whiz kids whose novels I admired.

By the time I finished reading, I knew that in my book, there wasn't much essential being.

Soft stuff, true soft stuff, seemed to be the hardest trick to pull off.

That morning, Paris was not partial. It was frigid, gray, and wet. The sun came up. The city's colors colluded. No birds, no green. Rachel made breakfast and I left for work wearing a scarf, my coat, and a sky-blue baseball cap.

On the Métro, I thought, I'm no writer, I'm barely a *rédacteur*.

Let the hills ring: Sarkozy married Bruni in a modest ceremony attended by few guests. According to *People* magazine: "Acting as witnesses for the couple were French businessman François

Bazaire of the LVMH Groupe and Mathilde Agostinelli, communications officer for the Italian luxury goods firm Prada."

Something smelled off to me. When a luggage/fashion executive acted as one witness, and the other was Prada's head publicist, wasn't it likely—*wasn't it obvious to everyone*—that the marriage of the Italian supermodel to France's top divorcé had been arranged as a marketing exercise to benefit Europe's economy?

Mid-February, a coworker's cousin set up a *parfumerie* in one of the conference rooms. She was a big girl in three shawls. Evidently she made and sold her own perfumes. Some idiots, Doo-Doo and others, went in and spritzed themselves, so the whole office stank. For the rest of the day I had a jarring headache.

"Are you okay?" Olivier asked in the afternoon, peering from behind his monitor.

My head was resting on my desk.

"Do you remember," I said, "the day in autumn when I ate my lunch here?"

"Ah, you do not like the smell of the perfumes."

"I'm sorry," I said, "but it's too much. And this is not just an American thing."

Olivier laughed. "No, you're right. I have a headache, too. Let's open the window."

Olivier got up and opened the French doors to the balcony. A cold breeze blew in. Olivier announced loudly that if anyone wanted the doors closed, they could move to another room, but he and his American friend needed to be able to breathe, thank you very much.

25

Back in October, Rachel had experienced a knee injury after running in Buttes-Chaumont. In December, we'd both gotten the flu. After the flu, Rachel caught a head cold in January. After the cold, *une gastro* knocked us down for a long weekend.

Vertigo came last. Rachel woke up one morning, tried to sit, and fell over as if she'd been spun around in a food processor.

"What's the matter?" I said.

"I have no idea," Rachel said. "Every time I sit up, the room spins. Not just the room, but me, too." She squeezed my hand. "It's scary."

Behind the wall, a power drill screeched. There was nothing trompe l'oeil about it: as of February, we now had construction on all six sides of our apartment. Upstairs, downstairs, north, south, east, west.

I didn't say it, but perhaps a drill had reached her inner ear.

The American embassy's website gave us the number for an ear, nose, and throat doctor (ENT) on Rue Royale. The doctor herself answered the telephone. She said she could see us before lunch. Doctors were like that in Paris—they answered their own phones and often they'd see you within two hours, frequently in offices that were part of their own apartments.

We went through the doctor's living room to reach her study, on wood floors smoothed down to leather. Large windows overlooked a sunny courtyard with boxed fruit trees. Rachel could barely walk. The short trip from the Métro station to the doctor's building had been an ordeal of stops, starts, and spins. At least it's nice out, she'd said.

That day, Paris was awash with gold light.

"And you haven't changed your medication recently?" the doctor asked Rachel after she'd done a few tests. Birds chirped outside with full hearts.

"No," Rachel said.

"Well, you should probably see an ENT."

"You're not an ENT?" I said.

The doctor typed on her glossy white laptop, all its cords neatly hidden from view.

"I can recommend one, in the eighteenth," she said. "He knows all the treatments. And he speaks English very well." She telephoned and obtained us an appointment for two hours later.

We took the Métro up to the eighteenth arrondissement. By that point, Rachel's symptoms had settled down. As long as she didn't jerk her head, she could walk. Both of us were starving. The second doctor's street was mostly offices, but there was a chain steak restaurant on the corner, the French equivalent of Sizzler. Inside, the bar was strung with promotional St. Patrick's Day advertisements.

"Look at that," Rachel said, pointing out the window after we'd sat down. The sidewalk was bustling, the sky was cloudless—Paris, the all-access picnic. "This could be our perfect day."

"What about the vertigo?" I said.

"Oh, forget the vertigo," Rachel said. "We're in Paris, we're having lunch together. Imagine if this is what Paris was."

At the ENT's office, we sat in the waiting room with a pair of grandparents holding gossip magazines that they scanned and passed back and forth. They looked seventy, maybe eighty. I wondered if they remembered the Paris of horse slaughterers, the Paris of *patrons* behind aluminum bars and flowers brought home from Les Halles.

A stooping giant summoned the grandparents into his examination room, patting them in through his door. Twenty minutes later it was our turn.

"Yes, hello," the ENT said as we walked under his arm.

We sat in chairs opposite his desk.

"You are . . . Rachel?" the doctor said, consulting his notes. He looked up, hesitating to smile. "And you are feeling?"

He did not speak English well. He ordered Rachel to sit on an examining table, and said things like "Good, yes?" while shoving her down until her eyes filled with water. Then he flipped her the other way. He said, "You feel sick? You make sick now?"

"No," Rachel said, "not now."

"Hmm, maybe bad," he said.

The doctor did some more tests, then filled out Rachel's *dossier* while she sat up on the table and tried to regain her balance. "All right, come down from there," the doctor chided after a minute.

Really he was probably six-four, but he looked even bigger. He wore a sport coat with shoulder pads that protruded like epaulettes.

The doctor rubbed his hair and sat down at his desk. He said he wasn't sure what type of vertigo Rachel had, but she had it, and she'd feel better soon if she adopted a daily routine of balance exercises. He passed me a sheet of drawings: stick figures engaged in tumbling.

"So that is all," the doctor said abruptly, and stood up. He extended a long arm to shake hands. "But do not be afraid. This is not," he said, "you know, a thing forever."

One Sunday, under ivy on Rue de Beauce, in the Marais, Rachel and I discovered an art gallery specializing in novelists. Each painting in the window was of an American writer popular in France. Rachel waited while I gawked at a hangdog Paul Auster;

a gouty Jim Harrison; a famished Joyce Carol Oates; T. C. Boyle and his emergency pull-cord lock of hair.

Inside me was a volcano, and on top of it, six thousand trivial feelings.

I'd begun writing my novel again, starting over from page one, but I wasn't hopeful about it.

Work at the agency, however, was going much more smoothly. Me speaking French sufficiently, me brainstorming, me presenting in my French-English hash. And no longer was I writing about how to care for your baby; now I wrote scripts for little movies that were purportedly advertising, yet in which neither brand nor product was mentioned. Was it so bad? Wasn't it actually rather fun?

But was my dream now to rise in French advertising?

I didn't know how long it would last. I didn't know how long I wanted it to.

Every day was an improvisation.

I was so tired.

A few days later, I saw a gastroenterologist for a stomach bug. His office was around the corner from the agency, high above the eighth arrondissement, on a tony street. The rooms were white, accented in camel, furnished with black modern chairs. Very luxe, but expensively grungy. The doctor himself wore Joey Ramone hair to the collar of a black leather jacket. He was half gnome, half roadie; he was probably Johnny Hallyday's personal physician. The doctor smirked to begin our appointment, expecting it to disappoint him. I told him about my stomach bug. Hearing my accent, the doctor asked where I was from. He sat up when I said New York City. He said, You moved from New York to Paris? Isn't it better to go the other way around? I said, Yes, I've heard that opinion. For ten minutes he made himself plain: Paris was done; oh, how he hated it. He wanted to know, didn't I find Parisians to be so conservative and snobby? He had a doctor friend, he said, with a practice in Miami, who was constantly bragging about his great American life. Did I know the East Village? For example, what a loft cost there nowadays?

The gastroenterologist asked what I did. I said I was a writer. He asked if I'd published a book he could read. I sighed and explained that I worked in advertising. Ah, but this is not writing, the doctor said, swishing his finger. Then he also sighed. He leaned back, his chair creaking, and asked me if I knew the work of William Styron.

26

Long ago I joined Morrissey's fan club to be alerted whenever Morrissey modified his touring schedule. It wasn't for me; I didn't hear my first Smiths song until 1999. During Rachel's and my courting period, when we told everything on ourselves, Rachel had said she needed to see Morrissey before she died. She was a fan. A big one. She'd already seen Al Green in concert, her other musical obsession, and he'd thrown her a rose. Now what remained was to see Morrissey onstage.

About a week later I'd joined his e-mail list.

Morrissey, the e-mail said, would play the Olympia theater in Paris very soon.

When tickets went on sale, I set the alarm for 4:25 a.m.

The night of the concert, we paused outside. "I don't want to rush this," Rachel said. I took her picture under the marquee. The Olympia was a famous Paris theater where Édith Piaf had performed. Rachel bought a T-shirt at the concession stand before going inside. During the show, everyone sang along. Rachel was relaxed. She was happy. Just like her, people around us knew the words to every song. Afterward, I offered to splurge on a cab, but Rachel said we'd spent enough money that evening; the T-shirt had cost more than I spent on lunch for a week.

On the Métro home, Rachel said, "That was probably one of the best nights in my life. Not just Morrissey, but the whole thing. Doing it here."

Paris, too, loved Morrissey. The initial applause, when he'd appeared onstage, was a wild, long-lasting roar. Morrissey addressed the crowd in French. He'd always loved France, loved Paris; then again, who didn't? Ecstatic applause from all of us who agreed. Then Morrissey announced a new song, one he'd never performed before, the lead single off his new album—he hoped we'd like it.

It was called, "I'm Throwing My Arms Around Paris."

Sometimes, some blips in time, the world seems extremely synchronized.

Days of winter were short. Thankfully, they were nearly done. Many people, including me, still wore scarves around the office. Cold in Paris was both a physical and a mental state. It explained why Parisians wore scarves in June, because winter haunted them. Still, sometimes women's legs would flash bare on the crosswalks. And a few flowers burst early in sidewalk planters.

A friend who was an editor at *The New York Times*, Sam, flew into town for Fashion Week. Sam was very tall, Ivy League, handsome in the bones, with a long face and wide shoulders. He invited us to a party thrown by the *Times*'s style magazine at a building adjoining the Grand Palais. When we arrived, Sam looked wrung out. He said he'd drunk too much wine the night before with some girls from *Elle* or some other magazine, girls in their twenties who were bunking at the Ritz, partying between shows—and could they *drink*, Sam said, wobbling his head.

We went into the party, following Jarvis Cocker from Pulp through coat check. Inside, we stood in an enormous, crowded ballroom with a soaring ceiling; above our heads was air and smoke for thirty feet. The scene was wild and homogeneous. Loud music, and many recognizable faces—a hundred takes on the same beautiful. People wafted into embraces, smoking cigarettes despite the recent ban.

So many uneasy women, I thought, for so much champagne.

We stood near Suzy Menkes, fashion critic at the *Herald Tribune*, who was talking to Karl Lagerfeld, boss of Chanel, for about five minutes. They occupied the room's only pool of empty space, which their assistants had carved out for them by ringing them like guards.

I shouted over the noise, "Is it me, or does Suzy Menkes look a little like Charlie Chan?"

"Shhh, she's very powerful," Rachel said darkly.

The room was crammed with fashionable Paris society: editors, models, designers, and their help. It was very noisy. Rachel and Sam talked about life in Paris; meanwhile, I couldn't take my eyes off Karl Lagerfeld. He resembled a short, dead Iggy Pop.

"Karl Lagerfeld looks like Beethoven," I shouted.

Rachel said, "Who's that kid from *Peanuts* with the statue on his piano?"

Sam snapped, "The fuck you guys talking about?"

"Exactly, a bust," I yelled, "Karl Lagerfeld is a bust."

A few minutes later, we were sitting on low leather cubes, which put us at supermodel knee level. Girls wandered by in colored tights, their legs the hues of different ice creams.

Rachel whispered, gazing, "This could only happen in Paris."

Sam asked me about my job. I explained how between my novel, my job, and my work editing the Web magazine, I was busy from about five in the morning until ten p.m., at which point we had dinner, something Rachel had cooked or takeout sushi. I told Sam how, at our nearby sushi restaurant, I'd become friends with the manager, a Moroccan guy my age who now gave me free beer when I ordered.

Aside from weekends, I said, I might as well have been living in Minneapolis.

Sam laughed. "But you're kidding. You do hear yourself, right? Wait—you're not joking? *Dude*," he said.

Sam folded up his legs so a supermodel could walk by. She

had on purple tights and a doll-size leather jacket. We knew her face from magazines; in real life she looked just as haunted. Did the fashion industry get them prestarved from orphanages?

Then again, who'd ever let Karl Lagerfeld near children?

"Listen to me: what the fucking ever," Sam said. He was watching the supermodel diminish. "You're in Paris," he shouted, standing up; "life is wonderful. Quit being a bitch and let me know when I can have your job, okay?"

We watched Sam set out to go hunting. First he had to stop and kiss hello to some girls just arriving, whom he knew from the previous night—none older than twenty-two, each wearing a skirt and stilettos, and all seeming at home, each girl inclined to her BlackBerry or iPhone, her face illuminated by a message.

Of course, Sam was right. No one heard you when you said you were sick of Paris. "Sick of Paris" meant your mind was rotten. You *were* a bitch. To paraphrase the *Simpsons* episode when a "Yahoo Serious Festival" came to town, "sick," "of," and "Paris" were three words that made sense alone, but not in sequence.

Besides, what did I have against champagne for sale in gas stations? Or chocolates from Patrick Roger? What about Parisian construction workers' way with sandbags? What about the solace of Place de l'Estrapade? What about the Arts et Métiers Métro station, and André's Lacoste rotation, and how excitable Parisians became about *charcuterie*?

Tecktonik kids, I couldn't forgive myself to ignore Tecktonik kids.

The weekend following the *Times* party, we walked by some teenagers standing outside a post office in the Marais, brooding in T-shirts, sweatshirts, and tight black jeans. All of them were busy texting until one boy put his phone down on top of a mailbox. He pressed some buttons and the phone bleated out a song. Suddenly, all of them were dancing, twirling their arms like *West*

Side Story re-created—the toughs revealing their Martha Graham training—only here it was set in Paris, with android moves.

During winter, I learned that exiting a Métro station in the morning sounded different when there weren't tourists around. At the staircase at Rennes, or Rue du Bac, or Franklin D. Roosevelt, the person in front would hold open the door for you to exit, bracing it against the wind from the street. You thanked them, *Merci, Madame, merci*. Next, you held it open for the person behind you, who'd rush forward to grab it, *Merci, Monsieur, merci*, and so on, so that each morning during winter, for maybe an hour before nine a.m., there was a continuous murmur of people giving thanks.

27

We received telemarketing calls at all hours from snappy Frenchwomen, whom I held in high regard. I named them Marianne. All the ones I spoke to sounded very French, and I made a rule to engage them.

For example, Marianne might call at breakfast. “Hello, this is Orange, your cellular communications company—”

“Yes, hello,” I’d say brightly.

Marianne wasn’t surprised to be interrupted. “Good morning, sir. This is Orange—”

“Please,” I said, “for one moment, slowly?”

“Hello?”

Sometimes Marianne was patient with me, sometimes she was confused.

“Yes, hello,” I said.

“Okay,” said Marianne.

I said, “My French is not very good.”

“Oh no,” Marianne said, “it’s quite good.”

“Oh, thank you.”

“I can speak slowly,” she said.

“That would be super,” I said.

“So,” she said, “today I am calling with an exercise of marketing.”

“Can you repeat that, please?”

“An exercise of marketing?” Marianne said.

"Thank you."

"No, it's all right," she said, laughing, "thank *you*."

Sometimes, though, Marianne called when it was inconvenient. During dinner or when I was in a rush to leave the house. Then I'd say something confrontational, like "Where are you calling from?"

"Excuse me? Sir, that is privileged information."

"But I live in Paris, and you know this," I said. "Is my information not privileged?"

"Excuse me?"

"It is," I explained, "the same concept."

"Sir," she said, "I will arrange for someone to call you back."

"Will it be you?" I said.

"Sir, Orange will solicit your participation when a time is more convenient."

Marianne was always pawning me off.

As March became visible, I'd stretch my hour at lunch to ninety minutes, occasionally two hours, and work on my book. I also started devising an advertising campaign in case Paris slipped in global popularity and the Hôtel de Ville needed slogans.

Paris—*Sex without the messy stuff.*
Paris—*Where refinement meets retirement.*
Paris—*Society's life raft has room for YOU.*

At work, the task of advertising was to make new the mundane. To find the perfect metaphor. Each week, in addition to my scripts, there'd be half a dozen small Louis Vuitton projects to complete, for which Pierre would hand me a brief, I'd go to a conference room, and an account manager would say, "We've got a purse to advertise. Here's what's new about it. Can you have a slogan done by tonight, tomorrow lunch at the latest?"

Most of the time a purse was just a purse. But the challenge was not unenjoyable.

Paris—*End zone of Western civilization.*

Other days, when no one was looking, I'd open the file for my novel on my computer and work on it furtively, pretending it was a client's copy deck. Since February, I'd been doing it more and more. I was back at my first job, age twenty-two, hiding my writing behind a Netscape window when a boss came nearby. As though I were committing a crime, getting high on my own supply.

Lindsay and her new boyfriend, Christian, the guy with eating issues, finally visited. Christian was a men's fashion designer who'd learned English in Cape Town and spoke with a South African accent. He arrived smoking—Lindsay had told us he smoked four packs a day. Didn't drink alcohol, didn't eat food, didn't bathe either, though he didn't look worse for it. Christian had a pudgy, friendly face and wore a green military jacket over a blue collared shirt, plus jeans and boots, with sticky hair. He could have been a Spanish poet, I thought.

Christian and I talked about bunkers. He was interested in them, he said, as suitable second homes. They spoke to him romantically; he said he was all for barricading oneself in. Christian explained that he often went on scouting trips looking for a bunker he could fix up for a summer home, even swap it for his big apartment on the Boulevard Saint-Germain.

"It could be gorgeous," he said. "You put in, how do you say, aprons?"

"Curtains," Lindsay said. "But please, Christian, your apartment here is amazing, you could not give it up."

"Maybe I prefer a bunker," Christian said, and laughed, hugging Lindsay while he chewed on her neck.

"Well, count me out," Lindsay said, pushing him away. "Oh yeah, a couple of concrete walls, slits for windows, what could be more romantic?"

According to Lindsay, Christian was from a Bordeaux wine family *ancienne*—he wasn't in line to the British throne, but he was suitably impoverished. At twenty, Christian had been wealthy from an inheritance, but he'd burned through all his money during the nineties, and now he had zip. He subsisted on an allowance from his grandmother while he tried to sell French workmen's jackets reconstructed as blue blazers.

We talked about Paris, having that in common.

"You know, Paris is tough," Christian said in English. "I would not want to live here if I could choose a different history."

He said Paris was probably the worst European city after London. "London is the worst. Weather is shitty. You cannot walk around. People are closed off, and they hate Jews. None of this will change." But Paris was too expensive, he said, too conservative, too self-protective. "Paris had, like, the nineteenth century. But look, we are all very lucky at this table—we're white, you see? Paris is the most hard on immigrants. And immigrants are really important, I think, to the life of a city."

The sunset put a purple glow into the courtyard. Rachel asked Christian where he would prefer to live. He said Berlin, for the art and music, or back in Cape Town.

I said, "Why not New York?"

"Same people who live in Paris live in New York," Christian said dismissively. "Manhattan is for shopping now, same as here."

"But you can still love it," Lindsay said. "I happen to love Paris."

"Yeah, of course, baby, it depends," Christian said. "*You* can be happy in Paris. And me, I'm happy that you're *in* Paris. And sometimes I am happy when I *think* about Paris." He thought about that for a moment. "Now see," Christian said, "if you're connected to reality, then no. But some people are not. I know a guy, he lives here eight years. Australian guy, absolutely mad about Paris. Barely speaks French, but he's completely in love. *C'est normal*. He's happy. You can do that if you're disconnected, walking around all day, staring at buildings, living in the fantasy. But reality is, it's a tough city to live in. For people who actually live and don't have money. It's not like the movies."

After midnight, Rachel and Lindsay watched dance videos on YouTube, and Christian and I talked more about bunkers while he smoked out the window. The sky was black and pearly—a bowl set to dry upside down. I told Christian I'd received a good book in the mail about bunkers, Paul Virilio's *Bunker Archeology*. I'd lend him my copy.

"You know," Christian said, "what people do not realize, you can find really good real estate near nuclear facilities. Big discounts, like *les soldes*, all year. No one realizes this. We should go together sometime, we can go for a drive."

That night, Rachel and I agreed in bed that it had been a successful dinner party, even if one guest (Christian) hadn't eaten dinner. But there was news on that front: Lindsay had informed Rachel that Christian *did* eat, except he ate only chocolate, and ate it only in bed, alone. However, he'd recently taken his first bite of chocolate in front of her, and Lindsay thought it was a good sign for their relationship.

The next morning, I was taking out the garbage when Asif pulled me into his kitchen. His ten-year-old daughter was doing homework at a folding table next to the stove.

"Nadira," Asif said, "please say hello."

Nadira kissed me on both cheeks. Then she frowned while her father explained that I was from New York City. She said she thought New York was very beautiful from some pictures she'd seen.

I said, "Is it more beautiful than Paris?"

"*Je crois—*" she started, but Asif told her to speak English. Nadira coughed and covered her mouth. She said in English through her fingers, "I think New York is more big than Paris? And more dirty. But I think I like that."

Asif asked Nadira what she'd said, and she translated it into French while turning in a circle. "You see how smart she is?" Asif said to me. "She is learning English *and* German in school. They're good, Paris schools, really good. She will be a doctor someday."

His comment upset Nadira. She yanked on her father's arm and bugged her eyes, reprimanding him in French faster than I could understand. Asif laughed. "She says she does not want to be a doctor. I said, what is wrong with being a doctor?"

"What do you want to be?" I asked Nadira.

"I want . . . to fly a plane!" Then her dress irritated her because it was too stiff to swing properly, and she tore at it. "Or maybe a doctor," Nadira said. She shouted with exasperation, "I am too young right now!"

We went outside. In the courtyard, the walls were warm. Spring was coming. Around Asif's door was a sector of plants. Asif pulled cigarettes from his pocket. I could see that someone had carefully ironed his shirt. Nadira kicked a soccer ball, using garbage cans for goalposts.

"She lives with her mother," Asif said. "Not close by."

He watched his daughter pensively. He made a play for the soccer ball, but Nadira slipped around him. Asif came back to me and smoked, standing with one of his legs thrust forward, heel quarter-turned like a fashion model in pose.

"She is my treasure," Asif said. "She's all I have on this earth."

Asif stared hard at me. Tears sprang up in his eyes.

"You don't have children, you don't know," he stated. He took my hand a moment later, as if we were going for a walk, and clenched it. He accused me, "But don't you see?"

•

When it was sixty degrees in March, I sent e-mails to friends in Chicago, "Hot and sunny here in Paris, how are you?"

One morning, it was at least fifty degrees at breakfast. But then the temperature dove. The air hardened, and people chipped their steps. Clouds filled the sky like they were blown in from a horn. By the time I was halfway finished with my lunch at the park, I looked up and saw that it was snowing, huge flakes falling on my nose, whitening the benches.

I glanced at Stephen King, but he didn't notice anything. He had his headphones on, and I noticed he'd outgrown my moniker: now he was reading Stieg Larsson, like everybody else. Five minutes later, gone were clouds, gone was snow. Back to a blue-gray Paris sky and warm breezes. At the office, people didn't believe my story. None of them had seen the snow. Only Tomaso believed me, though he said I was *très mignon* (very cute), "*toi et tes rêves de neige*."

Olivier scoffed: "This is only in the movies."

I'd heard Parisians say it never snowed in Paris. But they were wrong, and Olivier was wrong, and now I could prove it. It just snowed very quickly, and a person needed to pay attention.

28

Man, I was dying for a prostitute. Just one would do it. One prostitute who wasn't fourteen or a sex slave. We could shoot her, then go back to the hotel and get some sleep, and that would be grand.

Keef had said that back in the day, when the Rolling Stones rented a studio in Soho, he'd chat up girls who were listening through the window. Working girls, you understand. Vincent, the film director Pierre had hired for Louis Vuitton, and his collaborator, Lucas, a composer and sound engineer, both thought it was important that we capture London's contemporary prostitutes, in Keef's honor. But it seemed Soho had only young prostitutes, miserable girls selling their flesh from doorways, and it was depressing in fifty ways, never mind unsuitable for a global luxury brand's ad campaign.

To reach that evening, Vincent and I had come over to London a few days earlier on an early morning train, talking the whole way about Barack Obama, whom Vincent, like many Parisians, found magical. He was interested in America, Vincent said, for its lack of self-awareness, in contrast with France's narcissism—Parisians loved a show, and America was persistently entertaining. Probably the United States was too racist to elect Obama, Victor said, but if not, what a gesture, to elect a black! This would never happen in France, he said.

The day we arrived, we met up with Lucas at St. Pancras Station. Our location scout and driver picked us up, then we set off to film. Time gradually slowed for several days. It dragged and slurped and stopped. That's how filming worked, Vincent said. "You wait, you wait, and you wait. You eat badly. You wait more. Then maybe you get one minute of film, if the light is good."

Lucas said in English, "It is always catastrophe."

Our project was to capture London in seven short films, interpreting the memories of Keith Richards. We'd already interviewed Keef, and back in Paris I'd turned the interview into a script. By the time we were searching for prostitutes, we'd been crisscrossing London for days, from Hampstead to Battersea. Mostly we sat in traffic. Winds and rain battered the car. At one point, we had a long conversation about whether London or Paris was the greater sushi restaurant, given the amount of ambient techno music piped into public spaces. London won. After that, the location scout and I played a game of battling.

"Who'd win in a fight," he asked me, "New York or Los Angeles?"

"Los Angeles," I said. "New Yorkers don't have time to fight."

Our scout was a young Welshman who'd recently graduated from film school. To meet ends, he trawled London for advertising companies in need of British settings and chauffeured their teams around town. He also worked, he said, as a concierge for an elite credit card program—meaning he fielded calls from traveling Arabs and Russians looking for prostitutes.

In America, I said, we called that luxury humor.

The Welshman was also an antiroyalist. I told him about the French guy I knew who aspired to be the burger king of Paris, since he was unlikely to assume the British throne. The scout said, "Oh yeah, there's loads of them. They know exactly how many people have to die before they're in court. We've got a bit of history with France, intermingling."

I proposed a quiz to the Welshman: "Imagine it's you and one hundred five-year-olds. You're locked in a gymnasium. The children are overcome with a desire to kill you. How many could you put down?"

"Can I use one of them," he said, "as a weapon against the others?"

"Sure," I said. "But remember they're a mob."

"Right. I can't let them get me on the ground."

A minute later we gave the game over to the Frenchmen in the backseat.

"Who wins," I said, "Coca-Cola or Uma Thurman?"

They were staring out the windows. Vincent, the director, said in English, "That is not a game." He started coughing. "Okay, come on," he said a moment later, "it is so Anglo this game. It is not a game. How do you judge this? It is a soda and a woman. How do you decide?"

"It's simple," I said. "One wins, one loses. Just pick."

Vincent refused. He sighed. "It is nothing a French person would think is a game. It is so stupid."

I asked him to suggest a French game that we could play instead.

"Okay, okay, here is a French game," Vincent said. "We will talk about something for a little while. It will be about nothing. We will talk and talk and talk about it. Sometimes I will make the other side of the conversation, just to say you are wrong. And then we will stop."

Lucas agreed, this was a classic French game.

Vincent and Lucas were business partners as well as friends. Vincent directed artsy films—I'd seen one and liked it quite a bit, about a lonely man who wandered through a forest listening to the sounds of branches snapping—but his films didn't make much money, and to feed his family he directed commercials for fashion companies.

For his part, Lucas composed lovely ambient music—film scores for films not yet dreamed. But he didn't make much money doing that, either, so Lucas did all the sound engineering and scoring for Vincent's commercial work.

Both Vincent and Lucas were in their early forties. Both handsome, short-haired, and temper-driven. Vincent tended to brood, mostly on the future. He had squashed ears from playing too much rugby. He was an intellectual bruiser, a seeker, not someone who overremembered. When Vincent spoke, he barked, and when he laughed, he scrunched up his nose and raised his eyelids in gleeful surprise. His wife, a beautiful Dutch fashion designer, was the spitting image of Jean Seberg.

Lucas was the more inscrutable, mysterious—more outgoing while also holding back. He had reddish blond hair, small eyes, and a long ridgeline of a nose that drew from a prominent brow. He was constantly smoking, laughing, parrying with Vincent. But above all he seemed despondent. Prior to composing, Lucas had been a comedian.

It was around ten p.m. on our third evening, after our location scout had gone to bed, that we were searching Soho for a luxury-appropriate prostitute. Just one.

As we walked, Vincent brought up our conversation from the car.

"See, this is a thing I hate about the French," he said in English. Both Vincent and Lucas preferred to speak English with me so they could practice. Lucas also said he found my French accent indecipherable. "The French," Vincent said, "they are too—*comment tu dis*—too 'proud.' "

At that moment, a bouncer/pimp started giving us the eye. We walked faster to mask our intentions, not that it did much good. Lucas was trailing behind us, carrying a fuzzy microphone on a pole, shouting out to Vincent whenever he found something interesting.

Vincent said, "French people have a problem being proud. If we are in public? We don't say we like anything. We are not assholes—we are, you say, defensive. Oh, hey, look," Vincent barked, nodding ahead. After the next intersection were some doorways we hadn't seen yet, a few of them with women in lingerie who looked well past sixteen.

Vincent put his camera at waist level, covered by his shoulder bag, to shoot out the side. My job was to play the john. "You go before me," Vincent said. "Not speed, be normal."

We did three passes, me inspecting girls and Vincent filming them from the neck down. Each building had blinking neon for eyebrows. Entrances where there weren't girls had little handwritten signs taped up inside, "Busty" or "Gorgeous BRUNETTE" or simply "Upstairs."

Then we noticed another bouncer getting off his stool, coming toward us. Did I look too indecisive? Vincent and I sprinted down an alley. We heard Lucas clanging behind us, his equipment bag slapping his hip.

Once we'd stopped, Vincent said to me, "*Donc*, Parisians? When they love something, you know, *interne*? Most they will say is, '*Enh, pas mal . . .*' Also, okay, this is what I wanted to say—" Vincent leaned against a wall fluttering with flyers. "French people? Don't like to admit when they are wrong."

I told him I was impressed we were still having this conversation. Lucas came running around the corner—what was the danger? Then Vincent darted away, to go film a stag party stumbling out of a club.

Lucas turned and said, "Wassup?"

"Vincent wanted to talk about Parisians," I said.

"I understand," Lucas said in English. "Hello."

Lucas's English had maybe two dozen words, culled from movies. He packed up his microphone while saying, "You two guys . . . are a mysterious ensemble."

I asked him what he meant. Lucas stared at me. He said, "I do not like you."

Yes, you do, I said.

"No," Lucas said. "You make *games* of me. I will keep an eye on you."

"Lucas, I do not—"

"Hey, guy!" Lucas shouted, backing away. "Don't come at me. I will fuck you!"

Then Lucas ran forward to slap me a high five. At the last second, he yanked his hand back, laughing, and went off to go find Vincent.

A newspaper slipped under my door the next morning said Eliot Spitzer had been arrested for soliciting prostitution.

Been there, I thought, done that.

We were awake at five a.m. on our last day in London because Vincent wanted to re-create one of Keef's stories, about him walking home one morning in the sixties through Hampstead Heath. Keef had said it was the most beautiful he ever saw London. A summer dawn, mist rising from the green, with Keef and the other wimpled addicts stumbling home through the Big Smoke.

We filmed on the heath, freezing in the dark. Vincent instructed me to act like Keef—stumbling—and I didn't need to pretend. Afterward, we filmed from a boat on the Thames, to grab some final establishing images from the shot list. Then our driver took us to St. Pancras and we said goodbye while the sky blackened over with rain clouds.

Inside the train station, we sat on our bags. Suddenly Vincent flipped out. He shouted at Lucas, "We're late! We must run if we want to make the train!"

Lucas took off sprinting. Vincent buckled over laughing. We weren't late, of course; we still had two hours to kill. But Lucas hated traveling, and Vincent liked to play practical jokes. I didn't think it was funny, so I ran after Lucas and told him it had been a joke, everything was fine. Lucas was furious. When he finally spoke, he said in English, "So you guys are an ensemble against me?"

"No, it was Vincent's idea. He's sorry," I said.

Lucas either didn't hear or didn't understand me. He was enraged: "Guy, you *fuck* with me? *You fuck with me?!*"

Several people turned, including security guards. One guard came our way, hand to holster. Lucas beamed at him and clapped his hands, bowing to the guard, and held up one finger.

"Hello, mister, it's okay!" Lucas said. "We have no problems. We are very gentle!"

The guard turned away, and Lucas wandered off to buy a snack.

On the train back to Paris, Vincent and Lucas discussed what they'd eat for dinner. A nice steak, definitely some good vegetables. In London, we'd mostly eaten pub food. Lucas said he believed he'd gained five kilos from too much shepherd's pie.

Lucas said, pointing at me, "You look fat." Lucas noted that the prostitutes in Soho hadn't been fat at all, to his surprise. If anything, Soho had been a *défilé*.

I asked Vincent to translate.

"A fashion show," Vincent said. "Where the girls *promenade*, how do you call it?"

"The catwalk?"

"You have this?" Lucas said. "A cat who walks?"

"This is not translated," Vincent told me, then he closed his eyes and went to sleep. Lucas followed suit. The high-speed train hurtled toward Paris, toward the light. In London, the vibe had been an awareness of one's place. In Paris, though, the feeling was exhibition, of what you had to offer.

THE REALEST

SPRING

—Moroccan muezzins call to me in a way the Eiffel Tower does not—Behaving badly can be appropriate in a Parisian office—American cotton is all the rage—African Americans interpret brandy like Chinese businessmen—Marianne's inquiries—I learn to dip my morning bread—Paris loves George Clooney the best—Officially, I'm French—

29

If you wanted a nice weekend holiday, try Morocco, coworkers said. But not Casablanca. Scottish Keith cautioned, "It's a massive business dump." Like many, Bruno pushed for Marrakech. He told me he enjoyed going there for *les tagines*, but also the women. At this, three guys giggled, turning in their seats. They were Bruno's lackeys, in Bruno's new office. He'd recently been assigned new accounts in addition to infant nutrition and transferred across the street to the agency's other building.

Bruno frowned when I didn't grasp his Moroccan orgy scenario, and went back to pouting and clicking his mouse. All week he'd been acting like a lord banned from court. Of course, he had been cast out, far away from André and Pierre. Boards were stacked behind him from a new job that Bruno hated: a campaign for a machine that puréed fruits and vegetables into baby food.

"You're really becoming a baby expert," I said.

"I don't want to talk about it," Bruno said. "So I hear you went to London."

"For a few days."

"It must be good to be Pierre's boy," Bruno said, and snorted.

Lots of coworkers had recommendations on where to go in Marrakech. They'd all been there before. Marrakech for Parisians was like San Juan for New Yorkers, Los Cabos for the Los Angeleno: a hop by plane to sunny digs—a former colony of sorts—that many neighbors called home, where everyone spoke your language. So why not. My birthday was coming up, and Rachel found extremely cheap round-trip tickets, plus a rooftop bedroom in a riad, in Marrakech's old city, for next to nothing.

At the Marrakech airport, our driver, a tall guy in tight jeans with a blue Toyota van, said he had friends and family working in Paris. He dreamed about visiting them. Paris was "the most beautiful city in the world." From the backseat, I daydreamed. The windows were full of palm trees, sand, and far-off mountains. The streets were choked with dust. We passed donkey carts and mopeds, and many people wearing blinking Bluetooth earpieces. The driver and Bruno wore the same Pumas, I noticed.

Our riad, a private hotel inside a home, was located within the old city's fortress. Our driver parked and led us down an alley—left, right, left—until he banged on a door set into a nondescript wall. The heavy door swung open to reveal a courtyard. Inside was silence, a fountain burbling, roses clambering toward the sun.

A teenage girl took us up to our little room on the roof, with views of the minaret and five mosques, thousands of rooftop antennas, and the Atlas Mountains in the distance.

The muezzins called in succession, like car alarms triggering one another.

All of it was blissful to me.

That evening, there were no streetlights, only moped headlamps. But it was very calm on the street, still hot, a dense black. But nothing sinister. We set out to find dinner, turning one corner, then another. There weren't any street signs. The air was dry. A man passed us wearing a yoke, towing a two-wheeled wooden cart of pastries. People were out talking, eating in the dark. Not a Westerner in sight, but many boys sitting on bicycles, illuminated by a store's single lightbulb. Three or four women here or there.

Eventually we found a bistro recommended by a coworker (our directions from the riad were "second left, third right, then your fourth left, second right . . ."), and inside were thirty white people wearing formal outfits, in a garden under lemon trees strung with lights.

It was the most exotic aspect of the trip so far—real colonials in the wild.

For three days, I was thrilled by the minute. Inside red-clay towers, we found three-star restaurants. Teenage boys hung their arms around each other's hips, and older men held hands. Businesswomen wore shawls with blue jeans. We were fluid in traffic and tutored by our foreignness. That a family of five could share a single moped was proved multiple times.

And judging by the amount of people who texted while driving mopeds, you'd think cell phones were moped remote controls. In the souk, shielded by threadbare ceiling cloths, were European ladies dragging their daughters behind them in a hunt for bargains. Both fat mothers and skinny daughters bare-armed and pink in an extremely visible desecration of the local culture's preference for women to cover skin; but Moroccans ignored them, as if they were ghosts.

And when we got lost, or didn't move for half a minute, a boy would appear and request we follow him, to who knows where. Marrakech was a tourist city just like Paris—snake charmers in lieu of accordion players, but still the same, if not more purely about its business. Mercantile, abrasive, and more welcoming. *Please, come into my stall, sit, have some tea, now buy something.*

If cities like Paris and Marrakech had realized tourism was their most profitable enterprise, why should they resist? Why not play up the image, act the part the visitors wanted, cater to their whims and pocket the cash?

My Parisian friends might counter, Well, to play a part may look like an act of preservation, but it also can be self-annihilating.

Anyway, I found myself very comfortable in the heat, in Marrakech. I told Rachel, “For no good reason I feel like I’m home.” Sunday, I turned thirty-one, and for dinner we ate a delicious meal of chicken and lemons that our housekeeper cooked for eight hours in the laundry room. We drank expensive French wine for cheap, breathing air that smelled like a spice market. From the roof, we saw several falling stars.

The next afternoon, we flew back to Paris and arrived after dark. It must have just rained—the city was black and slick, paved with gold reflections. Our cabdriver from the airport sang along to the radio playing a live recording of a punk band. The band was singing in English:

Fire, fire, fire,
Paris is burning

30

A new neighbor joined my desk group at work: a contemplative Parisian art director named Chaya who wanted to improve his English in exchange for helping me with my French.

By that point, my fluency had gained turf. But I still had trouble. Proper nouns were pains in the ass; I'd think someone had conjugated a verb in the subjunctive, but they'd simply mentioned an eighties French sitcom I didn't know. And slang went right over my head. Chaya and I decided on a system where I'd post words or phrases I didn't recognize, and Chaya would attempt to translate them into English.

Une bouffe—a meal.
Pourri—nasty, rotten.
J'ai le spleen—I'm bummed out.

We soon covered the wall behind my desk with sticky notes. When I put up "*Faut pas pousser mémé dans les orties*," Chaya had trouble. He said in English, "This means, I think, Do not push the grandmother into the garden." He consulted his French-English dictionary. "Sorry, not garden, 'nettles.' What is this, nettles?"

"Something British," I said. "Anyway, what the hell? Why would I do this?"

"You do not *do* this," Chaya said. "It is . . . to illustrate an idea. It means you push your chance."

"Your luck?"

"Your luck? Ah, okay. *Faut pas pousser mémé dans les orties*: Do not push your luck."

"Or your grandmother," I said.

Five minutes later, Marc stopped by with a suggestion for the board: *Chier dans la colle.*

"It means," Marc said, " 'to shit in the glue.' But you do not want to do this."

I asked Chaya to explain. He thought about it for a moment. "You know when a project here goes slowly? This is the glue. Then when some people—" He looked around, then whispered: "When some people is asking stupid questions, and it goes *more* slowly in meetings? This is the shit."

"It's a metaphor," Marc said. "The glue is the scenario—it's life. So when the scenario is already, how do you say, sticky?"

Chaya nodded. "Then you make life worse when you put your shit in it."

We all dwelt on this wisdom.

"Okay, next," I said. "BCBG—the clothing chain?"

"Ah, no," Marc said. "BCBG, it means 'classy.' Sort of. You would say 'preppy,' maybe? *Bon chic, bon genre.* It's kind of passé."

Soon, according to Chaya and Marc, I was much more Parisian for using my new lingo. Sort of a tough guy now, Chaya said, me telling people where not to shit, pushing their grandmothers around. In two weeks, we'd added:

Ta gueule! Shut up!
Qu'est-ce que tu racontes? What the hell are you talking about?
Quel con. What an ass.
Laisse tomber. Leave it alone.

Ça arrache la gueule! That burns my mouth!
J'ai les dents du fond qui baignent! My teeth are soaking in something liquid, and it might be vomit!

Among other things to learn: when entering an elevator in a Paris office building, it was customary to say hello, even if you didn't know the other people. Then perhaps you'd mention the weather. When exiting, you wished the other passengers good day.

I explained to coworkers that this behavior did not occur in the United States. One girl said, "That is because Americans are very cold."

In our office, it was also obvious that men were in charge. Well, no surprise. But French businessmen were different from American businessmen—and not just when it came to black cocks and Jews. French businessmen, at least in advertising, were uniquely moody; conniving men who were easily wounded, doing deals or not. They fell in love constantly—with women, with objects—and they did it with their bodies and souls. Perhaps it was a balance exclusive to our one office, but the attitude was, boys will be boys—boys will be spoiled, indulgent, grabby *garçons*. As Julie would say, men in our office got to play both Doctor *and* Madame Bovary. And meanwhile the women held careers, cooked dinner, raised the children, and dressed like the world's best, and still they trotted around Paris unrecognized, exhausted, losing out to their inherited *rapport de force*.

During a meeting in early April, I called one of our bosses a stupid ass. He wasn't in the room and he *was* a stupid ass, but Pierre was shocked; he was also impressed by my fluency. In the hallway afterward, Sabine asked, "Where is this coming from?" Sabine was another project manager on Louis Vuitton. I told her about Chaya's sticky notes and slang lessons. Sabine frowned. She said she didn't like the new me very much; I was becoming obnoxious, "just another one of the boys"—another man she was required to coddle. Sabine said she'd speak to Chaya about tempering my instruction.

Basically, Paris office life was an old boys' club with female lifeguards.

31

At the beginning of April, a new American Apparel store opened around the corner from Rue Béranger. Parisians lined up for the ribbon-cutting. No matter that there was another American Apparel branch ten minutes away, and several already in Paris. Such was the rapture that season for American cotton.

Same week, at a birthday party for one of Pierre and Chloe's sons, Rachel asked Pierre's teenage niece about her T-shirt, "*C'est American Apparel, non?*"

"*Ah oui!*" the girl gushed. "*Moi, j'adore American Apparel. Mais pour moi, c'est trop cher.*"

Rachel explained to her that, in the States, their clothes were cheap. The niece went wide-eyed. *Vraiment?* The niece touched Rachel's arm. She said, Do you know anyone, oh please, who could ship me some jeans?

The next celebrities for Louis Vuitton were Sofia and Francis Ford Coppola. To make Francis more comfortable during his interview, we'd hired Harold Pinter's stepdaughter, a magazine editor, supposedly an old friend of the Coppolas, to visit Francis on the set of his latest film. One night, strategizing together, Harold Pinter's stepdaughter reached out and pinched the sleeve of my T-shirt. She said, "Oh, I love this, this is *gorgeous*, is it American Apparel?"

"J. Crew," I said.

"Oh, is it *really*," she said, making a note.

On the whole, Pierre was the man of the hour at the agency. And healthier, too: smoking less, working until three a.m. less frequently. His Louis Vuitton work had won several big awards. The client was so pleased, Pierre was being fêted. The client had even begun recommending him and his team to other companies, which led to us winning a big campaign for one of France's premier brandy makers, because, they said, Pierre knew how to market French luxury better than anyone; he'd mastered telling "the story of French luxury's DNA."

The brandy marketing boss visited our office to introduce his project. He was a young guy in an old man's sport coat. He was maybe twenty-five—but an old twenty-five. Very grave. His chief dilemma, he explained, was to reconvince the world to love France.

For centuries, the brandy boss said, the country's essence—its way of living, language, and *la vie de bohème*—was the best. France's perspective, fashion and flesh, books and cuisine, had all been coveted, with earth trusting Paris "to export the true meaning of luxury."

But times had changed.

Sure, the boss said, in some sectors—for example, bespoke clothes and fashion-label perfumes, high-end wine and some liquors—France still ruled. For the most part, however, what the market deemed luxurious was being determined elsewhere. "Frequently in Chinese knock-off shops," he added.

His present dilemma, the boss said, mostly had to do with consumers. And it wasn't so bad. The world thought differently about Paris, fine. At the same time new markets were emerging. Traditionally, he said, brandy was considered "something old Frenchmen drink by the fire in their slippers." The room nodded. Of course, he said, old Frenchmen in slippers still drank brandy—the room laughed—but there was a newer, bigger customer base. Specifically, "the blacks of America," both those economically rising and economically struggling, as well as "China's nouveau riche."

The room looked surprised.

Both groups were challenges, the boss said. Regarding the former, surely, he said, we'd heard this from other clients? Seen other luxury businesses struggle with unsought fans? "The rappers and their champagne?" The room recognized the reference: the previous year, Louis Roederer's managing director had caused a scandal by saying in *The Economist*, about some rappers' fondness for his wine, "What can we do? We can't forbid people from buying it."

"My point of view is that customers are customers," the brandy boss said. His team was, at that moment, devising new products "preferred by American blacks," that is, fruity cocktails. Meanwhile, Chinese businessmen drank brandy straight like wine.

A collective gasp.

"That's a joke," someone said.

"But that's not normal," someone said.

"No, trust me, it's true!" the brandy man said. "You've never seen anything like it." For example, he described how a businessman in Guangzhou might plonk down ten bottles of expensive brandy if he was hosting a big dinner, to demonstrate his wealth, and everyone would hit it hard while they ate.

Around the table, there were many little puffs of incredulity.

At the end of the meeting, the brandy boss invited us down to an ancient village where his brandies were still distilled—"so you can understand our DNA even better." Well, why not, Pierre said. A week later, Pierre, an art director named Louise, and I traveled by high-speed train to appreciate brandy better. We tried our best. On a gorgeous day, as the sun shone down especially for us (it felt that way), we drank two brandy cocktails in the morning in a rustic bar, three or four glasses of wine at lunch in a fancy dining room, and about ten varieties of brandy during a long tour of a scientific-looking tasting room, two musty wine cellars, and an appointed château in a landscaped vale, with a ride in the afternoon on a river boat.

By nightfall, I understood the genetics of brandy a little better. But really what I knew was that I liked to pass out on high-speed trains.

Vincent and Lucas telephoned Pierre to let us know they were ready to show their London films. Titles finished, music composed, and the knife of value applied to their editing. We rode over on Pierre's scooter, with me borrowing a spare helmet from André, a pink mushroom cap he kept beside his desk for whenever a cute girl needed a lift.

"*Très mignon*," André said when I put it on.

Vincent and Lucas's office was above a park in the eleventh arrondissement, in a family neighborhood of old white buildings and iron fences. Pierre and I climbed some battered stairs and rang the bell. Angry shouting from inside: Vincent yelling for Lucas to get the door, Lucas screaming he wasn't ready.

After a minute, Vincent appeared.

"Listen," Vincent said, "Lucas . . ." He shook his head. "Don't test him." Pierre laughed, but Vincent put his hand on his chest and said, "No joke, be careful."

Their studio was clogged with movie and photography equipment. Paint flaked off the walls. There was a room of computer monitors and gear, with windows overlooking the park, and posters from Vincent's movies. At the end of a hallway was the room where Lucas composed. He was just coming out, frowning and smoking. Lucas waggled a finger at us. His room was not for public viewing. Pierre chided him and tried to push past, but Lucas shoved him back, saying, No, fuck off.

While Vincent loaded the films we joked around, talking about deadlines. But I couldn't help my curiosity. I ambled back and pushed open Lucas's door.

"Guy," Lucas shouted behind me, "what are you doing?"

"Don't do that!" Vincent shouted from the other room.

"Oh, come on," Pierre said behind me, and pushed past. We got a glimpse of some keyboards in the dark, then Lucas came running and slammed the door.

His face was red. He stammered, "I told you no, and what do you do?"

Pierre and I backed up, hands in the air.

Lucas shouted, "What did I ask? What one thing? Do I come into your office and touch your shit? I asked you not to. This is how you treat me?"

Vincent hushed him, but Lucas didn't hear. He kicked a wooden chair so hard it smashed against the wall.

"Lucas!" Vincent shouted.

Lucas left and slammed the door behind him.

"Hey, he told you not to go in," Vincent said. "Where is the respect?"

"I'm really sorry," I said.

We spent half an hour watching their films. They were beautiful, especially the music. Lucas didn't return. I sent him an e-mail that afternoon to apologize. He wrote back late that evening to say there were no hard feelings. After we presented the movies to Louis Vuitton, who loved them, Lucas and Pierre visited for a debriefing and to begin planning our Coppola work. Everyone embraced with *bises*, and Lucas called me a Fucking Guy, then he told me I looked fatter.

That weekend, a friend of ours from New York visited Paris. Danny was in town for a wedding, and we took him shopping because he'd forgotten to pack his suit jacket. In one boutique, when he came out of the dressing room, Rachel told Danny he was looking great, very slim. He said thanks, that he'd been trying to lose weight, and had recently begun tracking his body mass index in a spreadsheet on his laptop.

I asked if that meant he was exercising more. Danny said no, he didn't associate exercise with weight loss. Good for health, sure, but exercise didn't necessarily help the pounds fall off.

"You realize how Parisian that sounds," Rachel said.

"Well, you don't have to live in Paris to be Parisian," Danny said.

Rachel said a minute later, "You know, I locked a woman in a machine yesterday."

I said, "What the hell?"

"I was trying to help her," Rachel said. "An old woman at the gym. I'd seen her there before. She didn't know how to use a leg-lift machine. So I helped clamp down her thighs. Ten minutes later, I'm going to change and she's still there, locked in place, humming to herself. She didn't know how to get out. She was just sitting there, watching the world go by."

"Now, that's very Parisian," Danny said.

32

Marianne called during breakfast. During lunch. She wanted me badly, and I was all like, No, and she was all like, Well, I'll call back. One day, going into a meeting, I answered my cell phone without checking the caller ID.

"Hello, this is Orange, your mobile phone company. Would you—"

"No, I would not," I said in French. I stopped outside the conference room and covered my other ear with my hand. "Please stop calling. Already I said no. I am going into a meeting. Your company calls me six times a day."

There was an air of deep affront.

"Well, do you know why we call you?" Marianne asked.

"Yes," I said, "to pose me the question of participation. In an exercise of marketing."

"And do you know why I am calling you today?"

"You are calling about an exercise of marketing?"

"Sir, are you going to let me explain?" Marianne said testily. After a pause, she continued, "Good. Today I am calling because Orange would like to invite you to respond to a few questions to improve your service."

"Yes, exactly, I know," I said. "But I do not have time for this. I told you that. I do not want to have this conversation."

"But why?" Marianne asked.

"Because I said no—because right now is *my* time!"

My own vehemence surprised me. I added, "Have a good afternoon."

"Fine, we will call you back," Marianne said, and hung up.

See, against Marianne, the Parisian man was powerless. Against the all-powerful apparatus, against French bureaucracy and *dossiers*, man could struggle, but ultimately he would yield. And I still hadn't received my health-insurance card.

Much to Rachel's and my disappointment, Lindsay announced that week the end of relations with Christian, the bunker-loving menswear designer. Lindsay said it from the landing outside our apartment. She did not remove her jacket.

"So, he loves me, he loves me not? Nope. He loves me—oh, he *loves* me. Far as Christian's concerned, my heart is a bunker he can hide inside for eternity. However," Lindsay said, sitting down at our kitchen table, "now he points out we must end things. Cut the rope. Because, first off, he can't commit. He reminds me he told me this from the beginning, that he can't commit. Though really, what man can? Anyway, as part of breaking up with me, Christian reminds me he is not the marrying type. And of course it's killing him to tell me this. I mean, the man can cry. I'll give him that. God, can they cry."

She laughed. "Eating chocolate in bed, who does that? Anyway, he knows he has problems. Living among the birdcages—*he collects birdcages*. I mean, he gets it, he's not blind. But that's the worst part: none of them are. So he's enjoying his prenup. You know, like, 'Lindsay, I told you in the beginning, I am not a commitment guy, I have told you this since we met, so you cannot blame me for what I must tell you now.' But given the chance, what Frenchman is a 'commitment guy'? Ask any Parisian guy to quit being an oversexed little monster, and he freaks out. *Mais non! Tu demandes trop!* You're every woman who tried to entrap them, including their mothers. Especially their mothers. So one minute it's 'Baby, I love you, save me from my machismo.' But as soon as you start feeling anything, the tragedy vanishes and it's all kaput."

Lindsay's long eyelashes had tears she brushed away. "And you know what?" Lindsay said. "I think I really liked him. Isn't that sad?"

33

April in Paris meant lots of workmen walking around clutching baguettes. Occasionally they'd have a little plastic Franprix bag with a can of beer inside, maybe a cake or a yogurt. But if none of those things, there'd still be that baguette clasped delicately with a square of wax paper, the rod of lunch.

I asked Chaya to define France, what it meant to be French, specifically Parisian. What symbol said France most of all? He didn't pause: "The baguette. Or the Eiffel Tower. But this is a recent development."

Olivier nodded agreement.

Julie, my former neighbor, was visiting Françoise at her desk. She jumped in: "The baguette, of course. But Paris most of all. To be Parisian is to be the most French. Paris is the complete idea of France."

Françoise said, "Well, this is a very Parisian way of thinking."

I said after a moment, "What about raclette?"

"Raclette?" Olivier said. He peered at me in confusion. "How do you know about raclette?"

"I know things about cheese," I said.

Olivier laughed until he doubled over. "No, please—Americans do not *know* about cheese—Americans?—oh my god!"

By the beginning of April, I'd finished another draft of my novel. Passed it to Rachel. She read it in a week and said she liked it a lot—it was much further along—but it still wasn't quite there. I flipped the pages myself, stewing; by the last page, I agreed. So back to the revision board and early mornings . . .

At the office, in addition to my Louis Vuitton and brandy work, Pierre had asked me to help him develop a pitch for Jacquet Tartine, a French sliced bread that was narrow enough to fit into a mug. It was American sandwich bread on a diet—bread a person could soak in his morning coffee. I said I was having trouble with the concept. I asked Pierre, "You dunk your bread into your coffee?"

"You who?"

"You, France," I said.

"Of course," Pierre said. "Everyone dunks. Come on, you don't? Really?"

For once, André's mouth was closed. He was a baguette man, he said; this sliced sandwich bread should go back home, stateside.

Another sign of spring: tourists were back in high numbers. Riding the Bateau-Mouche, or queuing for the Musée d'Orsay. From the agency's balcony above the Champs-Elysées, we watched them pose outside their favorite stores for pictures. Most popular was my client, Louis Vuitton, whose headquarters were across the street. Tourists would wait for pole position, then stand next to the best window display. Frequently they posed while holding up whatever they'd just bought inside: a handbag, a pair of jeans, some shoes.

Also popular for backdrop were two other French brands still found on the Champs-Elysées: Cartier, up the street, and Montblanc, the pen manufacturer, which was actually a German company, but it sounded French, which seemed good enough for the tourists.

First, someone would get a picture with Cartier's window display, then he might rotate slightly for a photograph with the Arc de Triomphe.

With spring came new movie posters—mostly French movies set in Paris about people struggling to fall in love—and new advertisements on the boulevard, often starring George Clooney. George Clooney was Paris's most popular American that spring, its *ami préféré*. Back when we arrived, he had welcomed us with a Nespresso from a billboard near the airport. Now, in addition to his coffee work, George Clooney was endorsing Omega watches and *Leatherheads*, a movie in which he played a quarterback. He was everywhere, America's most palatable export—the United States as France would like it to be: worldly, cosmopolitan, unthreatening. Probably because George Clooney tended to endorse things that kept his hands out of trouble.

Rachel was waiting on a crowded sidewalk one afternoon to cross the Boulevard du Temple when a little old woman began lurching. She was a traditional French grandmother, in brown shoes and a navy coat. A step forward, a step back. Two feet away, traffic rushed by in front of them. The woman flung out her arms. For a second, Rachel didn't recognize what was happening. Then she realized the old lady was experiencing a dizzy spell. Rachel reached out, snatched the woman's arm, and pulled her back. A truck buzzed by. The woman leaned on Rachel. A man grabbed hold of her other arm. She got her feet under her and began thanking them both in French—*Merci, Madame, merci beaucoup—merci, Monsieur*—turning left and right. The man, Parisian, told the woman not to worry; he inquired if she would get home okay. Then the two of them began a conversation, while Rachel listened, smiling and nodding—the old woman was still gripping both their arms—but Rachel didn't say a word. She told me she hadn't wanted to make the situation any harder for the woman; revealing that she wasn't a native speaker might complicate things. Rachel's comprehension by that point enabled her to grasp almost anything said in French, but in an emergency situation, when it mattered most, the words weren't at her tongue. It was upsetting. Disempowering. Rachel said goodbye and crossed the street. Grabbing the woman's arm had been enough, but somehow not quite.

"Hello, is this Rosecrans Baldwin?"

"Yes."

"Good evening. This is Orange, your cell-phone company."

"Yes," I said, matching Marianne in French. "About an exercise of marketing, I understand. You called yesterday. You called again this morning."

"Excuse me?"

"You telephone me every day. You want to know if I would like to participate."

"Ah, I understand," she said, "you do not speak French. Excuse me, someone will call you back."

"Excuse me?" I said. "I *do* speak French." And someday, I'd hire an accent coach. "I understand exactly what you are saying. Completely. And I would prefer that you stop calling."

"Ah, oh," Marianne said, a little crestfallen. "Okay. But if you could please—"

"Excuse me," I said, "but, I am sorry, will you promise me something, please? That you will stop calling me? Will you make sure that I am deleted from the list of people you invite to this exercise of marketing?"

"But you understand, this is Orange, your mobile phone company?"

"Yes," I said, "and I would like you to promise me that you will not call me anymore."

"Me personally?"

"You, Orange," I said.

"Sir, you do not want to be called by your own phone company?"

"Exactly. I would like you to tell me that I am deleted from this exercise of marketing."

"I think it is better," she said, "if we call you back."

"No," I said. "In fact, I would like my name to be taken off the list. Can I be deleted from the list?"

After a moment: "No."

"Then will you tell me that you will not call me again?"

A long pause. Marianne said in a quieter, more delicate tone, "I can only tell you that I will personally not call you again."

"But someone else will call me."

"Yes," she said.

I said, "Can I speak to your manager, please?"

"Sir, a representative will call you back tomorrow."

"Excuse me," I said, "can I speak to your manager, please?"

She snapped, "No, you can't do that!"

"I can't speak to your manager?"

"What? Of course not! No, it's impossible."

"Then can I speak to someone else, please?"

"No, excuse me," Marianne said, hurrying off the line.

"Excuse me, what is your name?" I said.

But she was gone. She never called again.

34

May was stuffed with hot weekends. We'd wake up Saturday morning and the sun would be a heat lamp. Trees bloomed white and pink. With the whole day to ourselves, we'd consider walking across the city. Or maybe I'd go play tennis on one of the public courts beside the tenement buildings just outside the Périphérique—it was nearly impossible to book a court within Paris proper—and, if so, perhaps Rachel would phone Olivia, they'd go to the Palais de Tokyo and see the latest contemporary art expo, then maybe we'd all get lunch.

But on the day we decided to move back to America, we couldn't figure out what to do, so we stayed in bed listening to Asif drink with some friends in the courtyard, then Rachel said, "Hey, what about Giverny?"

Giverny was half an hour from Paris by train. We caught the train, arrived in Vernon, then set out along a path through woods and fields. From the station it was about a three-mile walk to the tiny village where Monet had found his water lilies, full of blue lilacs and stone houses with wooden shutters. Occasionally someone passed us on a bicycle, or a tour bus honked around a corner, but mostly it was quiet, with a long green view dotted with yellow. Next to our path, flowers rippled in the marsh, bent by a stream going through the grass.

At some point, Rachel said, "We need to figure this out."

"What exactly?" I said.

It came out halfheartedly; I knew exactly what she was talking about. We'd been building up to it separately for several weeks. Our adventures in Paris had often been disconnected, but when a big idea loomed between us, it would be in both of our heads. Rachel usually was the first one to put it into words.

"How long we're going to be in Paris," she said.

Two people jogged by with a dog, all three panting softly.

"Do you not like it anymore?" I asked. Technically it was a lob of a comment, and I wasn't proud of it. But I didn't want to reach the question that came next.

Rachel said, "It's not like we moved here to live in Paris forever. Of course there are things I still like. And there's a lot I don't." She added, "*We* don't, I thought."

"No, no," I said distractedly, "I think you're right."

"Wait," Rachel said, "who said anything about being right?"

We stopped in a small turn, where someone had built a bench. Rachel said after a long silence, "I mean, do you see us here for several years?"

It took me a minute. "I guess I just hadn't thought about leaving yet," I said. It came out more heated than I meant. I sat down, nervous and angry. I was transparent—in a way where I was the only one who couldn't see through myself. We walked again for a little while, going in silence next to a soccer field and through some woods.

Then Rachel said in a nervous, sad rush, "You know I'm not the chick who lives in Paris and, whatever, while her husband's working she decides to learn how to make pastry from scratch. I can't *be* someone else," she said.

"I'm not asking you to," I said. "I can't do it either."

"But do you want to work in advertising?" We stopped again. "We barely see each other during the week. When we do have time together, you're recuperating from lack of sleep. Meanwhile, either

I'm at home with the noise, or I'm out in a city where I barely speak the language—and it would be one thing if we could afford for me to take classes again, but—"

"I know," I said, "I see."

Rachel said after a long moment, "We had a dream of living abroad. We accomplished it. What about your professional dreams? What about mine?" She paused. "I don't think they'll happen if we stay in Paris."

And that was it, the truth. The sun bombed down. Up ahead was an outdoor pizza restaurant, more like a campsite, a small kitchen in a lean-to with plastic tables and red parasols provided by Badoit. It was empty except for a waitress who seated us by a creek, almost on top of it. The cook got up from fishing, sank his pole in a holster near the bank, and shouted, *Bienvenue!* The pizza was out of this world. Mine had wild mushrooms sautéed in garlic. We split a bottle of rosé, and we'd drunk most of it by the time we asked ourselves, sitting in the green and red shade, Did we really just decide to leave Paris?

End of June, my manuscript would be done. Assuming it was ready, my agent would send it around to publishers in July. I said I wanted to wait until then before I gave Pierre my three months' notice.

"Do you feel comfortable saying that?" Rachel asked.

"I do," I said.

That afternoon, we visited a museum up the road and napped in a field overlooking tulip gardens. By the time we got back to the train station, I was light and joyful. The heat seemed to inflate the air. People fanned themselves with tourist maps. We took a bench in the sun and I lay down to nap.

A minute later, I was approached by an elderly couple with New England accents.

"Now, if only this nice young man will move over a little," the woman said loudly in English, bending over above my ear. "Oh, I'm afraid he's asleep."

Her husband shouted, "He's asleep?"

"Well," the woman said, "if this young man would be so nice as to move . . ."

"Is he going to move?!" yelled the husband.

"Maybe he will!" the old woman shouted.

"He doesn't speak your language!" her husband shouted back.

I sat up, we squeezed together, and the woman thanked me. Her old man withdrew a butterscotch from his shirt, a travel shirt of a thousand pockets. Then five American women came out of the station to wait for the train. They were winded from hiking, but had no trouble speaking at a volume that in France was reserved for emergencies.

How immense Americans made themselves when abroad, how bullying when we roamed. Some teenage French boys appeared. They overheard the women and started addressing them in English, with attempted Southern accents.

"Hello, how are you?" one boy said.

"Hello, misses, how is it going?" said another.

The women ignored them. They were debating over which brasserie to visit that evening. The boys continued their lesson plans anyway. "Excuse me, is Jane in the garden?"

"Jane *is* in the garden," another said.

"Do you have some milk?"

"The milk is in the refrigerator!"

I started laughing to myself. Maybe it was all the wine I'd drunk, or it was the Americans' ankle socks and their forward-facing backpacks, but I couldn't stop.

One of the teenagers caught my eye and winked, taking me for a coconspirator.

On the day we'd decided to leave Paris, I became French.

ART IS NOT A LUXURY

SUMMER

—Madame Tortoise joins our park—American versus Canadian accents—How to identify different nationalities in Paris—Sofia Coppola goes AWOL—Flat broke—The Marais has a shower scene—Prague, where bachelors shoot women—I join Lucas to California as his porter—American sitcoms are the fantasies of Parisiennes—My dream of human trafficking comes true—In Provence, the pure and the impure, mostly the pure—Movie posters are the voices and images of France—So much depends upon a salad dressing—

35

As summer arrived, the air was pollen-saturated. Buds cracked, flowers bloomed. People at the office carried around tissue packets, sniffling in the elevator. Paris was incandescent, alternating between sudden rains and bursts of sun. Each evening the light stretched later.

One Sunday morning, Rachel and I went for a walk in our neighborhood. People were strolling around carrying food to one another's homes. A furniture market was being set up on Rue Bretagne. We turned down an alley and found a two-man marching band serenading the block—an old man playing cornet and a young guy carrying a bass drum with a local politician's name written on its face. Then on Rue de Saintonge we saw Audrey Tautou, the actress from *Amélie*, going around a corner. She was wearing sunglasses, accompanied by a tall man in an undershirt and scarf.

Rachel said, "Funny how much smaller she is in real life. She was already tiny on the screen."

The next week, dozens of teenagers stopped traffic on the Champs-Elysées. They were screaming, singing, and carrying homemade flags. They wore tight pants and fabric flowers pinned to their chests, and were followed by sixty police officers on skates in riot gear—elbow, knee, and shoulder pads—like a Roman formation of Rollerbladers.

I asked François what the kids were protesting. We were standing on the balcony. He squinted, staring at me, then looked into the sun. "That it's May," François said. "They're celebrating being French, that they're young.

"You will never understand, I'm sorry," François said, laughing.

A new regular joined the lunchtime group. She was probably in her mid-eighties, slightly taller than Sarkozy. And formal: she wore pearls to lunch. Her hair was a winter garden. Each day, she read a newspaper at her nose for an hour. Before that, however, she'd lay down an orange napkin on the lawn, and on top of it she'd leave a salad of red pepper, haricots verts, and some greens, and next to it she'd place her pet tortoise.

Her tortoise was the size of a five-pound chicken.

The first time I saw Madame Tortoise, the tortoise ate its lunch, then went for a walk. There weren't many people around, so it was easy for him to cross the park uninterrupted and climb one of the hills to the base of a big tree. Total voyage took fifteen minutes. Under the tree, he turned a slow circle, stopped, and took a nap—just another one of the park's natural features.

The next week, I got to the park a little late, and Madame's tortoise had already gone on his walkabout. This time, though, some businesspeople were sitting under his tree. The tortoise wasn't bothered. He was a punk, a mean little dinosaur. He pushed in and nudged a lady's rump, and she looked back and screamed when she saw his beak crank open.

Madame Tortoise heard the noise and slowly rose to reclaim her pet.

That took doing: Madame Tortoise wasn't much faster than a tortoise. It took her almost two minutes to reach the tree with her cane. When she'd arrived, Madame removed her glasses and peered down, paying no mind to the businesspeople—all of them had stood up—and made sure her pet was fine, then returned to her bench empty-handed.

Twenty minutes later, when the tortoise woke from his nap, the office workers moved their lunch bags so he could pass, and he clomped his way home. There, at the napkin, he ate some apple slices and went to sleep.

The everyday reality of Paris always trumped for *le plaisir*.

Despite or because of his marriage to Carla Bruni, Sarkozy's approval ratings were down. People didn't like how conveniently the wedding had played to his image, nor how he'd courted Bruni while also wooing the media. One of the weeklies, behind the plastic wall of every newspaper stand, ran a cover with a large headline: "Four More Years, Whore."

Lindsay said, "So I walked into a government office the other day to get a form notarized, okay? Three French policemen were standing inside, at a security table—"

"Cute policemen?" Rachel asked.

"Cute," Lindsay said.

"I love a uniform," Rachel said.

"Who doesn't? So the first one looks at me. He's smiling, he shouts at me, 'You're arrested!' "

We were eating sandwiches in Buttes-Chaumont on a Sunday afternoon, sitting on a bench overlooking a stand of flowering trees. Joggers ran past us; young families pushed strollers. Many teenagers wrestled each other on the grass. Lindsay continued, "So I said to him, 'Oh, good, I always wanted to go to a French jail.' The other cops start giggling. Then the first officer digs through my purse for a security check. And he takes out all of my lipsticks and lines them up in a row."

"How many lipsticks?" Rachel said.

"Like four lipsticks," Lindsay said. "Whatever, it's a lot. Anyway, the policeman looks at me now. He's smiling, he says dryly, 'You have a lot of lipstick.' I said, 'Well, lipstick is important.' He said he agreed that it was. 'It is *very* important,' he stressed, 'to *me.*' So he put all of them in a plastic baggie, pretending to confiscate them and keep them for himself. I said, 'Excuse me, am I not allowed to wear lipstick in here?' I mean, seriously, by that point one of the other cops is about to try some on. But a line of people had formed behind me."

A few seconds later, Lindsay said, "I mean, can you imagine that happening in the States? They'd shoot you. I swear, I love this flirtatious country."

On the Métro ride home from the park, Rachel and I composed a list of what we loved about living in Paris: Loved living within walking distance of most everything that made Paris great. Loved Parisians' way of lingering, and how commonplace sensuality was a habit in exchanges. Men reading in public. Women hogging their merchants' attention. We loved the Parisians' ways of saying exactly what they wanted, and also how this trait, combined with their anti-P.C. conceit, forced them to put too much of themselves on the table.

We loved the everyday beauty of Paris, its tidy deterioration. Loved our new friends, our few friends.

What we hated: stores closed on Sundays, the Métro shutting down at midnight; how people often settled for celebrating the city's blandest features; most of all, living in Paris without time to actually live there.

"And construction noise," Rachel said. "That I could do without."

At work, my friend Yassine asked for help understanding American stomachs. Yassine, who resembled Richard Ashcroft on a crash diet, was an illustrator who'd just returned from a business trip to Miami, where he'd seen much that needed explanation.

We were standing on the balcony during *un pot*, an office party, around nine p.m. The lights of restaurants leached color from the sky. Cars were idling, penned in by traffic—so many expensive black coupes brought to heel.

"The day I arrive," Yassine said, "I arrive early, and they took me out for breakfast."

"You know, it's smart to eat when you're jet-lagged," said Cédric.

"Yes, thank you," Yassine said. "So I was saying . . ."

Cédric was Yassine's buddy in the office. They'd grown mustaches together. Cédric had newly joined the company. Previously he'd been an architect. He quit architecture, Cédric had said, because architecture in Paris was too depressing, Paris being a movie set where nothing new was allowed.

Graphic design was the only artistic field in France that remained truly cutting-edge, Cédric said.

"So, I'm looking at the menu," Yassine said, "and there's two thousand options. They took me to a diner. Real vintage America, I mean, fantastic. They had seats like—how do you say, *boofs*?"

"Booths," I said in English.

"So I'm thinking, hey, this is the real USA. You know, like *Twin Peaks*?"

I thought, That sums up exactly how many Parisians perceive the United States.

"Anyway," Yassine continued, "I was too tired to read English. So on the menu I saw something called the 'French omelet.' Fine. After ten minutes out comes . . . listen, I can't describe it. It was an omelet. *In theory.* Ham, cheese, and herbs. Only it probably had five eggs in it, it was this big"—Yassine spread his hands apart twelve inches—"and look: it was served *inside a croissant*. Inside the goddamn thing! A croissant as big as a loaf of bread!"

Cédric needed Yassine to explain it again, it was too confusing.

Boof, Yassine said, pouting out his lips.

In addition to Cédric, a new woman was added to our section, a copywriter from Quebec named Niki. For her first two weeks, Niki was the laughingstock. Nothing tweaked a Parisian ear quite like the Québecois accent. Niki could say anything and there'd be snickers, much worse than what I suffered when I'd first arrived.

Chaya said that during his first meeting with Niki, he caught only about ten sentences. "Honestly, Rosecrans," Chaya said, laughing, "your French is much better than this." Pierre explained that people in Quebec were complimented by Parisians for speaking a French that was generally more grammatically correct, "but the accent is so bad, it doesn't matter."

At the end of a day, if Niki called out *à demain*—see you tomorrow—her accent made it sound like "ah du-mayne," and people would burst out laughing after the door closed.

However, Niki was forgiven once she turned out to be great at her job, plus she started bringing in desserts. Her fiancé was a pastry chef; they'd moved to Paris so he could finish his training. Soon leftovers from his homework assignments began to appear regularly in the canteen, with extra napkins.

Basically, good pastry was the most fluent French.

I liked Niki a lot. Like me, she was a Paris freak. We'd talk about museums, sharing tips on which to visit; which café was best if you were thirsty on Rue Soufflot. Sometimes I could tell that Olivier and Chaya and Françoise felt excluded from Niki's and my Paris, us with our ardor and knowledge of new *restos*, and them peering in.

36

During summer—our second summer in Paris, our last—it became easy to identify tourists' nationalities on the street.

Italian women wore red eyeglasses and could match numerous shades of brown.

London men shaved daily and traveled in groups.

Russians wore, along with Arab women, the biggest sunglasses.

Australians were usually midway through travels; someday, they'd all get home.

South American teenagers, boys in beards, behaved hesitantly, posed artistically. You'd see one on a bench with a dark, blank air, like a television someone had left on the sidewalk.

Germans and Scandinavians walked Paris up and down, up and down, wearing trousers that cinched at mid-calf. Between them, in my experience, the Scandinavians were the more isolationist, the Germans were more eager to please.

And all non-American males were cool to carry purses, at the very least a petite shoulder bag, polygonally fashioned, that rested on the hip.

And the only thing Americans talked about was going home.

From the French side of my heart, I would say no one roamed Paris with more talk of home fires than us Americans. We missed our familiar conveniences. In urban lands, you knew us as the ones in bone-fishing shirts, hiking shoes, and trousers with many pockets. Even our sunhats had pockets. Should we pause, we'd rid our hands of foreign bacteria with gel. The world outside America was a jungle. We adopted a sagelike carriage and clasped our sanitized hands behind our backs—for our pockets were stuffed full of incredible resources: a camera, an audio guide, a Fodor's guide, a map, an iPod, and two cell phones, one smart enough to handle GPS. We knew how to travel. *We would wear your goddamn city out.* And possibly we did shrink from being bumped on public transportation, but we rode it. After all, *when in Rome.* Though have no doubt, we would be cautious. Our impermeability was vouchsafed by Gore-Tex, and we would not be fooled by your gratuity scams, Monsieur, so be forewarned: any refusal to serve us bread or water prior to *notre déjeuner* would be noted on TripAdvisor.com.

We'd conquered the world, we just wanted to see it unmolested. Not that we asked permission. Our m.o. was: you will not find grounds to say we are impolite before you've given us cause to be so. In fact, since we were leaving tomorrow anyway, might we try a little French with you, Mademoiselle Parisienne behind the bakery case? *Excusez-moi, où est la bibliothèque?* Oh haha—no, that was a joke, sorry, yes I'll have—Sorry?—No, I was—No I'll have, oh Jesus, THE CROISSANT, PLEASE—*LE CROISSANT*—Oh, for—WHAT—Thank you, no, excuse me, *merci*—Ah, no, nothing, NOTHING MORE—Hey, where's my wallet?—No, *you*—my chest pocket?—Is this a pocket?—Oh, it's Velcro—Okay, here we go—EXCUSE ME MISS HERE IS THE MONEY THANK YOU GOODBYE.

Sofia Coppola went AWOL, and geez, what a headache. The bosses panicked. Pierre was constantly on the phone. For several days, during a meeting an urgent *texto* might explode inside several BlackBerrys simultaneously, and Pierre, Marc, Marcel, or Sabine would need to go running out into the corridor.

Sofia Coppola had told the chiefs at Louis Vuitton she wanted

Marrakech as her city for the campaign. Then, unannounced, she flew there with a photographer friend. From Morocco, we learned she'd be doing the campaign herself, on Louis Vuitton's dime for a week's vacation, take it or leave it in so many words.

Of course they took it, but no one was happy. It was a moment for people to say they thought her film *Marie Antoinette* had been a turd.

Sofia Coppola returned to Paris, and Pierre and I drove over to Louis Vuitton HQ to view her photo albums. We took Pierre's scooter, me perched on the back wearing André's pink helmet. Downtown, practically on top of Pont Neuf, a yellow sun was hovering. We were escorted to a top-floor boardroom, with panoramic views. River, churches, blue sky, white clouds. About ten people were waiting. Then Sofia Coppola arrived, trailing handlers. She and her agent sat across from Pierre and me. The agent expressed an effusive hello.

Between Pierre and me, I think I was the more nervous. I'd spent an hour that morning trying to figure out what to wear, and had come up with nothing more than my everyday uniform of Tintin plays tennis—trench coat, sweater, jeans, and sneakers. For the duration of the meeting, only the four of us spoke—Sofia Coppola, her agent, Pierre, and me—while about fifteen people sat in chairs ringing the room as if it were an observing surgery. Mostly they were silent, except to laugh whenever Coppola laughed, *AHAHAHAHAHAHAHAHA*.

To start us off, the agent complimented André's helmet and called it chic. Then he said to me, "You know, your name is very strange."

Next, Coppola paged through her photo albums, telling the story of her vacation. She addressed her comments to the agent. The agent found her photos and anecdotes wonderful, hilarious. Occasionally, Pierre would lean forward, point to one of the pictures and say he liked it, then sit down again. I'd lean forward and say I agreed. Then Sofia Coppola would describe to her agent what was found in the picture, for example, a trunk originally owned by Diana Vreeland.

After about twenty minutes, Pierre and I explained how we intended to use her photos, and Coppola said it sounded fine. She was a little hesitant about the music, she said, based on the London films she'd seen, so she'd want final say on the sound track. Otherwise, all good.

Outside, Pierre stopped for a cigarette.

"Imagine how weird it must be," I said, a little buzzed from the meeting, "living in a bubble like that."

"What bubble?"

"The agent?" I said. "All those people?"

Pierre shrugged. "She's a major director. She has an Oscar. People ask her for things all day. She needs layers for protection. Maybe too much protection, okay. But did you like the photos?"

"No," I said, fastening the pink gumball on my head.

"No," Pierre said, "no one did. But everyone called them fantastic. That's the danger of the bubble." Pierre tossed his cigarette and nicked a parked car.

"But who knows," he said. "I really liked *Lost in Translation.*"

During a meeting the next day, Lucas worked himself into a huff about Sofia Coppola's music comment. Lucas said he couldn't remember liking the music in any of her movies, so perhaps he deserved final say about that.

Lucas demanded a meeting with Sofia Coppola. He was denied.

Since Coppola had done our Marrakech work for us, we spent the rest of the afternoon discussing San Francisco, the city her father had picked. A week later, I was at Louis Vuitton HQ again, this time doing Pierre's job because he was out sick: presenting to their global marketing chief to sell them on our Francis Ford/California idea.

Someone turned down the lights. "Ah, I love his little stories," one of the marketing guys said.

Up to that point, I'd always told my "little stories" in an English-French slurry to junior executives. Now, for the big boss, I went exclusively into French. I clicked through slides and described ideas. I made little jokes that I'd worked out beforehand. Then I got to the budget, a quarter-million euros. It was five times the size of any budget we'd previously proposed. My French faltered. The room was dark, but I could see all their faces.

One voice in my head: You're a cooked duck now. Another: Well, you try explaining how a Steadicam works.

Never mind that the pitch was outlandish.

That too much rode on my tongue.

I sensed panic going down my back like a lemon squeezed on my neck, which meant more panic was coming. I apologized about my French being terrible, but the global chief said loudly in the dark, "No, it's fine, please continue."

The guy resembled Kojak.

I wanted to say, But I don't know how.

But I did, in fact.

I slugged back into French and continued clicking. Words and sentences appeared in my hand like fish from a bag. I rode the Métro back to the office soaked to my shorts, but semiconfident. The Louis Vuitton people called that evening to say they'd buy the job. It had much less to do with my presentation and everything to do with the ideas that Pierre, Vincent, and Lucas had dreamed up, but I didn't tell Rachel any of that.

37

An old coworker of Rachel's named Alex visited Paris with his friend Caroline and crashed in our living room. Saturday night, Alex wanted to hit a famous gay bar he'd heard about in the Marais, but Rachel and Caroline were too tired from sightseeing to go out, so Alex and I went by ourselves—Alex to cruise guys and me to drink. Inside, the bar was full of hundreds of men. In fact, there *were* gay Parisians. Techno pumped the room to nearly popping. Alex pointed out the bar's main attraction, a shower booth installed above the liquor bottles where a beefy guy, lathered up, was playing with his penis. Semierect, it was the length of my forearm.

Alex bought us Coronas. "Pretty butch scene, don't you think?" he said. Some polished chests were revealed, but mostly it was *bobo* guys in office clothes or Lacoste shirts, a number of them with sweaters draped around their shoulders like any guy in Paris.

"The thing is," Alex said, "I was walking around today and I swear, in Paris you can't tell who's gay and who's straight."

"Your radar's messed up?" I said.

Alex laughed. "It's like they're homophobic and extremely gay at the same time. Seriously, either every man in Paris is gay or no one is."

It sounded right to me: straight Parisians tended to dress like gay Americans. But then what did gay Parisians dress like?

It came to me: Italians.

On Sunday, after Alex and Caroline had left for the airport, I finished writing my novel. I reread the last chapter and knew it was done. Rachel finished the whole thing by the following week-end and said I'd figured it out, it worked, it breathed the oxygen of its own little world.

38

Prague, it turned out, belonged to English stag parties: beery guys who marched in columns, carrying their dead—the doomed-to-marriage—on their shoulders. By day they caroused and turned pink in the sun. By night they stumbled around the city in matching shirts, hoisting neon beer bongs like rifles.

We went to Prague for a weekend because Rachel's parents were visiting for an academic conference, and they'd invited us to join them, on their tab. The castle city appeared to be under siege. There was plenty that was remarkable to be found in Prague, but mainly it was the British guys who interested me. At night, in the old city's dank noir, you'd see studs pinball between the alleys' walls and bank into corners to vomit.

Scottish Keith had told me what to expect. Ever since the rise of EasyJet and Ryanair, airlines that charged almost nothing for tickets, eastern Europe had begun catering to the stag-party industry. Brothels, artillery ranges, and beer halls with fine dining flourished near its smaller airports. I read ads from a Czech magazine in our hotel room: Walk-in humidors! Huge TVs! Escorts! Three floors with DJs spinning house/jungle/acid-rave!

There also seemed to be a lot of doubling- or tripling-up on services. For example, offering a wine cellar *and* an underground shooting gallery, in adjacent rooms. I found one establishment that offered strippers you could shoot with paintguns while they danced, and I was proud to say I didn't know anyone who would find that sort of thing desirable.

Rachel and I were standing in a blackened archway on our final night, waiting for a tram to pass—an empty streetcar, lit up all white, went by—when a drunk guy bumped into me, almost knocking me onto the tracks. He was wearing a rugby shirt with name and number, and was politely stricken in the way of a lost child. He wanted to know if we'd seen his mates, and tilted toward me his beer bong.

Around the time we returned to Paris, there was an article about tourism on the BBC's website that Keith e-mailed me. European hoteliers had been interviewed about their favorite guests. The Japanese placed first for being tidy and polite. Americans ranked in the middle—we were badly dressed, but eager to eat the local food. Brits ranked lower, for boorishness. However, the worst in the world, for being rude, cheap, and reluctant to speak the local tongue, were the French.

In an act of solidarity, Keith and I forwarded it to everyone.

Lindsay and Olivia visited our apartment for dinner during the last week of May. It had been a while since we'd seen them. Both needed to leave Paris every three months, since they didn't have papers, so Olivia traveled with her dance company and Lindsay went to Argentina, to see if Buenos Aires was a better place to live.

"You know they call it the Paris of South America," Lindsay said.

"Well, was it?" Rachel asked.

"Oh, no," Lindsay said. "I thought I was going to be shot. The lady next door was mugged on our stoop the second day I got there. I mean, they say the steaks are great, the boulevards are beautiful, but chrissakes, I'm a vegetarian, I don't drive."

Lindsay said she'd begun dating a new guy, a good one. No

more fetishist chocolate-eaters who preferred bunkers to Saint-Germain, no more wannabe drug dealers or their friends. This guy, Lindsay said, had a daughter, and maybe he wasn't completely separated from the girl's mother, but he was handsome and he had a good job.

He also kept a bag of green apples under the seat of his scooter.

"So that's one quirk," Lindsay said. "He's eating constantly. Cracking into them. I asked him, While you're driving? He said, What's the problem? Anyway, it makes him gassy. But at least this one eats food."

Lindsay went home after dessert, but Olivia lingered. She took a discerning bite of pear tart, then pushed it away. We offered her a cognac and she accepted, which was unusual because she rarely drank more than a sip of wine. We found out why: after a few minutes she revealed she'd been broken up with that afternoon by her most recent boyfriend, a Parisian dancer she'd been seeing for the past two months. Dumped *par texto*.

Olivia read us part of the guy's message, translating from the French: *You know I was always serious about you. I'm really saddened by this. It's very hard.*

"Like I'm the one dumping him," Olivia said. "I mean, who cares how sad *he* is? What's wrong with these guys?"

In the courtyard, Asif was laughing loudly, proposing a toast to friends who were drinking rum with him, sitting at a plastic table outside his door. I thought, Do you never tire?

The first of June arrived and Yves Saint Laurent died. From every newspaper, every *affiche*, his glory was proclaimed, and Paris mourned.

A photograph in many papers showed Pierre Bergé, the designer's longtime partner, holding the arm of Carla Bruni-Sarkozy at the funeral. Bruni, a former Yves Saint Laurent model, looked to be braless in the picture, wearing a gray top under a black jacket, with one nipple hard.

Everyone in Paris by then had seen Bruni naked. As François had shown in the office, much was available on the Web. But this was different. It was classier, an accident. I couldn't imagine Michelle Obama or Jackie Kennedy going so confidently, fashionably defiant into the public eye.

France perhaps was a conservative society, but it wasn't necessarily a fearful one.

39

New York City was gigantic and noisy. Where was the fire? During a brief visit in June, every cliché that had ever been lodged against New York percolated inside me, and my acquired French radar went bananas. Staying at my sister's apartment, I saw a commercial for Pizza Hut that advertised a meal offering "three whole pounds of food." Three pounds of food?! And New York smelled fried where Paris smelled baked. It was a totality, an expression of many cities. Paris, on the other hand, was a village. So perhaps I'd become a village person.

My agent met me for breakfast. He'd drawn up a list of editors he thought might like my book. He'd begin sending the manuscript around the following week, if that was okay.

I asked, Had he seen that Pizza Hut commercial promising three whole pounds of food?

He said, Oh, so you're Parisian now?

When we parted, I was extremely happy. That lasted three minutes, to the benches on the corner of Fifth Avenue and West Sixteenth Street. Then the idea of my book going around made my nervousness enlarge—not nervousness, but the fear I remembered, fear like lampreys in the blood.

If this book was rejected, could I wade into the next novel's sea?

Anyway, those were my thoughts on the flight from New York City to San Francisco the following day, or those were the thoughts of several of the people who lived inside my head. The rest of us, who weren't thinking about publishing, could not believe how absorbed we were by this episode of *The Real Housewives of New York City*, which in fact had a lot to commend it.

In San Francisco, Lucas the composer panicked because Air France had lost his boom. I won't mention the cool-out music playing in the lobby of our hotel, or the potted boulders, or the scents spritzed into the air of the hotel's public spaces to help us chill, because Lucas was grieved. Without a boom, how would he carry his microphone? Why couldn't he make himself understood?

Ostensibly, Air France telephone support had no French-speaking representatives if you called them from within the United States.

We collected Vincent and went to the Mission District, where our hired crew worked out of a warehouse. Their production chiefs were Craig and Robin. That afternoon, Craig was showing Vincent how to use a new model of RED camera when Lucas showed up, having just woken from a nap.

"Be careful," Lucas whispered to Vincent, pointing at the camera, "it's a trap."

Craig said to Vincent, "I'm sorry?"

Lucas snapped at him, "Be gentle with my friend."

Vincent told Lucas to be quiet and apologized to Craig. "He means 'nice,' not gentle. *Gentil* in French is 'nice,' please excuse him, he is crazy from the plane."

"I am not crazy," Lucas said, sulking.

Craig squared up to Lucas. Lucas was about six inches taller.

"Lucas," Craig said, "will you be gentle with me?"

Lucas said after a moment, "I will be gentle, *comme un lapin*."

That evening, on Lucas's behalf, I called Air France. They

said they would need a day to look around Aéroport Charles de Gaulle for his boom, and they'd call us back.

In our interview, Francis Ford Coppola said he admired today's youth culture in San Francisco—the dot-com kids, the laptop vagrants. So we found a coffee shop in the Mission District popular with bloggers, and asked the manager to provide us with a hipster we could shoot.

The girl he chose, a tattooed barista with a one-gear bicycle—"your typical pixie with a fixie," Craig said—flipped out when she learned the name of our client. She couldn't believe it—oh, she couldn't breathe from excitement! "Look, look," she said, showing Vincent how she'd emblazoned the Louis Vuitton logo on the stump of her tamper, to render it more luxurious.

Day two, Air France informed us they'd located Lucas's boom, but now we needed to prove that Lucas was its owner. I said we possessed a luggage-claim ticket and a reference number—wasn't that enough? This was not enough, they said, because they needed to open a *dossier*, which meant Lucas needed to fax copies of his boarding pass, claim ticket, and passport to the luggage-claims office at Charles de Gaulle.

Unfortunately, the woman said, she did not have the fax number at hand, so I'd need to call back the next day.

The next day, I got the number and faxed the documents. They called back to say that the fax had been received and we would be informed when Lucas's *dossier* had been assembled, at which point they'd proceed returning the boom to Lucas's possession, assuming it was his.

Lucas said he was about ready to renounce his French citizenship.

•

Day four, driving up to Coppola's winery in Napa Valley: Craig the production boss driving, Lucas in shotgun, me and Vincent in the back. Vincent was frowning out the window, trying to nap, while I took notes as Craig and Lucas got to know each other.

Craig, pointing to cows in the distance: "These are?"
Lucas: *"Les vaches."*
Craig: "Well, in English, we say 'dogs.' "
Lucas: "Dogs?"
Craig: "Dogs make milk. Milk makes cheese."
Lucas: *"Fromage."*
Craig: *"Fromage."*
Lucas: "The dogs, they are *agile*?"
Craig: "Small dogs, *agile*. Big dogs, no."
Lucas: "You fuck with me?"
Craig: "Actually, you want to say, 'You fucking with me? You fucking with *me*?' "
Lucas: "Ah . . . 'Craig, you fuck my wife? You fuck my *wife*?' "
Craig: "DeNiro."
Lucas: "DeNiro. Craig, tell me, my English is not too 'fade' for you?"
Craig: "The fade is just right."

Five minutes later
Lucas, pointing out the window at cows: "Dogs are gentle."
Craig: "Not boy dogs. Bulls. Danger. Stay away."
Lucas: "Ah . . . Danger. Not gentle."
Craig: "Lady dogs, gentle."
Lucas: "What is, 'Stay away'?"
Craig: "It means, 'Do not touch.' "
Lucas, screaming out the window: "Dogs, stay away!' "

Five minutes later
Lucas: "Craig, you tell me."
Craig: "What should I tell you?"
Lucas: "About Robin. Robin is beautiful. Why you . . . stay away?"
Craig: "What did you say?"
Lucas: "Uh-oh! Danger?"
Craig: "You want to know why I stay away from Robin."
Lucas: "Be gentle."
Craig: "Well, I'm married."
Lucas: "Yes. But you do not say Robin is beautiful?"
Craig: "Robin *is* beautiful."
Lucas: "Robin . . . stay *a lady*."
Craig: "Yes, Robin remains a lady."
Lucas: "Craig, tell me, you fuck your wife?"
Craig: "This has gone far enough."
Lucas: "Danger?"
Craig: "*Les vaches manger les fromages.*"
Lucas: "What? No, this is not making sense."

Close to our final night in San Francisco, Craig's friend Robb invited us over for dinner; he'd heard the French visitors were amusing. Robb made us pizzas by hand—with dough he'd prepared that evening; herbs he'd grown on his deck; sauce from tomatoes he'd plucked from his garden. There was his own beer to drink, home-brewed, and after that espresso, which Robb admitted was derived from coffee beans he'd roasted himself the previous weekend.

Vincent and Lucas were amazed.

That week, I'd spent a lot of time battling winds with a Lastolite EZ Balance Collapsible Light Balancing Disk, or squatting in a harness strapped to the outside of a camera truck, and I'd had some time to think. Basically, San Francisco was beginning to appeal to me. Back in New York, I'd always hated San Francisco. Most of the San Franciscans I knew were too contented, devoting their lives to their lifestyles; they all had terrific accessories and zero self-doubt. But from the truck, San Francisco seemed much more like Paris than New York did: neighborhoods crumbed over land. Rather than one big meal, a buffet.

In Paris, a great similitude prevailed—every roof a constant blue-gray—in the same way that unruliness governed New York City. I found myself wanting more time in San Francisco to figure out its organizing principle—was it bliss between quakes?

Though, to be honest, all I could think about was my novel sitting on five editors' desks.

"This is how to live," Vincent said after dinner, patting his gut. He was staring at some Victorian houses on a hill, at the fog combed over their foreheads. Vincent fumbled the door to the patio, lit a cigarette outside; then thunder boomed and he came scuttling back, just as the view became curtained with rain.

"In Paris," Vincent said, pointing down at his cup, "no one has coffee like this. This is incredible. Hey, what is this grocery store we visited today?"

"Whole Foods," Craig said.

"Unbelievable. So beautiful. We have nothing like Whole Foods."

I said, "What about Monoprix?"

Vincent laughed. "Whole Foods, the fruit, *comment tu dis*, they are like jewels. Show me where in Paris food is sold like art."

"Bon Marché? *Mais non*," Lucas said, "*trop bobo*."

"Yeah, *trop bobo*, *trop luxe*," Vincent said. He told Craig that Bon Marché was a "luxury grocery store," which made Lucas shout at Craig: "Guy, art is not a luxury—never!"

But what about Picard? I said. Vincent conceded the point. He explained to the group the idea of a store selling high-quality frozen food. "Conceptually, it's strong. And in execution. I am surprised someone is not bringing Picard to the States."

•

Air France called the next morning to say they'd finished assembling Lucas's *dossier* and planned to put Lucas's boom on the next plane to San Francisco.

Unfortunately, a week had gone by and this was on our last day in San Francisco, as we were leaving for the airport. I suggested to Air France that they should hold it, since Lucas would be able to pick up his boom in Paris the next morning.

Air France said that this would also be a satisfactory conclusion.

Back in Paris, after a twelve-hour flight, Vincent, Lucas, and I went through customs together. On the way to baggage claim, a gorgeous woman walked out in front of us, wearing a flimsy white dress and a visible black thong.

"See," Vincent said, smiling, enlivened, "this is how in Paris we say, *bienvenue*."

40

A week after I returned from San Francisco, in July, we were invited to a dinner party near Rue Montorgueil. It was one of Paris's most charming streets—of shops and bistros, people dining outside and catching up with friends. The hosts' building, collapsing, had a deep courtyard hidden from the street, with fenced bouquets of trees in each corner.

The husband, a Brit, with a blue apron around his neck, was carving salmon into thin slabs, like bars of pink soap. His Parisian wife, Claudine, hovered at his neck. She told him she would probably do it thinner.

"Would you like to do it yourself?" he said. Gradually Claudine allowed herself, against her own protests, to be convinced to take over.

Claudine was fun and argumentative. She wore a low-scooped dress and white espadrilles. During the meal, she roused her guests with provocations, then retreated into disagreement. By the couscous, she was drunk. By the cheese, she'd retired.

Which was unfortunate. Rachel and I liked Claudine and her husband, but their friends were snippy expats originally from London. They had in common a feeling of *blah* toward Paris. They found it lacking—it wasn't New York or Rome—and they said they were always on the verge of going home.

"You've only been here a year, well, you wouldn't know," one woman said to Rachel. She spiked a knob of couscous on her fork. "It's sad, of course. But Paris wears off. And it's frightfully hard to make friends. Never mind the culture differences."

"Love Paris, can't stand Parisians. God, they're combustible," another woman said.

"Parisians just won't let you in," the first woman's husband said.

The first woman agreed, nodding: "People say Parisians are rude by default, and to be fair they aren't—but they are. It's their world, we just live here. Personally, we've been thinking about going home for ages, haven't we?"

Her husband asked me in a confiding whisper: "Hey, have you discovered Picard?"

The hostess, Claudine, turned up again around midnight. By that point, half the guests had gone home; the rest were leaving. Claudine was mildly offended and said she needed cigarettes. She vaulted herself into high heels. Rachel was chatting with Claudine's husband, the host, so I volunteered to carry Claudine's umbrella, and we set out on Montorgueil. Cafés were full. Water trickled down the street. Rain came down lightly while Claudine told me about her mother; she wept over some argument they'd had recently. Then she said in English, "Stop." She smelled something wonderful. She couldn't quite place it. We started walking again. "My poor shoes," she said—they were soaked. Five minutes later, the rain was done, the night was hot and muggy, the lamplight was full of steam. Claudine quit crying to turn philosophical, eager to discuss French culture versus American culture, Paris versus Anywhere Else, and the tragedy that was Amy Winehouse. We bought cigarettes and did a second lap. We were thirty feet from the courtyard when it smelled again of something great. This time we nailed it: seafood cooked in wine.

Claudine said, "Oh, I love Paris, don't you?" She added, "The beauty of Paris is very forceful, I've always thought so. You know," she said, as if this was all part of the same idea, "I think your wife's shoes are incredible."

An hour later, Rachel and I went home on the Métro. The train was prompt, clean, and quiet. It rounded corners with great whooshing sucks. At our station, we came up between Art Déco lampposts, into a city silent except for cars hissing through puddles. The statue of Marianne stood ahead of us, a glimmering guide.

Most of the top American TV shows were known to my colleagues. That summer, *The Wire* was a regular topic of discussion. Something this good, people said, could not be made in France. Its dramatic scope was too broad, there were too many different races and levels of society, and how surprisingly subtle it was for an American drama!

When *The Wire* box-set turned up at FNAC for the first time with French subtitles, coworkers rushed out to purchase it. Until then, the show's Baltimore accents had been incomprehensible for most.

"Worse than *The Sopranos*," Pierre said, "which was tough for us at first."

"Oh, I couldn't watch this," Chloe said. "It gave me headaches. So what is *Wire*—about technology?"

"No," Pierre said. "That show in Baltimore. We watched it last night. You went to sleep."

"Oh, yeah, this is terrible," Chloe said, laughing. "I am certain the show is good, but come on, these people are not speaking English."

"It's a unique accent," I said.

Rachel said, "It's like Québecois."

Chloe said, "You know, for me, I really love *Grey's Anatomy*. How do you call it: *a guilty pleasure*."

"Like pornography," Pierre said, laughing.

"Yes," Chloe said, "but for girls."

That same week, I gave Pierre my notice. André was out that

day; it was just the two of us in their office. Pierre was shocked and hurt. He'd seen it coming, he said, but still . . .

Pierre said, "I understand. You're working too much. Rachel's under construction—I mean, she's working at home, there's construction all around. How long will you give me?"

I said, "I was thinking three months."

"Okay, so through October," Pierre said.

The next morning, Louise the art director and I visited brandy headquarters for a new product launch. Something about a flask. The brandy boss met us in a conference room, with several of his coworkers. He was happy to see us, he said; his bosses, particularly those in China, were pleased with how our global campaign had turned out.

"Now, I think you'll like this," he said to me. "It's for the States. Very sexy."

"It's a sleeve!" a woman announced suddenly, like it was my birthday. "A sleeve for your brandy!"

"It's so cool," another woman said, from the end of the table.

Louise and I were each handed a bulky wedge of plastic molded like a flask of liquor. Then one of the women walked us through a PowerPoint presentation. The idea, she explained, was to cater to the inner-city "urban market" in America—those African Americans who tended to buy their brandy in corner liquor stores. Finally they could have some "bling bling" of their own—she actually said this—the company's new brandy-carrying case in lieu of the rather nonluxurious, traditional paper bag.

Brown bags being not French at all.

Also, she said, the sleeve would be manufactured in colors to match fitted baseball caps and special-edition sneakers.

"This is horrible," I whispered to Louise.

"I don't understand it," Louise said.

Twenty minutes later, Louise and I were given some bling-bling of our own, plus fifths of brandy to slip inside. We returned to the office, threw away the sleeves, and shared the brandy with our fellow creatives, who'd been planning on having *un pot* after work anyway. Oscar went out and got some cheese; Olivier contributed "a nice little white" from the Loire; Niki supplied a box of pastries. We snacked on the terrace while the sun set behind the Arc de Triomphe—just another typical worknight in Paris, impossible to export or replicate.

In the distance, the Eiffel Tower looked like an enormous sprinkler.

The following week, Louise got sick and stayed home with a cold. She updated her Facebook status: "*Super weekend . . . le chat et moi sous antibio!!!*"

Many coworkers wrote good wishes on her Facebook wall.

André's comment: "*Quel cochon cet antibio.*"

Another week after that, Chaya and I were working together, listening to Led Zeppelin over speakers plugged into my laptop, when my cell phone buzzed.

The caller ID said New York.

"There's an offer," my agent said.

I asked him to hold the phone. I went downstairs to the Champs-Elysées and stood next to a magazine stand where I bought my newspapers every morning, and I asked him to start again. He explained that of the five editors, two were interested in my novel, including the one I liked best.

The hand of mine not holding the phone seized into a fist.

When we hung up, I did it, I screamed.

I composed myself and called Rachel and asked her if she'd done that day's grocery shopping yet. Rachel said no, she was doing laundry at the moment; did I need something in particular? I said she should pick up some champagne. This was our code if the book received an offer to be published, that I'd tell her to purchase champagne and she'd know what I meant.

Rachel said slowly, "You want me to . . ."

"There's an offer," I said.

Rachel yelped and began weeping. Me, too. Once we'd calmed down, I made her promise not to tell anyone; I didn't want our families to know until the contract was signed, I said, in case the deal fell through somehow.

When I got home, after opening the champagne, Rachel explained that she'd told someone anyway: "Oh, I had to, please don't be mad. I was exploding with the news. I thought, Who can I tell who doesn't know anybody? So I went out to the wineshop, you know the one on Bretagne? It was that young guy who doesn't speak English, the nice one. Anyway, he asked me what I was looking for. I said, *J'ai besoin du champagne*. He showed me the champagnes, the twenty-euro bottles. Then he said, What's your price range? I said, *Cher, très cher.* So now he's excited, he took me over to the 'expensive champagne' section. He's going on about this one and that one, I didn't follow, I just told him we wanted a bottle *très sec*, so he picked out a bottle and it was a hundred and thirty euros."

My eyes bulged.

"I know, we can't possibly! But how often is your first novel published?" Rachel was tearing up again, but she talked her way through it: "Anyway, we're at the cash register and the guy asked, What's the special occasion? I didn't really know how to explain it. It's a celebration, I said, *C'est une célébration du business*. He said, *Ah bon?* And I said, *Mon mari*, my husband, *il a vendu un roman*, he sold a novel. But the guy didn't follow. I tried to be more clear: *Il a vendu son premier roman*—he sold his *first* novel. I repeated it a couple of times, but now he's giving me this weird look. Anyway, I kept saying it, then I tried adding that you're a writer, you wrote a book, *un livre*. Once I said that, he started laughing, and we cleared everything up."

Rachel added, "Because he thought you were involved in human trafficking. I wasn't pronouncing *roman* right, so he thought you were a slave trader, selling Romans. I was saying it like, 'A Roman, you sold a Roman, your first Italian from Rome.' "

That evening we celebrated by playing pool with Lindsay in a billiards club near our apartment, we three and some Asian teenagers. The felt on the tables was torn. Hot dogs spun in a wheel beneath a heat lamp. The joy was both microscopic and enormous. I was loose and light. I felt found.

41

At the end of summer, Paris purged. Pierre and his family went south, Lindsay visited friends in *la campagne*, and Olivia left for a dance tour of western France. Days went by without a single cloud in the sky.

Bruno stopped by my desk and told me to join him downstairs while he smoked. Outside, he complained for ten minutes about some account planner who had it in for him. Then again, everyone had it in for him. Did no one in his new office listen to his problems, was I the only one? Bruno confided he had a new vision of the future: forget Paris, it was time for Brazil. Brazilian women? Besides, entrepreneurship was impossible in France, Bruno said, everyone knew this, but in South America . . . His eyebrows hitched up. He had a friend who'd moved to São Paulo two years ago, now the guy owned a dry cleaner, a video rental shop, a photography studio, a modeling agency.

"You get a loan instantly," Bruno said. "France has no room for entrepreneurs, but down there? Come on, a modeling studio?"

He said, "Hey, so is there room on Louis Vuitton for me?"

"I don't think so," I said. "But it's not my decision."

He nodded. "See you," he said a moment later, and clapped me on the back of the arm.

One night, Rachel found an ad in a magazine for a hip-hop party near République. We arrived early, at eleven, and the club was empty. I ordered a beer that advertised itself as tasting like lager combined with tequila, and it tasted like Sprite with pickles; I should have known better. Then within twenty minutes a hundred teenagers appeared, and many young twentysomethings. At least two guys were wearing the same sweater that was featured that week in the windows of H&M. The music started up: nineties Diddy hits and early Wu-Tang Clan. At the same time, a B-boy crew arrived and opened up the floor. The headliners were two boys, identical twins, dancing in liquid ways to mesmerize the crowd; a few years later, they'd emerge as dance stars in France, going by "Les Twins." But for that moment they held the floor for only twenty minutes, until finally the music got too good, everyone started dancing, and the DJ threaded his way to that summer's big Kanye West hit, and we all flipped out.

Perhaps when by all appearances I shouldn't fit in, I was at my most comfortable.

I dreaded it ending.

A few days later, an e-mail came from Pierre inviting us to visit him and Chloe in Provence. I was happy to receive it, and not just for the obvious reasons: quitting the agency, I'd worried about damaging my friendship with Pierre. Rachel and I took a high-speed train south from Gare de Lyon, riding in the upstairs cabin, with a shaded lamp at our table. Farms and forests, villages and cows. A few hours later we were having dinner outdoors at a giant table at Pierre's parents' house in the country. A half moon rose behind the roof, like a pearl in black underwear. The breeze was soupy warm. A swimming pool rippled where some teenagers had gone swimming while coffee was being served, at midnight.

Pierre's parents owned a seventeenth-century farmhouse in Margerie, near Montélimar, a stone house with enough space to sleep thirty. There were landscaped gardens, a terraced courtyard, and handmade toys left around aging in the sun. The kind of place you drooled over imagining, that turned out to be real.

That weekend, twenty-six people were visiting, the whole

family plus friends and neighbors, everyone contented and bronzed. It was Pierre's sister Monique's birthday, and lights had been rented for a dance party: an outdoor nightclub with a cheese course.

After the coffee, Pierre put on Britney Spears, a remix of "Toxic." It seemed to be the family anthem. And even the teenagers weren't sullen for a moment, amid the olive trees and dark shrubs and the smell of hash (from the teenagers). Monique opened her husband's birthday present, a purple box of lingerie. She ran inside to change. Jérôme got out his camera. He bossed the children around to adjust lights—those children that weren't by that point sleeping on benches—and Monique returned to dance. It seemed like it might go all the way, but it did not. It was perfectly tasteful, if a little more exotic than we'd anticipated, and everyone agreed, old and young, that we should be lucky to turn thirty-seven and be so toned.

Margerie, the town, was not exotic, we saw the next morning. It had a church and a few stop signs; otherwise it looked abandoned. Rachel and I were among the first awake on Saturday, with Pierre's father and his friend Antoine. When we'd retired the night before, the two of them had been drinking scotch at four a.m. Now they were fresh, impatient, ready to go.

First Pierre's dad made us espresso from a machine in the kitchen that could have been a tractor engine. He was regally patrician: a chemical engineer with flowing white hair and a round brown stomach. He asked how we felt about helping with the shopping. No problem, Rachel said.

"Antoine is also coming," Pierre's dad said, laughing, "but Antoine is no help."

Antoine appeared to be wearing the same outfit as the night before, though a freshly laundered version: white linen shirt, pressed jeans, black sunglasses, bracelets and rings. He looked eternally Mediterranean—tan, rakish, retired. He was a former musician, part of a seventies French pop band that had charted a number-one single. Now, Pierre told us, he was a professional gambler, working the casinos of Marseille.

At the market, we strolled under blue and white tents, past basket merchants and charcuterie displays. The air was hot. The area's lavender had been cut recently and the breeze was sticky with it, like purple pollen. The whole market appeared to know Pierre's dad; they called him "the city guy." For each stall, there was a period of negotiation, a discussion of produce, gossip, and weather.

"They love him," Antoine said to Rachel, "because they love his money."

"Come," Antoine said, pulling us away, "let's go get something to drink."

We went to a sandy café next to an old church. The sun hit us full in the face. Men in T-shirts were drinking coffee or white wine. Antoine suggested glasses of Ricard and some fried cod nuggets to fix our hangovers. For ten minutes, we sat and baked in silence. No word would have improved the impression.

Back at the house, Antoine disappeared to nap. We didn't see him again until around eleven o'clock that evening, when he showed up, still in sunglasses, with his guitar. He passed Rachel a binder full of sheet music. She asked him what he knew. Everything, Antoine said.

"How about Al Green?"

He'd been strumming something by the Beatles. "Who is Al Green?"

"Come on," I said, "'Let's Stay Together'? How about Marvin Gaye?"

"Do you know Elvis?" Rachel asked.

Antoine pulled down his sunglasses. "Do *you* know Elvis?" he said. "Americans don't know Elvis."

"Try me," Rachel said. "How about Steely Dan?"

And that was how you unlocked Antoine's heart. He and Rachel stayed up until three a.m. singing "Treat Me Like a Fool" and "Hey Nineteen." I watched them sing, hearing their voices rise over plates being cleared, over Antoine's guitar, over our friends nearby in conversation.

Jérôme, Monique's husband, the mathematician, sought me out.

"So you're getting along," he said. "You speak French. You love Paris."

"I love it," I said.

"You like the work you do with Pierre?"

"It's good."

"The luggage, the babies."

"I don't love the babies."

"No, no, not the babies," Jérôme said. He was watching his wife, who had started to sing. He said, "So what, you live here forever, in France?"

"No," I said, "we go back soon."

Jérôme started laughing, assuming I was joking. Then he turned serious. "Listen, don't be stupid. Are you crazy? Look at what we have."

Jérôme's looseness was noticeably different from the afternoon, when he'd told me, with gloom in his voice, how stressed he was, stressed out *au maximum*. "I am working like crazy," he'd said. "This is what life has become. You get it? Don't ask me about work, not on vacation. When I'm in the country, I am not in Paris, I leave it behind—I eat, I sleep, I screw, okay? Do not talk about work to me.

"Anyway," he said, goosing my arm, "before you leave, you'll have to come to Marseille."

He started a Marseille booster's song. From various points in the dark other voices sang along. Later in the evening, early in the morning, we were blasting Sanseverino's cigarette song through the loudspeakers, and Jérôme got me by both shoulders, shouting, "Listen, Paris, it's all *assholes*." He got my eyes to make sure I would remember this forever: "I'm telling you, Marseille, listen, beautiful beaches, and the women? The world tells you we're criminals, okay, and it's true, but that doesn't change the rest.

"It's a crime," he said morosely, "if you think France is just Paris."

True enough.

God, I'd miss them.

42

Year-round in Paris, though especially during summer, posters went up in the Métro for what I called the country-idyll picture. There was *Le cœur des hommes 2*; *Trois amis*; *Je déteste les enfants des autres*. Different films, but the posters were the same: French people in the countryside sitting at a table outdoors. Dipping their legs in a pool. Fishing the river Tarn from a chair. The light would be full of shadows, and nearby was a bottle of rosé, above was the sun—there would be a walnut cutting board and some cornichons. People outdoors laughing, eating, pursuing a kiss. The posters were everywhere, pervasive in all seasons. Down in the Métro, below the drumming rain and the city's dead-end jobs, its bureaucracy and shopping malls, these posters were a reminder that to lose touch with the rustic table was to lose, to some degree, one's French soul.

The posters were interchangeable, but the idea did not change.

Then again, what did I know?

In an interview I read somewhere around that time, John le Carré said the only way to write about a place was after visiting it for a day, or after a long life once you'd moved there. Because a day's visit gave you notes: smells, colors, advertisements new and advertisements peeling, and the writer could play naïf.

Or, if a writer moved to a place permanently, he'd be granted perspective, assuming he kept his eyes open for many years.

But time between those two lengths didn't lend more certainty, just detail.

Summer wound down. Dinner parties became dance parties. Rachel and I cooked *ensemble*, and we shopped at Picard. From the market, we brought home flowers that we arranged the way people store umbrellas. We roasted chickens. We hit dive bars. We hit clubs. We hit bars "installed" as exercises of marketing, where champagne was €140, but for that price two people could sit in a pink plastic love seat designed by Karim Rashid—we watched this occur but did not experience it for ourselves. Outside his rooms, Asif grew peppers, tomato plants, bushels on latticework, herbs in barrels. In the evenings the smell of mint came in through all our windows. Slowly the light went out. We played gin. We played Feist on the stereo for guests, and Alain Bashung, and Ladyhawke's "Paris Is Burning," which was a hit that summer at the office, where parties were organized on the terrace at night. Some were going-away parties for coworkers; some were parties because we had a view from a roof overlooking the Eiffel Tower and the Arc de Triomphe, the view wrapping from Montmartre to La Défense.

The first verse to "Paris Is Burning" said: "Tell me the truth / Is it love / Or just Paris."

Also popular was the Friendly Fires' single "Paris," remixed by Aeroplane, with vocals redone by the Brooklyn band Au Revoir Simone, to sound spacier and, oddly, more French, if still with an American's outsider touch: "One day we're going to live in Paris / I promise, I'm on it / When I'm bringing in the money."

One night there was a party in the glass-roofed Grand Palais, and it looked to us on the terrace like fireworks were being shot off indoors, it looked like terrorists were blowing up a flower shop.

One week before Bruno took his summer vacation, he invited me out to lunch. The two of us had steaks and plenty of wine—

champagne followed by Burgundy—all Bruno's choice, Bruno insisting on sharing the wine so I wouldn't namby out.

Breast-feeding, Bruno said, was in roughly the same place as when I'd left it. His baby-food job had gone well, however, and he'd been commended for his work. But work and life were both dull and discouraging.

"And what I hear," he said in English, "is you going to California, London, making movies?"

Bruno laughed, then continued in French: "I don't say it's fair or not fair. It's not your fault, but you have an advantage. You know this, right? The advantage is coming from outside. You're not Parisian, not French. You get to bypass the system. And you know Pierre from before—you're on Pierre's special team. Listen, you think if I said to André, 'Hey, dude, I've got this idea for a big chicken,' you think he'd listen to me? Come on."

We talked for twenty minutes about troubles Bruno was having with a woman on his team, who'd reported him for arriving late and blowing off meetings. Bruno said, "You know me, when am I late? I work hard."

I asked him if he'd be satisfied living forever in Paris.

Bruno took a moment to think about it, then gestured with his cigarette at the Arc de Triomphe and the grand buildings of the eleventh arrondissement. "Look where we are," he said. "Old families. Rich people. In Paris, if you're not rich, not from an old family, you're stuck. So of course you're not satisfied. Who wants to be stuck? But at least I'm stuck in Paris.

"Hey, now," he said, "it's dessert time, get something, let's eat."

We ate some kind of savory ice cream with herbs and salt, a wonder in every bite.

43

Rachel's and my friend Charles from New York visited Paris to see us and also to see a Brazilian guy. Charles and the Brazilian had met in New York, where Charles fell for him hard. But the Brazilian told him he wasn't interested. Still, the Brazilian told Charles that he was moving to Paris soon, and if ever he was in town . . .

"So I'm reading the signals right, yeah?" Charles asked me when I met him at his hotel. "Seriously, there's a chance here? This isn't just a lark?"

Charles was six-four, his hotel room was five-eight. In the lobby, he said *bonsoir* enthusiastically to the landlord, who did not look up from his newspaper. We went out for dinner with Rachel, then home for a nightcap, until finally Charles left to go meet the Brazilian at a gay bar.

The next morning, I offered Charles *pain au raisin* from my favorite *boulanger* around the corner, but he was too miserable and heartbroken to enjoy it.

"I should have known what to expect. He lives in Paris, he's got a goddamn scooter, of course I'm going to fall for him. Anyway . . ."

Charles let out a mournful sigh.

"We had great conversation. At the end, he says he has to get up early in the morning for work, so he says, Can I give you a lift? Just really nonchalant. I'm like, *Uh, I came all the way to*

Paris to see you, of course I'll take a lift. So we're bopping around Paris on his Vespa—I mean, kill me now—afterward he drops me off at my hotel. I'm like, let's stop pussying around. So I said to him, 'You know I've got a crush on you, right?' And he says—he's still sitting on his scooter at this point, only now he's got a big look of disappointment on his face—he says, 'Uh, I thought we worked that out in New York.' "

Charles got up, put on his jacket, and said, "But you know what? I'm totally over it, let's just go be in Paris."

Charles remained crusty for half an hour, until we were stopped by a woman who said she was a photographer from *GQ*. She said she wanted to shoot Charles for an upcoming issue of Paris street style. It wasn't exactly a Singer Sargent portrait, but it would do, and Charles cheered up. In the République Métro station, buying tickets, he was cut twice in line, but he didn't care in the least.

I explained that queuing rules were a bit looser in France than in the States.

"No, believe me, I get it," Charles said. "It's like black people in a Chinese restaurant in Bed-Stuy."

"You can't say that," I said.

"The hell I can't," Charles said. "I'm black, I live in Bed-Stuy, I love wontons, what's your problem?

"Hey, is it me," he added, "or did Parisians ditch berets for Yankees hats?"

Two French guys were going by in fitted New Era caps.

"Look what Jay-Z hath wrought," Charles said.

That night, outdoors at Café Crème for dinner, we told Charles about our big plan: returning to the States and moving to the woods, assuming we could swing it. Of course, Charles said. "This is obviously what you should do."

For Charles's last day in Paris, we took him to the Palais de Tokyo museum, where the main exhibit was an installation where visitors could shoot paintballs at the artist. Better than shooting strippers, I thought. But the exhibit wasn't running; the sign said the artist could be shot only on weekdays. So we decided to leave, though first we'd get something to drink from the museum café.

I was waiting in line, two people away from the register, when a woman cut to the front. She apologized loudly, but she needed to ask the cashier a question. Specifically: What was the secret ingredient in her salad? Because the sauce, she said, had been extraordinary.

The cashier said, Which salad?

The woman grabbed one from the refrigerated case. "Was it dill? Oregano? Something spicy? Or were the tomatoes dried rather than fresh?"

She apologized to the six of us in line. "It really is a tremendous salad," she said.

The cashier said she didn't know.

"Well, do you think we might inspect it?" the woman asked.

So the two of them picked through the salad. Lettuce, haricots verts, croutons, red onion, cheese. They tasted each thing, each time the woman saying, "No, no, that's good but that's not it."

The cashier excused herself to the kitchen and returned with a chef, a tall man in a short toque. The woman put it to him: "I'm really sorry, excuse me, but what is in your magical salad? Not the lettuce, not the onion, there's something else, something in the sauce. I'm dying to know what it is."

The chef tasted the salad. He said he agreed, it was a good salad, but he was sorry, he hadn't been the one to prepare it, he mostly did sandwiches.

"For me, it's the sauce," he said. "There's a really nice kick to it. Is it pimento?"

"That's exactly what I thought," the woman said, turning to smile at us all.

The chef suggested the woman try calling the manager. This led to the cashier finding the manager's mobile number on a note taped to one of the refrigerators. She dialed the number and handed over the phone.

"Hello, I am in your café at the Palais de Tokyo," said the inquiring woman. "Thank you, yes, it's a very nice café." Gradually, she explained her question. A moment later she smacked her forehead and started laughing, "Pepper *oil*, of course!"

"Ah, pepper *oil*," the chef said, nodding, and thumped his fist into his hand.

The woman in front of me said to the cashier, *That makes a lot of sense*, and she got one of the salads for herself. The woman on the phone sighed with relief, apologized again for the interruption, and thanked us all.

We said no problem, we were glad to know the truth ourselves.

After fifteen minutes in line, I returned with Charles's bottled water and explained why it had taken me so long.

"Dude, Paris," Charles said. "Honestly, nothing comes close."

44

Final week of August, Rachel and I took two of my allotted five weeks of vacation and went to the North Carolina coast with Rachel's parents. We sat on the beach and read books, drank vodka on the rocks, and ate fried clams. I rented a surfboard and rode slush. One night, we were drinking at a bar, just the two of us plus two sunburned white guys, one skinny, one fat, and a black woman with dreadlocks wearing sunglasses on a thin lanyard, drinking a brown cocktail with an orange slice. The skinny guy said to the fat guy, "Hey, what do you call someone who speaks three languages?"

"Dunno."

"Trilingual. Now what do you call someone who speaks two languages?"

"Bilingual," the woman said.

"Exactly," the skinny guy said. "So what do you call somebody who speaks only one language?"

"Monolingual?"

"Nope." The skinny guy was already laughing at his punch line: "*English.*"

The bartender said, "What?"

"Shit. I meant—"

"You meant *British*," the woman said, tapping her chin.

"No, no," the skinny guy said, "here's what I'm saying." He

took his time: "What do you call a guy who only speaks English? Wait. So you've got someone who just speaks their own language, except—"

The bartender interrupted, "This joke sucks."

The fat man said, "You barely speak English yourself."

"I said hold on!" the skinny guy shouted. His face became red. "Now, if you'll let me find my place."

The bartender said, "Just drop it."

"Oh, and how many languages do you speak?"

"Man, I don't speak dick."

The fat guy and the dreadlocked woman bumped fists and started talking about Barack Obama, who was on the TV. The fat man said he was voting for Obama, the woman said she was, too. The bartender said he didn't want to throw his vote away if a black man was unelectable in America, which wasn't him being racist, just realistic, he said.

I watched the skinny guy retell the joke to himself, head down, concentrating. He got to the punch line and said under his breath, "What do you call someone who only speaks one language?"

"American," he whispered a few seconds later. He smiled, looking up. He tried to tell his friends, but they were watching television, so he went to the bathroom.

During our flight back to Paris, a man sitting across from me showed his *USA Today* to one of the flight attendants. The front page said something about a public-sector strike being considered in Paris.

Man: "They're always at it, am I right?"

Flight attendant: "That's their way."

Man: "Well, it's a part of their culture. My kids don't understand protesting. Not like us. Baby boomers, we knew what protest culture was. We did something."

Flight attendant: "The world was a different place."

Man: "My kids don't march for shit. I'll tell you what, they'd march for cheaper cell phones, is about it."

SOMETHING IS ADDED TO THE AIR FOREVER

FALL

—How to write a Parisian theoretical manifesto—Vincent and I adhere to a dress code—Count on France to sexualize children's cinema—Rachel and I learn how to dress down Parisian women—Chez le Photographe du Business Travel—We'll always have (a certain foamy emptiness)—Last suppers—Bruno wants to play pool—

45

In September, fall came early to Avenue George V, with trees turning henpecked, their leaves shedding tips. Store windows changed to autumn displays: leather coats and baskets of apples. It was the best time of year to be in Paris. We took long walks in the Tuileries and visited the Orangerie, the museum where Monet's Water Lilies were kept. They looked alive, especially with so many trees outside turning yellow. We visited the Picasso Museum and sat for an hour in its garden, which by itself was worth the price of admission on an iridescent weekend morning.

One Saturday, with an odometer, we covered seven miles and barely left the city center.

So I was feeling extremely good the Tuesday that I picked up my pasta at noon, strolled down Rue Lamennais, and discovered, to my horror, that my lunchtime park had closed.

A newspaper article posted on the gate said the park was shuttered until further notice. The foundation that managed the grounds needed to rework its finances before it could afford the upkeep again. One man interviewed in the article said he and his coworkers were in mourning. He said he worked at a nearby advertising agency—I jumped, reading that, though I didn't recognize his name. He vowed to fight to reopen the park. It was a place, he said, that belonged to "old ladies and golden boys," that made people happy.

Next to the article hung a petition under plastic, signed already with twenty names.

Nearby was an island of pea gravel, with four benches. I found Stephen King sitting there wearing headphones, reading a newspaper. I sat on the other side of his bench and ate my lunch.

That afternoon, I was reading Jean Echenoz's *I'm Gone*, thinking about Paris being like an airport. Echenoz wrote,

> An airport does not really exist in and of itself. It's only a place of passage, an airlock, a fragile façade in the middle of an open field, a belvedere circled by runways where rabbits with kerosene breath leap and bound, a turntable infested by winds that carry a host of corpuscles of myriad origins: grains of sand from every desert, flecks of gold and mica from every river, volcanic or radioactive dust, pollens and viruses, rice powder and cigar ash.

Reading that, I was rather small.

Paris, I thought, was like a library book, something loaned.

At a party of Pierre and Chloe's that weekend, an artist friend announced he'd be having his first solo gallery show. Big cheers. The guy, Simon, was known for turning pornography into sculpture; he took a sex movie, paused it at the climactic moment, printed out the image, and diced up the print into squares, like pixels. Then he glued each pixel square onto a wooden block and assembled the blocks into a solid wall, so that, stacked together, they showed the frozen orgasm in a wooden-block re-creation.

Only Simon would also print out three other orgasmic moments, and paste their cut-up squares onto the wooden blocks' other sides, and make the blocks rotate in unison. So as the blocks turned, one of four orgasms was always coming into view, so to speak.

Around one in the morning, the liquor ran out. Pierre called a delivery service to send over more tequila, but everybody was short on cash, so Pierre and I, and some guy named Nicolas, whom I hadn't met before, went out to find an ATM.

During the walk, Nicolas said he was curious about Americans' ideas regarding anal sex. Was I actively pursuing it with my wife? Was I the type of American man who could discuss this?

"I used to be hung up about it," Nicolas said. "You know, too nervous to ask. This is a big crisis for men today: being men. Even in France, men are scared to say, Here is what I want. I met a woman years ago. She really liked it in the ass. So, I'm a gentleman, I wasn't going to ignore her desires. Once she introduced me to it, my life changed. What I'm saying is, if you like it and she likes it, what's wrong?"

Pierre got some money from an ATM while Nicolas was putting on a sweater, speaking through the fabric when it passed over his head: "It's just sex, it's natural, sex is good. Like I said, if she likes it—now this is paramount, of course. But why not?

"A woman wants *a man*," Nicolas said, squeezing my shoulder. "Believe me, if you want to be a man of the world, you need to try this," he told me brightly.

The following Monday, I was sitting outside my lunchtime park, not with Stephen King but with the smoking man, one half of the Puzzlers, when I overheard two twentysomethings discover the newspaper article pinned to the gate.

"Shit. Well, now that our park's closed—"

"What? It's not true!"

"Oh, and look, someone has already put up a manifesto."

"Oh good, the revolt of the *bobos*."

That month, manifestos were all around us. One weekend, near Montparnasse, Rachel and I were having lunch outdoors on the Boulevard Raspail when several fashion models came marching down the street, dressed like guerrillas in camouflage, passing out leaflets on behalf of Yves Saint Laurent. They were newsprint bundles with erotic photos of Naomi Campbell accompanied by the following in English:

> Fashion manifested. Fashion decontextualized, its net widened, the access great. Images for the world. Making connections, relations, associations. Giving beauty, prompting desire, inspiring change. Identities questioned, forged, explored, reforged . . . A contemporary spirit, a transnational dialogue, cultural hybrids. The new aesthetic of globalism.

After a year of advertising in Paris, I found it harder to tell the difference between bullshit and poetry. Sex fashioned as art, pornography, or manifesto. The next week, Rachel found the Naomi Campbell pamphlet on the bookshelf. "What's this?" I was about to say I thought it was important somehow, then realized what I was thinking and tossed it in the garbage.

46

The dress code for interviewing Sir Sean Connery arrived at the last minute by fax. Sir Sean lived in Lyford Cay, a massive gated community on an island in the Bahamas—white beaches, black staff, private school, private marina. The pamphlet said men in the compound were required to wear collared shirts at all times, tucked in at all times. Belts were mandatory. No denim, ever, no cutoff anything, and no visible logos of any type. Jackets would be worn for meals, ties with dinner. Sportswear was reserved for playing sports, no exceptions.

Vincent called to ask me if it was a joke. He said, "I have one nonjean."

I told him I had a pair of suit pants, that was it.

"Ah, mister, this is how you know you're a true Parisian," Vincent said. "But what is this about no sneakers, are we going to his wedding?"

Connery was Louis Vuitton's next star. Two weeks earlier, Pierre had asked me, "Would you mind going to the Bahamas before you quit?" Vincent and I arrived in Nassau at twilight. The air smelled tropical. From the airport, Lyford Cay was a twenty-minute drive, on a road lined with palm trees and chain fences. A hurricane looked to have wiped out hundreds of surrounding acres—there was little new growth or much to see aside from shrubs or the occasional cinder-block home half-finished, a cement mixer overturned in a yard.

We stopped the car after a mile and changed into our shoes, and tucked our collared shirts into our belted pants. Vincent wandered away to photograph a shank of rebar, and I tried calling Rachel to let her know we'd landed, but my cell phone was out of range.

To prepare for the interview, I'd been reading Sir Sean Connery's—we'd been informed to always remember the "Sir"—new autobiography, *Being a Scot*. Highlights included learning that he'd placed third in the 1950 Mister Universe Pageant. I wanted to ask him about that, though I feared he'd slap me. Vincent told me he'd have my back.

Next morning, the temperature was eighty-six degrees at breakfast. The sun broiled the grass. Vincent and I arrived at the shoot location early: a beautiful white house hidden in a leafy grove. We'd heard it was the former vacation home of Bill Paley, the broadcasting executive who built CBS. In the main house, no one but me and Vincent had on collared shirts, and few people wore shoes—they were too busy running in and out of the ocean to set up Annie Leibovitz's portrait, to be shot in an hour.

We found a team customizing a dock on a long white beach. There were a dozen assistants for the cameras, lights, and rigging. There were people for makeup, wardrobe, and hair. What "Annie" did or did not want was constantly being asked—"Annie" being said in a tone of anxious menace. "Did Annie say that?" "Did you hear that from Annie or from who exactly?" "Has anyone seen Annie please?"

A producer introduced Vincent and me to Annie at the catering table, explaining we were there to film Sir Sean once she was done with her shoot. Annie shook our hands and said, "So you guys don't need to be here right now, right?" and walked away, and her producer showed us to a guest bedroom where we might wait.

The shoot seemed to go well, from what we overheard on people's radios. But it was tense. Annie did not want people peering at Sir Sean. Annie wanted the RED camera. Annie did not want the RED camera. Annie needed more lenses brought down immediately.

The worst was when Annie was losing light. Her assistants looked like they were trying not to scream. Annie's producers, many long-haired women who appeared to have grown up riding horses, born to multitask in heavy winds, would command everyone to speed up, to pay attention. Radios beeped and crackled, antennas wobbling while the women walked quickly to and from the beach while tying up their hair. "Annie's losing light!" "We're losing it, people!" "Light's going now, people, let's go!" "We're losing the light!"

Sir Sean came to see us after lunch, after his nap. He was seventy-eight, a total charmer. He laughed and apologized for being late. Posing all morning in the heat, in outfits such as a wool tuxedo, had worn him out, he said. He asked for a glass of water, then vodka, then back to water. He was tall and grandfatherly, wearing a white shirt and ascot—skinnier than when he'd played a Russian submarine captain, but still handsome, unbowed.

And yet, I'll say this: Sir Sean appeared more nervous than me. Unlikely, considering my digestive response that day. But he answered fluffball question after fluffball question with first-class grace. For example, if I said, "If Edinburgh were an actress, who would she be?" he said, "Edinburgh, I think, would be an actor, and he would be me."

At one point, Sir Sean pointed at Vincent behind the camera. "Your man there," he said to me, "he's signaling something."

Vincent was waving a drinking glass in front of the lens, to get a wobbly look.

I said, "That's just for effect."

Vincent said, stammering, "Sorry, Sir Sean, it is an artistic effect, please."

"Oh, French, is he . . ." Sir Sean said. He laughed and leaned toward me. Our knees were suddenly three inches from touching.

His mustache, I noticed, had a million legs. "My wife's French, you know," Sir Sean stage-whispered. "She's an artist, a painter. You've got to love the French. I know I do," he said, leaning back, "always have."

Afterward, when Sir Sean went home, Vincent and I packed up our gear and wandered onto the beach. Annie Leibovitz and her shoot had disappeared. Wardrobe was gone, catering was gone. The dock was being towed away by an antique Chris-Craft boat. Annie and her producers were already on a plane, someone mentioned, back to New York for a *Vanity Fair* shoot in the morning. So Vincent and I spent the afternoon reading books on Bill Paley's beach, swimming in his ocean, and drinking his Kaliks—I'd found an unlocked minifridge full of beer beneath a picture of Truman Capote visiting the house, wearing tropical patterns.

I told Vincent that the day I met Pierre had been one of extraordinary good luck. He said same for him. For parting gifts, I stole an ashtray from the guesthouse, and Vincent bought a cap from the golf club, to give to his father. "He will not believe I was here unless I have something to show."

47

On the afternoon Vincent and I returned to Paris, Rachel learned her grandmother had died, her father's mother. More than a year earlier, right after we'd moved to Paris, Rachel's grandparents on her mother's side had passed away within a day of each other, and she hadn't been able to return for the funeral, to her regret. The evening I got back, Rachel talked to her family on the phone. After she hung up, she said the distance between them and Paris was acutely painful. She didn't know where she was, only where she wasn't.

Rachel flew back to the States for a week, and I worked later than normal and took long walks at night. I didn't want to be in the apartment alone because I couldn't focus with Rachel gone; I'd be going to brush my teeth and wind up taking out the garbage in my underwear.

We spoke at length on the telephone. I told her how much I wished I was there in North Carolina. This was true, though not complete; I wanted to be there, but I also didn't want to be by myself. When a person felt marvelous in Paris, the city amplified his feelings and fed him full. But when a person was lousy, the city shut down. He belonged underground, at best.

Which perhaps explained all the women crying on the Métro—many more than I'd seen in New York. No one bothered them underground. If anything, crying in public in Paris seemed to be the best way to guarantee you'd be left alone.

One night, I ate dinner at a restaurant on the Champs-Elysées by myself, and finished a bottle of red wine. Afterward, stumbling a bit, I went next door to see a Pixar movie. I thought it would cheer me up: a film for kids that was billed as adult-friendly.

The "adult-friendly" part at least explained the ads that played first.

Advertisement number one was for Magnum ice-cream bars: women in bathing suits worshipping an ice-cream god while sunlight beamed out from their vaginas. The second ad was for Häagen-Dazs, in which a woman, who sounded like a phone-sex operator, told us about the passion we'd feel for their new dark-chocolate ice cream; we heard this while half-naked black people blew kisses at each other. The third ad was for M&Ms—it was one big setup for a crotch-fondling joke. Finally, in an ad for Orangina, animals dressed like strippers did pole dances.

I was temporarily much cheered up.

In a changing world, count on France.

48

In the middle of September, Lindsay got a new apartment, a studio around the corner from Buttes-Chaumont. We visited and afterward took a walk around the park at nightfall, all of us wearing light jackets. Fireplaces burned. There were joggers zipping by, with reflective strips on their shirts briefly catching the light. For dinner we tried going to Le Faitout, one of our favorite cafés, where they served a breathtaking chicken with morels, but it was closed.

Open instead was a restaurant none of us had tried before, decorated like an American diner. It had booths, even a glass case for desserts, with rotating plates. Lindsay said once we sat down, "This could be the last dinner we share—I mean, in a diner, guys, really?"

Lindsay started crying, laughing at herself. She said, "I saw a friend recently from Chicago, this girl Sarah. She just moved here. I'm breaking her in. Her accent is horrendous. And her fashion—awful. I mean, God bless her, I love the girl, but we go to a party and she's wearing a yellow felt hat, a pink skirt, fishnet stockings. The French just tear her to shreds."

Toward the end of dinner, the waiter tried to clear our plates, but Rachel held him off, saying in French that she wasn't quite done, she needed another minute, though she'd love to hear about dessert if that was all right. He said, Of course, Madame. He described a molten chocolate cake. Rachel asked him about the preparation, was it really molten in the center? He assured her that it was. Well, Rachel said, she'd pass, but she'd have an herbal tea, did they have herbal tea?

She was glowing with fluency while I ordered coffee.

Lindsay said, "Hey, do you guys know my friend Gilles? He got in an awful motorcycle wreck last week. All his friends came over to help with his convalescence. I made grilled cheese sandwiches. Well, I swear, the French were awestruck. They were all, '*Waouh*, Lindsay, what a wonderful sandwich, now tell us, how did you make this? There is egg in here, is that right? Is there cream in the sauce? What exactly did you put into the sauce?' I was like, 'What sauce? What are you talking about, people, it's a grilled cheese!' But they made me go, step by step, in detail, through the preparation of this 'wonderful sandwich.' "

After dinner, we walked Lindsay back to her apartment. The evening was frosty. There weren't any stars out. Trees in the park bounced and jostled under the streetlamps.

"I'll tell you what," Lindsay said in her doorway. "About Sarah, my friend who just moved here? Next time we go out, I'm going to stand up for her. All those French bitches dressing her down . . . I'll go up to them, I'll say, 'Look, bitch, wash your hair; nice shoes.' "

The next afternoon was hot. Sunbathers turned out to quilt Buttes-Chaumont. After a run, I was sitting on a hill, stretching amid dozens of people, when a woman lying downslope from me suddenly slid off her bikini top and hitched down her bottoms, while also lifting up her knees so that I saw her Métro ticket—what Parisians called a woman's pubic hair when it had been trimmed to a rectangle.

I was reminded of Chloe's joke about women's pubic hair getting bigger these days in Paris, now that the Métro system had switched from tickets to Navigo passes, the size of credit cards.

Anyway, I moved and finished stretching near the Buttes-Chaumont puppet theater, a green hut covered in ivy. Then an old man started ringing a bell. Parents stirred, pushing their children toward the gate. I'd always assumed the theater to be defunct, but here was an actual Punch and Judy show. I went up to buy a ticket, then realized I didn't have any money on me. Probably better this way, I thought. Some things were better left undone. Plus, I wouldn't have wanted to give the wrong impression: the sweaty North American scum who, a second earlier, had been staring at a woman's pubic hair.

There should be a name for the syndrome that occurs when you're in Paris and you already miss it.

The next day our health-insurance cards arrived.

49

Pierre put me on a team to pitch a watchmaker in Switzerland. One final presentation, he said.

"Oh, I get it," Rachel said, "you've run through all of France's products, now you're expanding to the Swiss."

The watchmaker was headquartered near Neuchâtel, an hour from Geneva. We flew Air France. Even in economy there was free champagne and complimentary newspapers. For a snack: brown bread, herb butter, a large piece of prosciutto, two cherry tomatoes speared on bamboo, and two *macarons*, pink and pistachio. In Geneva, our boss Bernard rented an Audi and drove us to a three-star hotel on Neuchâtel's lake. We had individual suites. Each was constructed on top of its own dock—docks extending like fingers into the lake—with giant rooms, waffle-cloth towels, espresso machines. Holes were cut into each dock with individual fireman poles should we desire to slide down into the water. Bathrooms big enough for eight people to shower. And a television the breadth of a cow, with four channels of pornography (German, German, Czech, French), which was for some reason impossible to turn off at the moment the girl from reception arrived to deliver your complimentary toothbrush.

"You know what," Rachel said over the phone when I tried to calculate the horsepower of my bathtub, "just don't."

The next morning we drove through long tunnels, over mountain passes, and across ravines. In the watchmakers' boardroom, we told little stories under life-size murals of Tiger Woods, master of the global business class's favorite pastime. At the end, we ate lemon cookies, drank Nespresso, exchanged kisses, and shook hands. Then our team drove back to Geneva, returned to Paris, flying economy again on Air France—champagne, newspapers, and this time tuna tartelettes, tomato tartare, and chocolate ganache tarts—so that we arrived back in Paris in time for cocktails. Did everyone want cocktails? Should we get cocktails? *Un vers, deux vers?* Where should we go for cocktails, the third, the eleventh, the ninth?

Nothing spectacular happened in Geneva. No one commented on it. We didn't even win the account. But no biggie. This was doing business in Europe, the ordinary business of luxury. And no one noted the extraordinary luxury of simply doing it, because they'd do it the following week, and the next.

But I knew I'd never do it again.

"Listen, this is a ton of bullshit," my friend Greg said. "What are you talking about right now?"

Greg was a partner at a New York advertising firm. I'd called him to ask if he knew of any copywriters who'd be interested in moving to France.

"Look, how did you even get this job?" Greg said. "I mean, *I'm* tempted to take it. You realize accounts like this don't exist. Right now I need to oversee some antacid copy, we're hung up with the client's legal team—*that's* advertising. I really have no idea what you've been doing over there."

I explained how, on the previous evening, Louis Vuitton had sent our team to Asnières, outside Paris, where the luggage was still hand-sewn, so that we would better understand their luxury DNA. We'd been shown Karl Lagerfeld's custom trunk, designed to store his iPods—he traveled with dozens of them—and afterward we drank champagne where Kanye West had sat two weeks earlier while discussing his plans to intern and learn the fashion/luggage craft.

A Louis Vuitton boss told me, "Mr. West is nice, you know. A true gentleman. *Very* creative. He's someone who is building brands right now."

After my call with Greg, I got stuck trying to devise a tagline to sell some new belts. I told Niki, the copywriter from Quebec, that I could really use her help; I asked if I could have some of her time.

She said she wasn't sure she understood.

I said loudly in French, "I said I need your time."

Tomaso whispered, "*Oh yeah.*"

Olivier said, "Me, too, please."

Someone shouted, "*In his mouth.*"

Tes temps—your time. *Tétons*—nipples. My final note for the wall.

50

We ate last dinners throughout October. We went to Chateaubriand and ate the foam. Pierre and Chloe took us for cocktails to Chez Janou, a tiny cottage in the third arrondissement, not far from Place des Vosges. Chloe was astounded we hadn't been there before. "But this is where all the Americans hang out, like La Perle for hipsters. How do you live here all this time and not know Chez Janou?"

For dinner afterward, we went to Les Côtelettes, a new traditional French restaurant nearby where we ate *andouillettes* and *boudin noir*, then afterward we hopped in Pierre's car and drove to a new club called Cha-Cha, near the Seine. Techno blared, people texted, dancers danced. Due to the ban on cigarettes, the owners had built a glass box inside where people could smoke, into which Chloe disappeared, introducing herself to people with swooping *bises*. On the top floor was a private party. Floating down the stairs, the music sounded much better, so Rachel tried to sneak in, but the bouncer told her he needed a password. She spent ten minutes testing different pieces of her vocabulary. The bouncer humored her, but he wouldn't allow her passage. Whatever the password was, we did not find out.

At the office, Marc the project manager returned from a week in California relaxed and happy, no longer burnt out by *la stresse*. He showed around a photograph of him eating a cheeseburger the size of his head; it was the only thing he would talk about from his trip.

In Paris, October was extremely fine. The next week I called in sick with a *gastro*—I lied—and Rachel and I spent two days roaming Paris, reliving our first week, before I began work. We went for long walks and said goodbye to our favorite markets, garden stores, the Village Voice bookstore, the Red Wheelbarrow bookstore, and WH Smith. It smelled like toasted spices on the street. The light on the riverbank was one long glaze down Ile St. Louis, and the light was constant and stationary, like Paris itself.

I'd been wrong with my "city of clouds" idea. Paris was the city of light, like people said, but its light was the kind that was kindled internally.

End of October, Rachel's birthday fell right before we flew home. We went out for dinner and dancing on the Champs-Elysées. Christmas lights were being strung up, but they weren't lit yet. Around midnight we ended up at Regine's, a nightclub where Lindsay knew the owner, tucked into a street behind where I went to work every morning.

At the same club, back in February, I'd almost been turned away one night for wearing sneakers and jeans. Luckily, that evening, for Rachel's birthday, I had on a suit.

The bouncer let in the girls, but stopped me.

"Sorry," he said. "Too formal."

"He's with me," Lindsay said. "I'm friends with Regine. What is the problem?"

"There's been changes," the bouncer said. He waved his hand over me like it was a security wand. "The club's got a new look."

"How about he loses the tie?" Lindsay said.

I took off my tie and untucked my shirt.

"Next time," the bouncer told me, "wear sneakers."

Downstairs, the club was packed with guys in sneakers, girls in hoodies. After twenty minutes, Lindsay and I went outside to split a cigarette. A line of hopefuls stretched down the block. One young guy, handsome and cool, ducked under the velvet rope and asked us for a light.

"Wait a second," he said in French after a puff, "the two of you are together? That's a paradox."

"Why a paradox?" Lindsay said.

"Well, you're beautiful and tall. Then you," he said, turning to me and contemplating, throwing back his hair, "you're not very tall."

Lindsay said, "Is he beautiful?"

"He's wearing a suit," the guy said. "He's proper. Like if you're visiting Granny on Sunday. But you," the guy said to Lindsay, "you're one of us, you know?"

Harsh but true. The guy was dressed in skintight lumberjack clothes, and Lindsay was wearing a green plaid shirt she'd bought that afternoon at H&M.

Then he said to me, "Look, I'm sorry. You're beautiful. Please, can I see your teeth?"

I opened my mouth.

"*Waouh*, man, honestly? You have great teeth." He took his time, peering in, apparently oblivious to my fillings. "Really beautiful." After I closed my mouth, he said, "Now I can see you guys together. It is the contrast, very subtle."

There didn't seem to be anything else to say, so I said, "You have a good head."

"Thank you," he said, smiling. "Look, do you mind if I come downstairs with you?"

No problem, I said. I told the bouncer that the guy *avec la bonne tête* was with us. The bouncer didn't like it, but he allowed him in anyway; after all, he was wearing the right clothes.

51

The truth was, we snuck out. There was no honest way to say goodbye. We inventoried our apartment, packed our duffel bags, and walked Paris from end to end. We ate another dinner with Lindsay at a little restaurant near Montmartre. We read French newspapers. We closed accounts and left forwarding addresses.

Vincent the film director e-mailed me: "See you in Obama land."

Three nights before leaving, the agency threw me a goodbye party. There were four cases of champagne, a case of liquor, and four platters of charcuterie. People gave me goodbye *bises*. They said they'd heard from Pierre that I was having a novel published—the idea was met with disbelief. Where had I lived my secret life?

They also asked where I'd be moving. I explained that we were returning to the United States, to the woods of *Caroline du Nord*. No one could grasp this—me with cows and pigs, "with a big truck and a big gun?"

I explained it was more like we were moving to the countryside, *la campagne*.

"*Ah bon*," people said reverently, nodding, "*la campagne*."

Around two, when the party was still loud, I told people I was going out to find more champagne. Instead I rode the Métro home and crawled into bed. At four a.m., a text message woke me up, Pierre writing to say that he and some people were going out to find something to eat, did I want to join them?

That same day, prior to the party, Bruno had taken me out for lunch. "Please," he'd said, "you should at least see my neighborhood one time before you go."

"Of course," I said. "*Avec plaisir.*"

Bruno drove us on his scooter up to the seventeenth arrondissement. We ate on Rue Jacquemont at La Tête de Goinfre, a restaurant dedicated to pork. Bruno did all the ordering. First came an amuse-bouche of sausages and pickles, plus champagne. Next, a charcuterie platter meant for four people that we split, of more sausages, hams, pâtés. Then a 1.5-kilo steak to share, plus *pommes sautées* and a green salad, with two bottles of Côtes du Rhône. One hour, two hours. We talked about office politics a little, not much. Dessert we skipped, but we ordered calvados and coffee. Mostly Bruno wanted to talk about his family, his girlfriend, a recent fishing trip, some upcoming plans to visit Lisbon.

He asked me, Don't you like the restaurant? Isn't the food exceptional?

I did, I said. It was.

This is true Paris, Bruno said. Family Paris. Shame it had taken me so long to see it.

I agreed, I apologized, we toasted.

On our way back to the office, Bruno proposed billiards. Fantastic! I yelled into his helmet. Now time had no influence. In Paris, the past was all around you, but from the back of Bruno's scooter, the present was boisterous and pulsing. We buzzed past markets I didn't recognize. Down streets I'd never seen. For eighteen months, people had told me Paris was finished, a city fading, cauterized by tourism and a reluctance to change. But I hadn't seen it. I knew too many Parisians now—passionate, self-aware Parisians. The day that Parisians stopped being so Parisian, then maybe. But the Parisians I knew were nowhere near done.

What my friend Bruno taught me about being Parisian: never let the heart languish.

Bruno drove us to the Académie de Billard Clichy-Montmartre. Bruno shouted at a stoplight that he had wanted to show it to me for some time. It was an architectural wonder inside, Bruno said, with a glass ceiling and ancient tables. And it was beautiful, from what I saw, though I got to see it only through the window. Bruno went inside to book a table, but a clerk said the hall was members-only.

We stood outside and Bruno smoked.

"Imagine if the Germans had bombed everything," Bruno said. "Maybe no one would like Paris." We shivered from the cold. "Next time you're in Paris, we go," he said, nodding to the billiards hall. Then Bruno remounted his Yamaha, tiptoed it backward into the street, and waited for me to board.

That night at the party, Bruno found me late and stubbed his thick fingers into my chest, shouting over the music, "Hey, you remember the billiards from today? So beautiful. Look, from lunch?" Bruno pulled up his shirt to show me his brown gut. He laughed. He shouted, pointing, "I gotta start a diet soon!"

Then he clenched my arm. He had something he wanted to tell me. He said, "Wait, I'll get us more to drink, I'll be right back, okay?"

Bruno disappeared into the crowd. I ducked out the entrance. I told people on the staircase I was going out to find more champagne. From the bottom of the stairwell I heard Sabine's voice above me: "Where does he expect to find champagne at this hour? Hey, did he say goodbye to any of you?"

But that was the thing. I couldn't figure out how to say goodbye. I would not—not to Bruno or any of them. Saying goodbye to Paris was something a person did when he knew he was dying. Otherwise, Paris was forever one day soon.

ACKNOWLEDGMENTS

The author is grateful to Sean McDonald and PJ Mark, without whom this tale might not have come to the telling; Frederic Bonn and Zoe Deleu, who opened the door; Marilyn and Michael Knowles, who opened their home; and the MacDowell Colony, for its generosity.

The author also wishes to thank Emily Bell and everybody else at FSG, everybody at Janklow & Nesbit, Jennifer Murphy, Asha Thomas, Geoff Kloske, Megan Lynch, Kate Lee, Frédéric Guelaff, Mathieu Baillot, Leslie Baldwin, Andrew and Melissa Cotton Womack, Jonathan S. Paul, LCD Soundsystem, Katherine Ortega and the Mafiosos, and Jim Coudal.

Above all, Rachel Knowles, my love.

To everyone the author encountered in Paris, especially his colleagues who didn't imagine winding up in a book, a mountain of gratitude.